Before you judge this book by its cover, listen to the CD. It's real music... Hip-hop, R&B, Alternative. I'm totally serious... Good music doesn't need to be brainless, and music that uses your brain doesn't need to be lame. The people who put this CD and guide together are independent recording artists and teachers who love music and love words... You need words to write songs.

We just figured that there's a better way to study, and why not listen to beats while you're getting something done. So, the music includes 'vocabulary' words that you'll need to learn for school, tests, life; but you won't notice them until you read the lyrics. We call them 'Money Words,' or 'Word$' in shorthand at Native, the New York City production studio where we recorded and mixed the tracks.

After you listen to the CD, the exercises will back them up, and you're set. And, in case you don't already know, a 'synonym' is "the same thing as," and an 'antonym' is "the opposite of." If you need help, get it at www.defmind.com.

So, grab your CD player, get something to write with, and don't stress.

-k

Printed materials and music Copyright © 2004 Defined Mind, Inc.

All rights reserved. No portion of this book or the accompanying compact disk recording may be reproduced – mechanically, electronically, or by any other means, including photocopying without written permission of the publisher.

Published by
Defined Mind, Inc.
166 East 92nd St.
New York, NY 10128
www.defmind.com

Book Design: Keith London
Cover Illustration: Arna Bartlett, William Hermany
Imagedog Media, New York, NY

ISBN# 0-9763767-0-9

Manufactured by Book-mart Press in The United States of America
Initial Concept: Lorraine Goodman
First printing November 2004

Defined Mind
Vocabulary Accelerat[or]

Keith London
&
Rebecca Osleeb

Published by
Defined Mind, Inc.
New York

Knowledge is a State of Mind™

I OWE A LOT OF PEOPLE, SO THIS IS FOR:

My Soul Mates Robin & Dakota,
For putting up with me for all of these years.

My Grandfather Jules,
Without whom this never would have existed.

Our Parents,
Also, for putting up with me for all of these years.

My Granny,
She would have loved this.

My Patron Saints:
Todd Retallack, The Patient
Rob Last, The Steadfast
The Clan Mazursky, Loyal & True
For making It possible.

The Great City of New York & Its Citizens,
For their Energy, Intellect, and Strength.

And, of Course,
The Students, Wherever You Are...

Contents

TRACKS 13

HOT 16
    "Hot" Listening Exercise 16
    "Hot" Lyrics 17
    "Hot" Dictionary 19
    "Hot" Synonym Matching 24
    "Hot" Sentence Completion 26
    "Hot" Crossword Puzzle 30
    "Hot" Synonym Sentences 32
    Middleton & Willie, Too "Hot" 36

ALREADY TAKEN 40
    "Already Taken" Listening Exercise 40
    "Already Taken" Lyrics 41
    "Already Taken" Dictionary 42
    "Already Taken" Synonym Matching 46
    "Already Taken" Sentence Completion 47
    "Already Taken" Crossword Puzzle 50
    "Already Taken" Synonym Sentences 52
    Five Minutes with Mia Johnson 54

SHINE 58
    "Shine" Listening Exercise 58
    "Shine" Lyrics 58
    "Shine" Dictionary 60
    "Shine" Synonym Matching 62
    "Shine" Sentence Completion 63
    "Shine" Crossword Puzzle 66
    "Shine" Synonym Sentences 68
    Pascarell's Defined Mind "Shine"s 70

WHY DIDN'T YOU TELL ME 74
    "WDTYM" Listening Excercise 74

CONTENTS

"WDYTM" Lyrics 75
"WDTYM" Dictionary 76
"WDYTM" Synonym Matching 80
"WDYTM" Sentence Completion 81
"WDYTM" Crossword Puzzle 84
"WDYTM" Synonym Sentences 86
"Why Didn't You Tell Me" This Was Tough? 88

GO! **93**
"Go!" Listening Exercise 93
"Go!" Lyrics 94
"Go!" Dictionary 96
"Go!" Synonym Matching 102
"Go!" Sentence Completion 104
"Go!" Crossword Puzzle 108
"Go!" Synonym Sentences 110
Rodney Willie Is Ready To "Go!" 114

SUPERGIRL **118**
"SuperGirl" Listening Exercise 118
"SuperGirl" Lyrics 119
"SuperGirl" Dictionary 120
"SuperGirl" Synonym Matching 124
"SuperGirl" Sentence Completion 125
"SuperGirl" Crossword Puzzle 128
"SuperGirl" Synonym Sentences 130
Hecker & Beers Launch "SuperGirl" 133

THE LETTER **138**
"The Letter" Listening Exercise 138
"The Letter" Lyrics 138
"The Letter" Dictionary 140
"The Letter" Synonym Matching 143

Contents

"The Letter" Sentence Completion 144
"The Letter" Crossword Puzzle 146
"The Letter" Synonym Sentences 148
"The Letter" Examined 150

UPSIDE DOWN 154

"Upside Down" Listening Excercise 154
"Upside Down" Lyrics 154
"Upside Down" Dictionary 156
"Upside Down" Synonym Matching 160
"Upside Down" Sentence Completion 161
"Upside Down" Crossword Puzzle 164
"Upside Down" Synonym Sentences 166
Mia Johnson Gets Inverted 169

MOVE IT 174

"Move It" Listening Exercise 174
"Move It" Lyrics 174
"Move It" Dictionary 176
"Move It" Synonym Matching 179
"Move It" Sentence Completion 180
"Move It" Crossword Puzzle 182
"Move It" Synonym Sentences 184
Blanding & Jackson "Move It" 186

EPHEMERAL DAYS 190

"Ephemeral Days" Listening Exercise 190
"Ephemeral Days" Lyrics 191
"Ephemeral Days" Dictionary 192
"Ephemeral Days" Synonym Matching 196
"Ephemeral Days" Sentence Completion 198
"Ephemeral Days" Crossword Puzzle 202
"Ephemeral Days" Synonym Sentences 204

Contents

Nina Zeitlin's "Ephemeral Days" 207

SUBLIME **212**
    "Sublime" Listening Exercise 212
    "Sublime" Lyrics 213
    "Sublime" Dictionary 214
    "Sublime" Synonym Matching 217
    "Sublime" Sentence Completion 218
    "Sublime" Crossword Puzzle 220
    "Sublime" Synonym Sentences 222
    The "Sublime" Piece 224

WIDE OPEN SPACES **229**
    "Wide Open Spaces" Listening Exercise 229
    "Wide Open Spaces" Lyrics 230
    "Wide Open Spaces" Dictionary 231
    "Wide Open Spaces" Synonym Matching 236
    "Wide Open Spaces" Sentence Completion 238
    "Wide Open Spaces" Crossword Puzzle 242
    "Wide Open Spaces" Synonym Sentences 244
    Nina Zeitlin Longs for "Wide Open Spaces" 248

COMPLETE CHAPTERS DICTIONARY **252**

COMBINED CHAPTERS EXERCISES **292**
    Combo Synonym Matching 292
    Combo Sentence Completion 295
    Combo Crossword Puzzle 298
    Combo Synonym Sentences 300
    Article Excerpts 304

"HOT" – ANSWER KEYS **320**
    "Hot" Listening Exercise Answer Key 320
    "Hot" Synonym Matching Answer Key 320
    "Hot" Sentence Completion Answer Key 322

Contents

"Hot" Crossword Answers 324
"Hot" Synonym Sentences Answer Key 325
Middleton & Willie, Too "Hot" Answers 327

"ALREADY TAKEN" – ANSWER KEYS 329
"Already Taken" Listening Exercise Answer Key 329
"Already Taken" Synonym Matching Ans. Key 329
"Already Taken" Sentence Completion Ans. Key 330
"Already Taken" Crossword Answers 332
"Already Taken" Synonym Sentences Ans. Key 332
Five Minutes with Mia Johnson Answers 333

"SHINE" – ANSWER KEYS 335
"Shine" Listening Exercise Answer Key 335
"Shine" Synonym Matching Answer Key 335
"Shine" Sentence Completion Answer Key 336
"Shine" Crossword Answers 337
"Shine" Synonym Sentences Answer Key 337
Pascarell's Defined Mind "Shine"s Answers 338

"WDYTM" - ANSWER KEYS 340
"WDYTM" Listening Answer Key 340
"WDYTM" Synonym Matching Answer Key 340
"WDYTM" Sentence Completion Answer Key 341
"WDYTM" Crossword Answers 343
"WDYTM" Synonym Sentences Answer Key 343
"WDYTM" This Would Be Tough? Answers 344

"GO!" – ANSWER KEYS 346
"Go!" Listening Excercise Answer Key 346
"Go!" Synonym Matching Answer Key 346
"Go!" Sentence Completion Answer Key 348
"Go!" Crossword Answers 350
"Go!" Synonym Sentences Answer Key 351

Contents

Rodney Willie Is Ready To "Go!" Answers 353

"SUPERGIRL" – ANSWER KEYS 355

"SuperGirl" Listening Exercise Answer Key 355
"SuperGirl Synonym Matching Answer Key 355
"SuperGirl" Sentence Completion Answer Key 356
"SuperGirl" Crossword Answers 358
"SuperGirl" Synonym Sentences Answer Key 358
Hecker & Beers Launch "SuperGirl" Answers 360

"THE LETTER" – ANSWER KEYS 362

"The Letter" Listening Exercise Answer Key 362
"The Letter" Synonym Matching Answer Key 362
"The Letter" Sentence Completion Answer Key 363
"The Letter" Crossword Answers 365
"The Letter" Synonym Sentences Answer Key 365
"The Letter" Examined Answers 367

"UPSIDE DOWN" – ANSWER KEYS 368

"Upside Down" Listening Answer Key 368
"Upside Down" Synonym Matching Answer Key 368
"Upside Down" Sentence Completion Ans. Key 369
"Upside Down" Crossword Answers 371
"Upside Down" Synonym Sentences Answer Key 371
Mia Johnson Gets Inverted Answers 373

"MOVE IT" – ANSWER KEYS 375

"Move It" Listening Exercise Answer Key 375
"Move It" Synonym Matching Answer Key 375
"Move It" Sentence Completion Answer Key 376
"Move It" Crossword Answers 377
"Move It" Synonym Sentences Answer Key 378
Blanding & Jackson "Move It" Answers 379

"EPHEMERAL DAYS" – ANS. KEYS 380

Contents

"E. Days" Listening Excercise Answer Key 380
"E. Days" Synonym Matching Answer Key 380
"E. Days" Sent. Completion Answer Key 381
"Ephemeral Days" Crossword Answers 384
"E. Days" Synonym Sentences Answer Key 384
Nina Zeitlin's "Ephemeral Days" Answers 386

"SUBLIME" – ANSWER KEYS 388
"Sublime" Listening Exercise Answer Key 388
"Sublime" Synonym Matching Answer Key 388
"Sublime" Sentence Completion Answer Key 389
"Sublime" Crossword Answers 391
"Sublime" Synonym Sentences Answer Key 391
The "Sublime" Piece Answers 392

"WIDE OPEN..." – ANSWER KEYS 395
"WOS" Listening Exercise Answer Key 395
"WOS" Synonym Matching Answer Key 395
"WOS" Sentence Completion Answer Key 396
"WOS" Crossword Answers 399
"WOS" Synonym Sentences Answer Key 399
Nina Z. Longs for "Wide Open Spaces" Answers 402

COMBO EXERCISES ANSWER KEYS 404
Combo Synonym Matching Answer Keys 404
Combo Sentence Completion Answer Key 407
Combo Crossword Answers 409
Combo Synonym Sentences Answer Key 409
Article Excerpts Answers 412

DEFINED MIND CD & CHAPTERS TRACKS

1. **HOT - Keith Middleton & Rodney Willie**
   Lyrics by Rodney Willie
   Music Written & Performed by Keith Middleton
   Avon Marshall – Vocals
   Rodney Willie - Vocals
   Produced by Keith Middleton
   Technical Producer - Craig Chang

2. **ALREADY TAKEN - Mia Johnson of The Mia Johnson Band**
   Lyrics by Mia Johnson
   Music Written & Performed by Mia Johnson & The Mia Johnson Band
   Mia Johnson – Guitar, Vocals
   Rocco DeCicco – Guitar
   Jeff Hiatt – Bass Guitar
   Tom Walling – Drums
   Produced by Dave Logan & Craig Chang

3. **SHINE - Joe Pascarell & The Machine**
   Lyrics by Joe Pascarell
   Music Written & Performed by Joe Pascarell & The Machine
   Joe Pascarell – Guitar
   Ryan Ball – Bass Guitar, Vocals
   Todd Cohen – Drums
   Produced by Joe Pascarell

4. **WHY DIDN'T YOU TELL ME - Nina Zeitlin**
   Lyrics by Nina Zeitlin & Matt Kelly
   Music Written by Nina Zeitlin & Matt Kelly
   Nina Zeitlin – Vocals
   Joe Mendoza – Guitar & Bass Guitar
   Mike Pandolfo– Instrumentation
   Produced by Mike Pandolfo

5. **GO! - Keith Middleton & Rodney Willie**
   Lyrics by Rodney Willie
   Music Written & Performed by Keith Middleton
   Rodney Willie – Vocals
   Additional Vocals – Keith Middleton
   Produced by Keith Middleton
   Technical Producer - Craig Chang

TRACKS cont'd.

6. SUPERGIRL - Adrianne Hecker & Lyle Beers
Lyrics by Adrianne Hecker & Lyle Beers
Music Written & Performed by Lyle Beers & Mike Pandolfo
Adrianne Hecker – Vocals
Produced by Mike Pandolfo

7. THE LETTER - Keith Middleton & Rodney Willie
Lyrics by Rodney Willie
Music Written & Performed by Keith Middleton
Avon Marshall – Vocals
Produced by Keith Middleton
Technical Producer - Craig Chang

8. UPSIDE DOWN - Mia Johnson of The Mia Johnson Band
Lyrics by Mia Johnson
Music Written & Performed by Mia Johnson & The Mia Johnson Band
Mia Johnson – Guitar, Vocals
Rocco DeCicco – Guitar
Jeff Hiatt – Bass Guitar
Tom Walling – Drums
Produced by Dave Logan & Craig Chang

9. MOVE IT - F.A.M.E. Ent.
Lyrics by Edmund Blanding & Troy Jackson of F.A.M.E. Ent., with Keith London
Music Written & Performed by Leon Gaines
Troy Jackson – Vocals
Produced by Craig Chang

10. EPHEMERAL DAYS - Nina Zeitlin
Lyrics by Nina Zeitlin & Matt Kelly
Music Written by Nina Zeitlin & Matt Kelly
Nina Zeitlin – Vocals & Instrumentation
Rick Briskin – Guitar
Produced by Dave Logan & Mike Pandolfo

Knowledge is a State of Mind™

11. SUBLIME – Joe Pascarell & The Machine

Lyrics by Joe Pascarell
Music Written & Performed by Joe Pascarell & The Machine
Joe Pascarell – Guitar, Vocals
Ryan Ball – Bass Guitar
Todd Cohen – Drums
Produced by Joe Pascarell

12. WIDE OPEN SPACES – Nina Zeitlin

Lyrics by Nina Zeitlin & Mike Pandolfo
Music Written by Nina Zeitlin & Mike Pandolfo
Nina Zeitlin – Vocals
Vera Pandolfo – Backing Vocals
Joe Mendoza – Guitar & Bass Guitar
Produced by Mike Pandolfo

Produced by Native LLC
Recorded @ Native, New York, NY, July - October 2004
29 West 17th St., NYC 10011
www.nativemusic.net

KEITH LONDON, EXECUTIVE PRODUCER

Thanks to: The Artists who jumped at the chance to put their hearts & souls into this recording; Robin, for not divorcing me while I created An Alternate Reality; Dakota, for giving the studio scene a great Allman Brothers' cover vibe; Rebecca the Genius for ditchin' pitchin' hoagies to work in the Penthouse or Style on the studio couch; the visionaries 'el-K' & The Johnny Zed who gave us the muscle to put it together; JT for Insight & keeping me on the right track; Nina for her Passion & hooking up the studio; Dave, Craig & Mike for buying in & getting it done; Michele, a Woman of Action; Steven Beer, Bill Gladstone, Bob Strickland, & Katherine Brennen for Street Cred; Todd Retallack, Rainer Jenss, Rob Last, Sue Maz, Markus Malarkus, Mike Sweeney, Bob Emerson & Rodger Hood for their backing &/or Wise Counsel; Bennett, for telling Sue to 'Just Do It;' Jason, for rollin' the dice on hot dogs at his Bar Mitzvah; Jules, Jemi, Dick & Fran, for Blood is Thickerer; & of course, The Reverend Gil, without you, Mia & The Band would still be hanging out on 17th St. waiting for the elevator.

KEITH MIDDLETON & RODNEY WILLIE
HOT

"HOT" LISTENING EXERCISE

Listen to "Hot" all the way through at least once. Then listen to the song again, and in the spaces provided below, list the Word$ that you hear.

NOTES:

"HOT" LYRICS

by Rodney Willie

Got an e-mail that was sent to me
'bout a party happening this week
It said we're required to be **sedentary**
While we're in class sitting quietly
But not for long we'll get you on your feet
We know you're tired of **uniformity**
Same old **monotony** can make you weak
We can **rectify** it
We've got the **remedy**
Raves of the party would **propagate**
Word was spreading quickly no could wait
The girl I wanted to take seemed to **vacillate**
She kept **wavering** on who she wanted to date
Her **fluctuation**, got so **frustrating**, I wasn't waiting
Said I'd go alone, then I got the message
From my best friend "Yo this party is hot!"
I hung up the phone

Hot
Temperature's changing
Hot
Ignited and flaming
Hot
There's no mistaking
Conflagration fires **razing**
It's so **exhilarating**, exciting, **invigorating**
Inviting and **stimulating**
I don't ever want to go

It was no **illusion**
It was real and I was there

What a beautiful **union**

"HOT" LYRICS cont'd.

Fusion of the crowd and music so amusing
In the **proximity** of a girl sitting in **seclusion**
Her I'm **perusing**, **pursuing** I'm using a **profusion**
Of **ungainly** moves that made her laugh
Said I be doing much better with a partner
So I took her hand and we started to dance…

Hot
Temperature's changing
Hot
Ignited and flaming
Hot
There's no mistaking
Conflagration fires **razing**
It's so **exhilarating**, exciting, **invigorating**
Inviting and **stimulating**
I don't ever want to go

It so **indisputable** what this jam will do to you
Its certain you gonna like it from your **follicles** to cuticles
When ever we perform, this song they want it
Marquee above the entrance got our name on it
It's got flames on it, opposite of being **frigid**
If you're frozen or under the **tundra** come get with it
It'll thaw you out in a New York minute
Soon as we **decree** for the DJ to spin it
Got it on blast
Perpetuate the party yeah we wanna make it last
Indefatigable crowd no they never get tired
Like they drunk a hundred cups of coffee all stay wired
Hot enough to cause a riot, someone go and get a hose
We gonna soak you up with water that'll **saturate** your clothes

Devoid of **uniformity** not the same old song
Not **monotonous** the hotness is gonna blaze on, Yeah.

It's blazing hot in here - Hot
Temperatures changing
Hot
Ignited and flaming
Hot
There's no mistaking
Conflagration fires **razing**
It's so **exhilarating**, exciting, **invigorating**
Inviting and **stimulating**, I don't ever want to go

So hot in here, make me want to sing
Oo, oo, ooo
So hot in here, make me want to sing
Oo, oo, ooo
So hot in here, make me want to sing
Oo, oo, ooo
So hot in here, make me want to sing

"HOT" DICTIONARY

Conflagration (n) – inferno, fire.

During the summer, when the weather is hot and dry, the Western U.S. is often beset by a conflagration of brushfires.

Decree (n) – proclamation, ruling, declaration; an official statement that something must happen.

The king issued a decree stating that his birthday would be a holiday.

Devoid (adj) – lacking, deficient, without. Antonym: plentiful (adj).

Amish homes are devoid of appliances because their faith forbids the use of electricity.

Exhilarating (adj) – thrilling, elating. **Exhilarate** (v). Antonym: boring (adj).

Sky diving is exhilarating.

"HOT" DICTIONARY cont'd.

Fluctuation (n) – flux, variation; to vary irregularly; to rise and fall. Antonym: stability (n).

> Fluctuations in the temperature this summer have made it hard to get to the beach; one day it's hot, the next day you need a sweater.

Follicles (n), **Follicle** (n) – small holes present in skin, the best known are those though which hair grows, "hair follicles."

> He went bald, so he bought a formula that claims to revitalize your hair follicles.

Frigid (adj) – freezing, cold. Antonym: hot (adj).

> She resides in Florida during the winter because she dislikes the frigid New York winters.

Frustrating (v), **Frustrate** (v) – exasperating, vexing, annoying. Antonym: soothing (v).

> It's frustrating when I'm hungry and I find a long line at the cafeteria.

Fusion (n) – synthesize; blend or join together. **Fuse** (v). Antonym: separation (n).

> She liked his music because he fuses different styles.

Ignited (v), **Ignite** (v) – 1. light, kindle. Antonym: extinguish (v).

> She used a lighter to ignite the firewood.

Ignite (v) – 2. to initiate an angry or controversial situation. Antonym: pacify (v).

> Tensions were ignited when the protesters' petition was rejected by the city.

Illusion (n) – delusion, chimera; false impression; figment of your imagination. Antonym: reality (n).

> When you see a magician saw someone in half it is only an illusion they've created.

Indefatigable (adj) – unrelenting, tireless, determined; never willing to admit defeat.

She is an indefatigable lobbyist for education reform.

Indisputable (adj) – unquestionable, certain. Antonym: disputable (adj).

It is indisputable that The Yankees have won more championships than any other team in the history of baseball.

Invigorating (adj) – revitalizing, energizing. **Invigorate** (v). Antonym: draining (adj).

He was refreshed after he went for an invigorating run in the park.

Marquee (n) – canopy above an entrance; a shelter above a theater entrance.

When it began to rain she ran for shelter under the theater marquee.

Monotony (n) – repetitiveness, sameness. **Monotonous** (adj). Antonym: variety (n)

Sometimes the monotony of long drives makes me tired.

Perpetuate (v) – preserve, continue, maintain; make something last. **Perpetual** (adj). Antonym: terminate (v).

The local preservation society is working to perpetuate the community's history.

Perusing (v), **Peruse** (v) – scrutinize, examine; to read with care. Antonym: skim (v).

She spends her entire Sunday perusing the newspaper for interesting articles.

Profusion (n) – overabundance, excess, surplus, many; large amount. Antonym: dearth (n).

International copyright laws are being revised to stem the profusion of counterfeit goods.

"HOT" DICTIONARY cont'd.

Propagate (v) – reproduce, spread. Antonym: confine (v).

> Scientists working with endangered giant pandas are encouraging them to breed in order to propagate the species.

Proximity (n) – nearness, closeness in relation, immediacy. Antonym: distance (n).

> We can walk to the movie theater instead of driving there because of its close proximity to the house.

Pursuing (v), **Pursue** (v) – follow, chase; to go after something.

> He is pursuing a career in acting.

Razing (v), **Raze** (v) – level, burn, devastate, destroy; tear down. Antonym: build (v).

> The conflagration razed the town.

Rectify (v) – repair, fix; to correct or resolve a problem.

> When the blackout occurred the power plant's staff met to determine how they would rectify it.

Remedy (n) – cure, medicine.

> The best remedy for a broken heart is to find solace in your friends.

Saturate (v) – soak, drench. Antonym: dry (v).

> Coming in from a long jog, her uniform was saturated with sweat.

Seclusion (n) – isolation, privacy, solitude. **Seclude** (v). Antonym: company (n).

> To avoid the press, the actress went into seclusion.

Sedentary (adj) – inactive. Antonym: active (adj).

> His doctor recommended that the he modify his sedentary lifestyle, get off of the couch, and join a gym.

Stimulating (adj) – inspiring; thought provoking. **Stimulate** (v). Antonym: boring (adj).

She found their conversation about the upcoming election stimulating.

Tundra (n) – rolling, treeless plain in the North American arctic and Siberia.

My parents went to Alaska to watch caribou roaming the tundra.

Ungainly (adj) – awkward, clumsy, ungraceful. Antonym: graceful (adj).

Penguins walk in an ungainly manner on land, however, they swim gracefully through the water.

Uniformity (n) – standardization, regularity, consistency. **Uniform** (adj). Antonym: irregularity (n).

Restaurant chains strive to maintain the uniformity of their food at all of their locations.

Union (n) – combination, amalgamation, merger. Antonym: separation (n).

At my aunt's wedding the Justice of the Peace asked, "Is there anyone who objects to this union?"

Vacillation (n) – indecision, uncertainty; inability to decide. **Vacillate** (v). Antonym: decision (n).

They couldn't make up their minds and vacillated between getting a cat or a dog.

Wavering (v), **Waver** (v) – hesitate, hesitancy, fickle; inability to decide or focus. Antonym: deciding (v).

The mayor rebuked wavering council members for their hesitancy to support his position.

NOTES:

_____

_____

"HOT" SYNONYM MATCHING

Match the following Word$ with their synonyms. Note the letter of the matching synonym in the space adjacent to the word.

Vocabulary Words | **Synonyms**

1. _____ Conflagration
2. __y.___ Decree
3. _____ Devoid
4. __al___ Exhilarating
5. __s.___ Fluctuation
6. __q.___ Follicles
7. __d.___ Frigid
8. __a4.__ Frustrating
9. __1.___ Fusion
10. _____ Ignite
11. _____ Illusion
12. _____ Indefatigable
13. _____ Indisputable
14. _____ Invigorating
15. __d3__ Marquee
16. __h.___ Monotony
17. _____ Perpetuate
18. _____ Peruse
19. _____ Profusion
20. _____ Propagate
21. __a9__ Proximity
22. _____ Pursue

(a) arctic plain
(b) spread
(c) standardization
(d) cold
(e) awkward
(f) continue
(g) kindle
(h) repetitiveness
(i) follow
(j) inspire
(k) soak
(l) fire
(m) excess
(n) hesitate
(o) inactive
(p) correct
(q) holes in skin
(r) isolation
(s) variation
(t) join
(u) unrelenting
(v) delusion

Vocabulary Words	Synonyms
23. _____ Raze	(w) indecision
24. _____ Rectify	(x) revitalizing
25. __a9__ Remedy	(y) declaration
26. _____ Saturate	(z) level
27. __(__ Seclusion	(a1) thrilling
28. _____ Sedentary	(a2) lacking
29. _____ Stimulating	(a3) canopy
30. __a__ Tundra	(a4) annoying
31. _____ Ungainly	(a5) certain
32. _____ Uniformity	(a6) scrutinize
33. __a7__ Union	(a7) combination
34. _____ Vacillation	(a8) nearness
35. __9__ Waver	(a9) cure

NOTES:

_____
_____
_____
_____
_____
_____
_____
_____

"HOT" SENTENCE COMPLETION

Using a form or tense of the Word$ in the Bank, find the words which best complete the sentences below.

WORD BANK

Conflagration	Decree	Devoid	Exhilarating	Fluctuation
Follicles	Frigid	Frustrating	Fusion	Ignited
Illusion	Indefatigable	Indisputable	Invigorating	Marquee
Monotony	Perpetuate	Perusing	Profusion	Propagate
Proximity	Pursuing	Raze	Rectify	Remedy
Saturate	Seclusion	Sedentary	Stimulating	Tundra
Ungainly	Uniformity	Union	Vacillate	Wavering

1. During the debate, his opponent found his remarks to be _____, making it difficult for him to debate against him.

2. He is following his dream by _____ a career in law.

3. An open, rolling plain, there is little vegetation on the _____.

4. Her _____ were damaged over the years by the constant dying and straightening of her hair.

5. The _____ that razed the forest is thought to have been started by a cigarette.

6. The presidential candidates are _____ their ideas by making speeches throughout the country.

7. She was _____ by her little brother's refusal to move his feet off of her books.

8. My backpack was _____ because it had too much stuff in it.

9. The Olympic torch was _____ during the opening ceremony in Athens.

10. The _____ stated that the country would be handed over to its new government.

11. She enjoys the college classes that she's taking, and she finds them very _____.

12. Her income is never steady; it usually _____ between $40,000 and $100,000 a year.

13. It's as though he's an immovable, _____ blob; he's always vegging out in front of the boob tube.

14. We have to get that boy out of the house; he'd find my new morning exercise program _____.

15. The numbing _____ of her life bored her, eventually leading her to quit her job to travel around the world.

16. Working to figure out what was wrong, the technicians were doing everything they could to _____ the problem.

17. My grandmother believes that the best _____ for a cold is homemade chicken soup.

18. His plan to ride a ferret across the country defies logic, and is _____ of any sense.

19. She is an _____ competitor, who gives 100% of herself during every game.

20. In some cultures women are kept in _____ and are rarely seen in public.

27

"HOT" SENTENCE COMPLETION cont'd.

21. While I'm editing the book I need to _____ the exercises to verify that everything makes sense.

22. Alaska isn't always _____; as a matter of fact, during the summer it can get quite hot.

23. The building's manager decided to replace the _____ over the main entrance.

24. The best thing about the location of my office is its _____ to my house.

25. The studio released its latest movie and inundated the press with a _____ of PR materials.

26. I've heard that hang gliding is _____, and that there is no thrill that can compare.

27. At the end of the day I'm tired, and my concentration tends to _____.

28. His music is described as a _____ of hip hop and alternative styles.

29. The novel 1984 is a cautionary tale that describes the monotony of a society based on _____.

30. The aim of the preservation society is to _____ the culture and traditions of their country.

31. She is _____ between taking a job that is closer to home and a job that offers more money.

32. The next door neighbors _____ their house and are building an

entirely new one on the same foundation.

33. The massive corporate merger is reported to be a _____ of equals.

34. Mirages are only _____ caused by the heat rising off of the desert sand, which distorts the view of the horizon.

35. The tie-dying instructions require you to _____ the shirt with water before you place it in the dye.

NOTES:

"HOT" CROSSWORD PUZZLE

Use the synonyms provided in the clues to identify the Words that complete the crossword puzzle on the following page. The numbers run top-to-bottom and left-to-right

Across

1. Light, kindle
2. Follow, chase
3. Delusion, chimera; false impression
4. Unrelenting, tireless, determined
5. Standardization, regularity, consistency
6. Freezing, cold
7. Overabundance, excess, surplus, many
8. Inferno, fire
9. To be indecisive, to be uncertain
10. A small hole present in skin
11. Preserve, continue, maintain
12. Revitalize, energize
13. Isolation, privacy, solitude
14. Proclamation, ruling, declaration
15. Flux, variation
16. Reproduce, spread
17. Canopy above an entrance
18. Cure, medicine

Down

1. Lack, deficient; without something
2. Awkward, clumsy, ungraceful
3. Unquestionable, certain
4. Level, burn, devastate, destroy
5. Synthesize; blend or join together
6. Treeless arctic plain
7. Repair, fix, correct
8. Exasperating, vexing, annoying
9. Inspiring; thought provoking
10. Combination, amalgamation, merger
11. Thrilling, elating
12. Nearness, closeness in relation, immediacy
13. Soak, drench
14. Hesitant, fickle; inability to decide or focus
15. Inactive
16. Scrutinized, examined; read with care
17. Repetitiveness, sameness

"HOT" CROSSWORD PUZZLE

31

"HOT" SYNONYM SENTENCES

In the following sentences, use correct forms or tenses of the Word$ in the Bank to match the underlined synonyms, and write the correct word in the space provided below each sentence.

WORD BANK				
Conflagration	Decree	Devoid	Exhilarating	Fluctuation
Follicles	Frigid	Frustrating	Fusion	Ignited
Illusion	Indefatigable	Indisputable	Invigorating	Marquee
Monotony	Perpetuate	Perusing	Profusion	Propagate
Proximity	Pursuing	Raze	Rectify	Remedy
Saturate	Seclusion	Sedentary	Stimulating	Tundra
Ungainly	Uniformity	Union	Vacillate	Wavering

1. Stock prices <u>vary</u> day to day.
   _____

2. During the long winters the <u>arctic plain</u> is barren and cold.
   _____

3. The <u>fire</u> spread quickly, and thankfully no one was hurt.
   _____

4. I enjoy reading the newspaper because I find it <u>thought-provoking</u>.
   _____

5. Her mother always said, "<u>Follow</u> your dreams."
   _____

6. He <u>lit</u> the campfire with a match.
   _____

7. "We will do whatever is necessary to <u>correct</u> the situation."
   _____

8. The researcher <u>scrutinized</u> the results of the study prior to making any announcements regarding its outcome.
   _____

9. She was an <u>unrelenting</u> protester against animal testing, and didn't end her boycott until the company agreed to release its monkeys.
   _____

10. When he does his homework, he likes to <u>isolate</u> himself.
    _____

11. She had made her dream come true; her name was in lights on the theater <u>canopy</u>.
    _____

12. It isn't always easy making choices, and sometimes I <u>am uncertain</u>.
    _____

13. I'm not sure that those dance lessons are helping him out very much; he's still looks pretty <u>awkward</u> when he does his routine.
    _____

14. I find it <u>exasperating</u> when people jostle me to get into the subway.
    _____

15. This summer she has a job in a factory putting popsicle sticks in molds all day, and she said that the <u>repetition</u> is going to drive her crazy.
    _____

16. As a result of his <u>inactive</u> lifestyle, he was 50 pounds overweight.
    _____

17. A native of southern California, he finds Massachusetts <u>cold</u>.
    _____

"HOT" SYNONYM SENTENCES cont'd.

18. The best <u>cure</u> for the flu is to drink lots of fluids and to get some rest.

   _____

19. He <u>hesitated</u> before asking her out on a date.

   _____

20. The community group was the result a <u>combination</u> of different factions from throughout the area.

   _____

21. When manufacturing consumer goods, it is important to have a measure of <u>standardization</u> to ensure that each item produced is the same.

   _____

22. Despite the <u>overabundance</u> of TV channels, I can never find anything to watch.

   _____

23. My dad says, "Of course you can't find anything good on, TV is <u>lacking</u> of anything intellectually stimulating."

   _____

24. Our parents bought our house based on its <u>being close</u> to a good school.

   _____

25. He was traumatized at the circus when he was a kid, and he now lived in <u>continual</u> fear of little dogs riding bicycles.

   _____

26. After the hurricane severely damaged the house, we needed to <u>level</u> it, and build a new one.

   _____

27. The plaintiff's lawyer stated, "Given the facts of the case, it is <u>unquestionable</u> that my client is innocent."

    _____

28. The special interest group worked to <u>spread</u> rumors about the competing candidate.

    _____

29. The sponge won't hold any more liquid, it's <u>soaked</u>.

    _____

30. We went to an interesting restaurant last night where the cuisine is a <u>blend</u> of Cuban and Chinese foods.

    _____

31. Four-foot-three inches tall and ninety pounds, he had no <u>delusions</u> that he was going to win a round against the World Heavyweight Champion.

    _____

32. My visit to the day spa was <u>revitalizing</u>.

    _____

33. My friend said that bungee jumping in New Zealand was <u>thrilling</u>, although I'm not sure that I'd want to try it.

    _____

34. The crazy king issued a <u>proclamation</u> stating that all of the country's citizens were required to wear their socks on the outside of their shoes.

    _____

35. If you look closely at your arm, you can see the <u>holes</u> in your skin.

    _____

MIDDLETON & WILLIE, TOO "HOT"

- Keith London

Brooklyn – Keith Middleton and Rodney Willie are two of the most exhilarating artists we've worked with yet. Igniting the scene with their profusion of beats and indisputable rhymes, they fuse music from around the world in a conflagration of genius and decree it their own.

I also need to acknowledge the indefatigable and stimulating Avon Marshall who sang the lead on this track. Devoid of any the self-consciousness that becomes so ungainly in a vocal booth, his talent is no illusion. Even as the temperature in the studio fluctuated, he stayed true.

Their music shatters the monotony that saturates the airwaves today, razing the state of uniformity that is so perpetually frustrating. Invigorating and a remedy to rectify the soul, it's impossible for me to be sedentary when I'm listening to their tracks.

Successfully pursuing their music careers and propagating their reputations, you'll see their names on a marquee, or when you're perusing the bins for CDs. Having worked in close proximity with them, I can tell you that they are the perfect union of talents, and there is no vacillating on this, with Rodney's mile-long dreds, his follicles are ready for prime time. Far from seeking seclusion on the frigid tundra, these boys aren't wavering, they're making it happen.

> Now, refer to the article you've just read to select the statements that best describe the author's remarks. Circle the letter that corresponds to the correct answer.

Question 1

(a) Keith Middleton and Rodney Willie are exhilarated.

(b) The author enjoys working with Rodney & Keith.

(c) Keith & Rodney get excited when they work with fire.

(d) The artists are exhilarated to work with the author.

Question 2

(a) The artists utilize fire as a metaphor for their music.

(b) Rodney Willie & Keith Middleton are pyromaniacs.

(c) The author is using fire as a metaphor to describe the intensity of the artists' music.

(d) Keith and Rodney use too many beats, and rhymes that you cannot question.

Question 3

(a) The artists combine different musical styles to create a unique sound.

(b) The author witnessed the artists using a blast furnace to forge new music.

(c) Rodney and Keith combine different musical genres by starting conflagrations.

(d) Keith Middleton & Rodney Willie are in a position to issue official declarations.

Question 4

(a) Avon is a tireless and inspiring performer.

(b) Avon leads Rodney Willie and Keith Middleton.

(c) The singer who provides the lead vocal track for "Hot" is never willing to admit defeat.

(d) The singer who provides the lead vocal track for "Hot" is unrelenting and thought provoking.

Question 5

(a) Avon does not use thaumaturgy to enhance his performances.

(b) The singer's awkwardness in the recording session indicated a lack of any discernable talent.

MIDDLETON & WILLIE, TOO "HOT" cont'd.

(c) The changes in the production studio's temperature caused Avon to be candid.

(d) Avon Marshall is a genuinely gifted performer, and he is very comfortable in the studio.

Question 6

(a) Keith & Rodney are drenched by sameness.

(b) Keith & Rodney write music that mixes it up.

(c) Keith & Rodney write music that breaks glass.

(d) Keith & Rodney compose music that is on par with other performers you hear on the radio today.

Question 7

(a) The artists' music forges it own path, breaking the typical boundaries present in today's play lists.

(b) The author is exasperated by the artists' music causing fires in places where standardization is the rule.

(c) The artists are continually vexed by the devastation caused by today's radios.

(d) Rodney and Keith want to encourage standardization and seek to preserve their exasperation.

Question 8

(a) The author finds the artists' music energizing, and believes that it can be used to cure illnesses.

(b) The author finds the artists energized.

(c) The artists want to be seated, but the author is insisting that they get up.

(d) The author finds the artists' music energizing, and regards it as a metaphorical cure for one's state of well being.

Question 9

(a) Rodney and Keith are spreading their music and following their reputations.

(b) The artists are making it in the music industry and are building their reputations.

(c) Keith and Rodney are following a career in music and are looking to reproduce their reputations.

(d) The author feels that the artists are followers working to spread their reputation.

Question 10

(a) The author expects the artists to perform publicly, sell their CDs in stores, and to become famous.

(b) The author expects the artists to put their names on a canopy, and anticipates that readers will scrutinize their CDs.

(c) The artists anticipate that you will soon be shopping for CDs.

(d) None of the above.

Question 11

(a) Rodney and Keith work too closely together, and won't make any decisions.

(b) Rodney's hair is very long, and consequently, his follicles belong on TV.

(c) The artists and author have worked closely, giving the author an appreciation for the artists' talents, and their preparedness for stardom.

(d) The artists have worked closely with the author and have expressed a predisposition for prime-time television.

Question 12

(a) Keith and Rodney are looking forward to their trip to Alaska.

(b) Rodney and Keith are working hard to achieve stardom.

(c) The artists aren't hesitant in their ambition to visit the tundra.

(d) All of the above.

MIA JOHNSON & THE MIA JOHNSON BAND
ALREADY TAKEN

"ALREADY TAKEN" LISTENING EXERCISE

Listen to "Already Taken" all the way through at least once. Then listen to the song again, and in the spaces provided below, list the Word$ that you hear.

NOTES:

_____
_____
_____
_____

"ALREADY TAKEN" LYRICS

by Mia Johnson

You are standing next to me
And at this **proximity**
You are **deleterious**
To my **tranquility**
I catch a whiff of your **aroma**
That is so **inimitably** you
And the **delirium** that follows
Is **tortuous** pure **ecstasy**

Cuz you are so off-limits
And I am really just not kidding
I repeat this like an **incantation**
Cuz I see you **inevitably** each day
No matter how **enamored** I am of you
It cannot change a thing in this world
Because you are, already taken by best friend

They've been together for three years
A **consummate** and **interminable** pairing
But now **conversely** their love appears
To be a **senescent** habit they're sharing

And I **intuit** your attraction to me
That you **laboriously shroud**
And we keep our **reticence synchronously**
Because it's perfectly **futile** to say it out loud

Cuz you are so off-limits
And I am really just not kidding
I repeat this like an **incantation**
Cuz I see you **inevitably** each day
No matter how **enamored** I am of you
It cannot change a thing in this world

"ALREADY TAKEN" LYRICS cont'd.

Because you are, already taken by my best friend

And this **amorous** way I feel about you now
Could just be
Some undue **infatuation**
Just not worth losing my best friend, to me
So I simply have to learn how to **acquiesce** in
This **awkward** situation

Cuz you are so off-limits
And I am really just not kidding
I repeat this like an **incantation**
Cuz I see you **inevitably** each day
No matter how **enamored** I am of you
It cannot change a thing in this world
Cuz you are already taken
Yeah you are already taken
Yeah you are already taken

"ALREADY TAKEN" DICTIONARY

Acquiesce (v) – assent; agree without protest. Antonym: protest (v), resist (v).

    He acquiesced to his boss' demands.

Amorous (adj) – affectionate; relating to love or romantic desire. Antonym: hateful (adj).

    The lovers amorously gazed at one another.

Aroma (n) – fragrant, pleasing scent. **Aromatic** (adj). Antonym: stench (n).

    The aroma of her perfume was sweet and exotic.

Awkward (adj) – 1. to be uncomfortable in a situation. Antonym: relaxed (adj).

    It was awkward to see my best friend at the mall with my older brother.

Awkward (adj) – 2. clumsy; difficult to handle. Antonym: graceful (adj).

The clown's giant shoes caused him to walk awkwardly.

Consummate (adj) – archetypal, standard, picture-perfect.

A skilled cook and decorator, he is the consummate homemaker.

Conversely (adv) – in opposition; contrary. **Converse** (adj). Antonym: analogously (adv).

He said that if he passes the final he'd receive a B in Algebra; conversely, if he failed the final he'd receive a D.

Deleterious (adj) – harmful, damaging. Antonym: helpful (adj).

Smoking is deleterious to your health.

Delirium (n) – confusion, disorientation. Antonym: clarity (n).

She was in a state of delirium after meeting her favorite movie star.

Ecstasy (n) – rapture, joy, happiness. **Ecstatic** (adj). Antonym: despair (n).

He was ecstatic when he won a trip to the Bahamas.

Enamored (v) – smitten; in love with; also idiomatically used in reference to appreciation for an object. Antonym: repelled (v).

Enamored with the dress, she decided to buy it for the prom.

Futile (adj) – useless, hopeless, pointless. **Futility** (n). Antonym: useful (adj).

It would be futile to engage Superman in an arm wrestling contest.

Incantation (n) – chant; singing magic spells.

The witch's incantation turned him into a toad.

Inevitably (adv) – certain, unavoidable. **Inevitable** (adj).

It was inevitable that airlines would lose business after they raised airfares dramatically.

"ALREADY TAKEN" DICTIONARY cont'd.

Infatuation (n) – fixation, obsession; an engrossing passion. Antonym: indifference (n).

He was infatuated with her and had pictures of her all over his house.

Inimitably (adv) – uniquely, distinctly; not able to be imitated. **Inimitable** (adj). Antonym: commonly (adv).

Snoop Dogg is known for his inimitable style.

Interminable (adj) – endless, incessant. Antonym: finite (adj).

Although the lame movie was short, it seemed interminable to the audience.

Intuit (v) – perceive, insight, instinct; knowing without logic. **Intuition** (n).

I can usually intuit when someone is not telling me the truth.

Laboriously (adv) – backbreaking, tedious, grueling; demanding a great deal of work or care. **Laborious** (adj). Antonym: easily (adv).

The designer laboriously hand stitched pearls onto the dress.

Proximity (n) – nearness; closeness in relation. Antonym: distance (n).

When driving, you need to judge the proximity of surrounding cars.

Reticence (n) – reluctance, unwillingness; inclination to silence. **Reticent** (adj). Antonym: willingness (n).

Being very shy, she was reticent to participate in the class discussion.

Senescent (adj) – aging; decaying over time. Antonym: youthful (adj).

The twelve-year-old dog was senescent.

Shroud (n) – 1. blanket, veil, cover; a draped material that envelops an object.

At the funeral the widow wore a shroud that veiled her face.

Shroud (v) – 2. hide, cover; shield from view. Antonym: uncover (v).
The leaves shrouded the driveway, making it difficult see the garage.

Situation (n) – predicament; circumstances at a given moment; a state of affairs.
Prior to arresting the protester, the police officer assessed the situation.

Synchronously (adv) – simultaneously, concurrently. **Synchronous** (adj). Antonym: sequentially (adv).
My favorite TV shows are aired synchronously, which forces me to miss one.

Tortuous (adj) – 1. arduous, trying, difficult. Antonym: easy (adj).
Immigrants find that applying for a green card is a tortuous process.

Tortuous (adj) – 2. characterized by curves. Antonym: straight (adj).
The winding mountain pass was tortuous.

Tranquility (n) – peaceful, calm. **Tranquil** (adj). Antonym: chaos (n).
Dotted with tranquil lakes, the Adirondack mountains are a great place to spend the summer.

NOTES:

"ALREADY TAKEN" SYNONYM MATCHING

Match the following Word$ with their synonyms. Note the letter of the matching synonym in the space adjacent to the word.

	Vocabulary Words	**Synonyms**
1.	_____ Acquiesce	(a) arduous
2.	_____ Amorous	(b) spell
3.	_____ Aroma	(c) endless
4.	_____ Awkward	(d) certainly
5.	_____ Consummate	(e) contrary
6.	_____ Conversely	(f) simultaneously
7.	_____ Deleterious	(g) agree
8.	_____ Delirium	(h) predicament
9.	_____ Ecstasy	(i) perceive
10.	_____ Enamored	(j) joy
11.	_____ Futile	(k) pleasing scent
12.	_____ Incantation	(l) nearness
13.	_____ Inevitably	(m) covered
14.	_____ Infatuation	(n) archetypal
15.	_____ Inimitable	(o) smitten
16.	_____ Interminable	(p) peaceful
17.	_____ Intuit	(q) aging
18	_____ Laborious	(r) uncomfortable
19.	_____ Proximity	(s) fixation
20.	_____ Reticence	(t) unique
21.	_____ Senescent	(u) affectionate
22	_____ Shrouded	(v) grueling
23.	_____ Situation	(w) reluctance

	Vocabulary Words	**Synonyms**
24.	_____ Synchronously	(x) useless
25.	_____ Tortuous	(y) harmful
26.	_____ Tranquility	(z) disorientation

"ALREADY TAKEN" SENTENCE COMPLETION

Using a form or tense of the Word$ in the Bank, find the words which best complete the sentences below.

Word Bank				
Acquiesce	Amorous	Aroma	Awkward	Consummate
Conversely	Deleterious	Delirium	Ecstasy	Enamored
Futile	Incantation	Inevitably	Infatuation	Inimitable
Interminable	Intuit	Laborious	Proximity	Reticence
Senescent	Shroud	Situation	Synchronously	Tortuous
Tranquility				

1. We live in close _____ to our neighbors.

2. Time never stops, and _____, everything changes.

3. She was in a state of _____ when she was accepted to Yale.

4. In the United States people drive on the right hand side of the road; _____ in Britain you would drive on the left hand side.

5. The hikers' route through the mountain pass was _____.

6. When the boxer regained consciousness after getting knocked out, he awoke in a state of _____.

"ALREADY TAKEN" SENTENCE COMPLETION cont'd.

7. The president of the student government _____ to the demands of the student body.

8. Professionals working in the fashion industry strive to create their own _____ style.

9. His father's stories about his childhood were _____.

10. Given the fact that she can't sing, it's _____ for her to try out for "American Idol," unless she wants to be on the "blooper" reel!

11. The hood of the explorer's parka _____ her face.

12. My mother became _____ with my father the first time she saw him.

13. I love the _____ of the ocean when the weather is calm.

14. She could _____ that I was worried about my upcoming exam.

15. Feeding a dog chocolate can be _____ to its health.

16. She was _____ with the her favorite band, and she listened to their CD constantly.

17. The _____ of freshly baked pastries filled the air.

18. She created an awkward _____ by asking me to help her cheat on the test.

19. It was _____ for me to see my dad dating after my parents got divorced.

20. The witches chanted an _____ around a boiling potion.

21. Always the _____ professional, she managed the meeting flawlessly.

22. After the banquet, he _____ washed every dish by hand.

23. She was _____ to speak in front of the class.

24. On some SUVs the front wheels move _____ with the back wheels.

25. The fourteen-year-old cat is _____.

26. The two lovers gazed at one another _____.

NOTES:

"ALREADY TAKEN" CROSSWORD PUZZLE

Use the synonyms provided in the clues to identify the words that complete the crossword puzzle on the following page. The numbers run top-to-bottom and left-to-right.

Across

1. Affectionate; relating to love or romantic desire
2. Reluctance, unwillingness; inclination to silence
3. Archetypal, standard, picture-perfect
4. Chant; singing magic spells
5. Confusion, disorientation
6. Nearness; closeness in relation
7. Clumsy; difficult to handle or manage
8. Peaceful, calm
9. Aging; decaying over time
10. Rapture, joy, happiness
11. Tedious, grueling
12. Certainly, unavoidably
13. Assent; agree without protest
14. Blanket, veil, cover (or) hide, cover

Down

1. Fragrant, pleasing scent
2. Perceive, know without logic
3. Useless, hopeless, pointless
4. Endless, incessant
5. Harmful, damaging
6. Fixation, obsession; an engrossing passion
7. Uniquely, distinctly
8. In opposition; on the contrary
9. Predicament, circumstances
10. Smitten; in love with
11. Simultaneously, concurrently
12. Arduous, trying, difficult

"ALREADY TAKEN" CROSSWORD PUZZLE

"ALREADY TAKEN" SYNONYM SENTENCES

In the following sentences, use correct forms or tenses of the Word$ in the Bank to match the underlined synonyms, and write the correct word in the space provided below each sentence.

WORD BANK

Acquiesce	Amorous	Aroma	Awkward	Consummate
Conversely	Deleterious	Delirium	Ecstasy	Enamored
Futile	Incantation	Inevitably	Infatuation	Inimitable
Interminable	Intuit	Laborious	Proximity	Reticence
Senescent	Shroud	Situation	Synchronously	Tortuous
Tranquility				

1. The bakery was filled with the <u>scent</u> of fresh bread.

   _____

2. If you don't have a CD player it's <u>useless</u> to try to listen to a CD.

   _____

3. She discovered an <u>affectionate</u> love letter in her locker.

   _____

4. The sorceress' <u>spell</u> made him fall in love with a chicken.

   _____

5. Her style is <u>unique</u>.

   _____

6. The <u>predicament</u> she found herself in was unsettling.

   _____

7. When two things occur at the same time they happen <u>simultaneously</u>.

   _____

52

8. She was <u>elated</u> when she found out that she had won the Nobel Prize.
   _____

9. Although she didn't tell him, he could <u>perceive</u> when she was mad at him.
   _____

10. Although my workout is only an hour long, it seems <u>endless</u>.
    _____

11. I am <u>obsessed</u> with romantic novels.
    _____

12. He <u>agreed</u> to their demands.
    _____

13. I am not <u>in love</u> with BMW's new designs.
    _____

14. Polished and poised, she was the <u>picture-perfect</u> professional.
    _____

15. They were the consummate odd couple; she was outgoing, and <u>in contrast</u>, he was very shy.
    _____

16. The bus was in such <u>close relation</u> to my car that it almost hit us.
    _____

17. After the accident, the driver was in a state of <u>confusion</u>.
    _____

18. When going on a first date I always feel <u>uncomfortable</u>.
    _____

"ALREADY TAKEN" SYNONYM SENTENCES cont'd.

20. I enjoy the <u>peacefulness</u> of a quiet afternoon.

    _____

21. It is <u>unavoidable</u> that children will grow up.

    _____

22. The old crumbling building is <u>decaying</u>.

    _____

23. He was <u>reluctant</u> to share his opinions with the class.

    _____

24. Often, the path to success is <u>arduous</u>.

    _____

25. The first snowfall of winter <u>covered</u> the hills.

    _____

26. Writing a novel by hand is a <u>grueling</u> task.

    _____

FIVE MINUTES WITH MIA JOHNSON

- Keith London & Rebecca Osleeb

Philly & NYC – We caught up with Philly's inimitable Mia Johnson and had the chance to discuss her tracks for DM. Although she's laboring through recording her first full-length album, she finally acquiesced to our requests for an interview. In particular, I wanted to talk about her ballad of futility in love, "Already Taken."

She sings about the consummate forbidden love, in which she is enamored with her best friend's man, and the awkward state that results. Reticent to discuss the object of her infatuation, she shrouded any clues by saying that the song was composed to capture "wanting what is difficult or impossible to get."

Notable for the musical tension, and conversely, the release of the track, "Already Taken" is an incantation that prompts memories of unrequited love. Ecstatic when taking in his aroma and delirious when in close proximity to him, her best friend's man is deleterious to Mia's former tranquility. The worst part is that she intuits he synchronously cares for her, even though his relationship with her best friend seems to be interminable and senescent. Inevitably, Mia sees that her amorous sentiment cannot be returned, and that she must move on. She turns a fine verse, and despite the tortuous events depicted by the song, her message is given with passion instead of despondency.

Although she has recorded two short CD's, Mia believes that her band's upcoming new album "will eclipse both of them in performance, sound quality, and production." While we're waiting, The Mia Johnson Band can be seen performing regularly at clubs across the country.

> Now, refer to the article you've just read to select the statements that best describe the authors' remarks. Circle the letter that corresponds to the correct answer.

Question 1

(a) Mia had plenty of time for the interview.

(b) She easily agreed to speak with the authors.

(c) After many requests, Mia agreed to do the interview with resignation.

(d) She was happy to take time away from her other projects.

Question 2

(a) Her current project is easy.

(b) Recording a full-length CD is grueling work.

(c) Recording a full-length CD is a tranquil experience.

(d) She wasn't occupied with any work other than recording "Already Taken."

FIVE MINUTES WITH MIA JOHNSON cont'd.

Question 3

(a) Mia isn't unique.

(b) Her style is widely copied and indistinguishable from other performers.

(c) She wants to leave Philadelphia.

(d) Mia has her own unique style.

Question 4

(a) She believes that love is readily attainable.

(b) Mia's song expresses the idea that there is "someone for everyone."

(c) "Already Taken" is a song about someone having stolen Mia's car.

(d) Mia sings about the difficulty of falling for someone who cannot reciprocate.

Question 5

(a) Mia is going to resign from her friendship.

(b) She acknowledges that she can't date her best friend's boyfriend.

(c) She recognized her love of sediment, and will hire a mover to bring it back.

(d) Mia decided to move out of her apartment.

Question 6

(a) Mia hates her best friend's boyfriend.

(b) She has no problem managing her situation.

(c) Her predicament has left her feeling uncomfortable.

(d) "Already Taken" describes how easy it can be to eat your best friend's lunch.

Question 7

(a) She did not readily discuss whom she may have written the song about.

(b) Mia was happy to tell the authors about the subject of her infatuation.

(c) The authors easily recognized the relationship that inspired the song.

(d) The song's lyrics are about things that are easily obtained.

Question 8

(a) Mia sings slowly.

(b) Her song only has one defining characteristic.

(c) "Already Taken" uses music to give the listener contrasting feelings.

(d) She wrote the music to soothe the listener.

Question 9

(a) "Already Taken" is like a mystical chant that causes the listener to remember.

(b) Mia is a witch.

(c) The authors can't remember anything.

(d) Her songs bring back memories of old friends.

Question 10

(a) Mia's lyrics describe how much she dislikes her best friend's boyfriend.

(b) Her girlfriend's boyfriend lives near her house.

(c) She sings about how badly her best friend's boyfriend smells.

(d) Mia is obsessed with her girlfriend's boyfriend, and the situation is awkward.

Question 11

(a) The boyfriend secretly likes her but can't break up with her friend.

(b) "Already Taken" describes a friendship that never ends.

(c) Mia needs to synchronize her watch.

(d) Her best friend has an odd scent.

Question 12

(a) The events discussed in "Already Taken" are readily resolved.

(b) Mia's storytelling reflects vitality rather than sadness.

(c) She's a depressing writer.

(d) Her song causes the listener to turn around.

JOE PASCARELL & THE MACHINE
SHINE

"SHINE" LISTENING EXERCISE

Listen to "Shine" all the way through at least once. Then listen to the song again, and in the spaces provided below, list the Word$ that you hear.

"SHINE" LYRICS

by Joe Pascarell

I feel **actuated**
I push through the **welter** of my life
Done with **vacillation**
I am **rabid** in my aim

No more **lurking**
Watch me
I will shine

Illuminate me

Don't **forsake** me
I am **resplendent** in the day
Scoff at all that's in my way
Captivated by this life
I will shine

Living in **seclusion**
Taking **solace** in my pain
Feeling like a **martyr**
I was **mired** in the **dregs**

No more **skulking**
Watch me
I will shine

Renovate me
Don't **forsake** me

I am **resplendent** in the day
Scoff at all that's in my way
Captivated by this life
Hold the fire inside
That's **inciting** me to shine

Illuminate me
Don't **forsake** me

I am **resplendent** in the day
Scoff at all that's in my way
Captivated by this life
Hold the fire inside

I am **resplendent** in the day
Scoff at all that's in my way
Captivated by this life
Hold the fire inside that's **inciting** me to shine
I am **resplendent** in the day

"SHINE" LYRICS cont'd.

Scoff at all that's in my way
Captivated by this life
Hold the fire inside that's **inciting** me to shine

I am **resplendent** in the day
Scoff at all that's in my way
Captivated by this life
Hold the fire inside that's **inciting** me to shine

I am **resplendent** in the day
Scoff at all that's in my way
Captivated by this life
Hold the fire inside that's **inciting** me to shine

"SHINE" DICTIONARY

Actuated (v), **Actuate** (v) – motivate; to put into action.
He was actuated by his drive to succeed.

Captivated (v), **Captivate** (v) – entrance, charm, enthrall. Antonym: repel (v).
The audience was captivated by her virtuoso performance.

Dregs (n) – sediment, muck, residue, remains, leftovers; what is left behind.
Finishing the entire bottle of chocolate milk, he drank it down to the dregs.

Forsake (v) – abandon, renounce, desert. **Forsaken** (v). Antonym: devote (v).
Religious leaders ask their followers not to forsake their faith.

Illuminate (v) – 1. enlighten, clarify; make something understood. **Illumination** (n). Antonym: obfuscate (v).
His novel illuminates the issues preceding The Civil War.

Illuminate (v) – 2. brighten. **Illumination** (n). Antonym: darken (v).
The footlights illuminated the stage.

Incite (v) – compel, spur, impel, provoke, goad; to cause. Antonym: soothe (v).
The jury's controversial verdict incited a riot.

Lurking (v), **Lurk** (v) – prowl, hide; lie in wait; move about stealthily or undetected. Antonym: parade (v).
He was seen lurking around the parking lot before the truck was stolen.

Martyr (n) – one who is subjugated; one who endures pain or suffers voluntarily typically to incite change. Antonym: oppressor (n).
She fought for women's rights all of her life and died a martyr for the cause.

Mired (adj) – 1. caught up; in a difficult situation.
She was mired in the conflict between her parents.

Mired (adj) – 2. trapped by a thick substance. **Mire** (n). Antonym: unhindered (adj).
His shoes became mired in the mud.

Rabid (adj) – 1. extreme, fanatical. Antonym: casual (adj).
He was a rabid Yankees fan, and never missed a game.

Rabid (adj) – 2. a state of infection with rabies. Antonym: healthy (adj).
The dog that bit her was rabid, so she needed a tetanus shot.

Renovate (v) – refurbish, restore. **Renovation** (n). Antonym: demolish (v).
They decided to renovate the hundred-year-old house rather than demolish it.

Resplendent (adj) – dazzling, stunning, glorious, brilliant. Antonym: dull (adj).
She was resplendent in her sequined gown.

"SHINE" DICTIONARY cont'd.

Scoff (v) – mock, ridicule; make fun of. Antonym: encourage (v).

The critics scoffed at the comic's attempt to play a dramatic role.

Seclusion (n) – isolation, privacy, solitude. Antonym: company (n).

Whenever he was depressed he avoided his friends and went into seclusion.

Skulking (v), **Skulk** (v) – creep, loiter, sneak; to move furtively or secretly. Antonym: parade (v).

The spy skulked through the city's streets hoping he wouldn't be detected.

Solace (n) – comfort, support. Antonym: distress (n).

After her husband left her she found solace in writing.

Vacillation (n) – indecision, uncertainty; inability to decide. **Vacillate** (v). Antonym: decision (n).

He vacillated between the candidates.

Welter (n) – turmoil; bewildering jumble; a confused mass. Antonym: order (n).

A welter of decade-old newspapers is piled in the garage

"SHINE" SYNONYM MATCHING

Match the following Word$ with their synonyms. Note the letter of the matching synonym in the space adjacent to the word.

Vocabulary Words	Synonyms
1. _____Actuate	(a) abandon
2. _____Captivated	(b) sediment
3. _____Dregs	(c) comfort
4. _____Forsake	(d) isolation

5.	_____Illuminate		(e)	lie-in-wait
6.	_____Incite		(f)	dazzling
7.	_____Lurk		(g)	indecision
8.	_____Martyred		(h)	caught up
9.	_____Mired		(i)	refurbish
10.	_____Rabid		(j)	sneak
11.	_____Renovate		(k)	confusion
12.	_____Resplendent		(l)	clarify
13.	_____Scoff		(m)	charmed
14.	_____Seclusion		(n)	fanatical
15.	_____Skulk		(o)	motivate
16.	_____Solace		(p)	goad
17.	_____Vacillation		(q)	mock
18.	_____Welter		(r)	subjugated

"SHINE" SENTENCE COMPLETION

Using a form or tense of the Word$ in the Bank, find the words which best complete the sentences below.

WORD BANK				
Actuated	Captivated	Dregs	Forsake	Illuminate
Inciting	Lurking	Martyr	Mired	Rabid
Renovate	Resplendent	Scoff	Seclusion	Skulking
Solace	Vacillation	Welter		

1. Her children gave her _____ after her husband's death.

2. The demonstrator was overrun by government forces and died a _____ for his cause.

"SHINE" SENTENCE COMPLETION cont'd.

3. Paparazzi often _____ in the bushes around celebrities' homes, waiting to ambush them.

4. He was so embarrassed after pouring a drink down the front of his pants that he _____ away from the party.

5. She was attacked by a bloodthirsty hamster when she was a child, and she's had a _____ hatred of them ever since.

6. Critics _____ at Henry Ford's early attempts to build a car.

7. He was fired for _____ co-workers to rebel against the new company rules.

8. The story and the beauty of the film _____ audiences.

9. She _____ between deciding to go to Florida and going to California.

10. The entire building was _____ after asbestos was found in the walls.

11. Their strong commitment to their community _____ them to volunteer.

12. I would never _____ my family.

13. The queen wore a _____ jewel encrusted gown.

14. Seeking _____, the reclusive star flew to a private island.

15. At the garage sale there was a _____ of CDs and cassettes to look through.

16. The diary she left behind _____ her thinking and clarified why she ran off with the guy who runs the deli.

17. As the horse pulled the wagon its wheels became _____ in the mud.

18. She drank the chocolate milk down to the _____.

NOTES:

"SHINE" CROSSWORD PUZZLE

Use the synonyms provided in the clues to identify the words that complete the crossword puzzle on the following page. The numbers run top-to-bottom and left-to-right.

Across

1. Compel, spur, impel, provoke, goad; to cause
2. Abandon, renounce, desert
3. Entranced, charmed, enthralled
4. Caught up; in a difficult situation (or) trapped by a thick substance
5. Dazzling, stunning, glorious, brilliant
6. Creep, loiter, sneak; to move furtively or secretly
7. One who endures pain or suffers voluntarily typically to incite change
8. Refurbish, restore

Down

1. Enlighten, clarify (or) brighten
2. Mock, ridicule; make fun of
3. Motivate; to put into action
4. Inability to decide.
5. Turmoil; bewildering jumble; a confused mass
6. Sediment, muck, residue, remains, leftovers; what is left behind
7. Extreme, fanatical (or) a state of infection with rabies
8. Prowl, hide; lie in wait
9. Comfort, support
10. Isolation, privacy, solitude

"SHINE" CROSSWORD PUZZLE

67

"SHINE" SYNONYM SENTENCES

In the following sentences, use correct forms or tenses of the Word$ in the Bank to match the underlined synonyms, and write the correct word in the space provided below each sentence.

WORD BANK				
Actuated	Captivated	Dregs	Forsake	Illuminate
Inciting	Lurking	Martyr	Mired	Rabid
Renovate	Resplendent	Scoff	Seclusion	Skulking
Solace	Vacillation	Welter		

1. He decided to <u>refurbish</u> the house.

   _____

2. Her diamond earrings were <u>dazzling</u>.

   _____

3. He <u>couldn't decide</u> between having smooth or chunky peanut butter.

   _____

4. His blue eyes <u>enthralled</u> the girls.

   _____

5. The girls <u>mocked</u> his attempt to join the field hockey team.

   _____

6. The professor <u>clarified</u> the themes conveyed in Shakespeare' plays.

   _____

7. The prisoner was placed in <u>isolation</u> after disobeying the warden.

   _____

8. I found the cat <u>hiding</u> in the bushes, stalking the birds.

   _____

9. In an effort to <u>motivate</u> the players, the coach gave an impassioned speech at half time.

   _____

10. She found <u>comfort</u> in her friends after losing her job.

    _____

11. I've been <u>caught up</u> in work at the studio.

    _____

12. The escaped convict was found <u>sneaking</u> around the city.

    _____

13. The professor's office was a <u>confusion</u> of books, papers and scientific bric-a-brac.

    _____

14. We arrived late to the sale, and the earlier shoppers only left behind the <u>remains</u> of what the store had offer.

    _____

15. She is a <u>fanatical</u> basketball fan.

    _____

16. He was <u>spurring</u> the crowd to riot.

    _____

17. Would you <u>abandon</u> your beliefs for money?

    _____

18. He went to prison for speaking his mind about the government, and <u>subjugated</u> himself for his beliefs.

    _____

PASCARELL'S DEFINED MIND "SHINE"S

- Keith London

NYC – Although Joe Pascarell has captivated audiences with his band The Machine for over 10 years, he has not forsaken his own art, and created the resplendent anthem "Shine" with Defined Mind. Here is the story of how fans everywhere lucked into Joe following his melodic muse.

Having started The Machine with Todd Cohen, Joe scoffed at taking a traditional career, but mired in the welter of youth, he vacillated between jobs while his aspirations evolved. He wasn't a martyr or in the dregs, but he wasn't incited by the rabid pursuit of fame and self-orientation that marks many performers, and it took time for his calling to take shape. Alternately a premier auto mechanic (he use to create and work on blown Porsches) and a landscaper, his path couldn't have been less clear. However, fortunately for us, he was still young when his talent made itself apparent to him and others, and people soon sought him out.

Joe was actuated by a love of the music and a desire to share it with audiences, but it took Todd to illuminate Joe's perspective. Their band was different from the ones that many of us were in when we were in school, more capable, more imaginative, tighter. It didn't take long for Todd to ask Joe to dedicate himself full time to making the band work.

With a renovated sense of purpose Joe invested himself wholly, and the natural comfort he has on stage ceased to lurk in the shadows. Never one seek seclusion or to skulk, Joe didn't try to find solace in the spotlight the way other artists do; his ease was simply the result of his passion for his craft, whatever the venue. Although he was always immensely grateful for the audience's appreciation of his talents, when he was on stage the world didn't distract him. It was always first and foremost about the music.

10 years later, it still is... "Shine" announces that Joe's focus is as clear as ever, and that his best work is still yet to come.

Knowledge is a State of Mind™

Now, refer to the article you've just read to select the statements that best describe the author's remarks. Circle the letter that corresponds to the correct answer.

Question 1
(a) Joe has held audiences as captives.
(b) His performances have enthralled audiences.
(c) He has a 10-year-old machine that captures audiences.
(d) The Machine hasn't captivated audiences.

Question 2
(a) He has abandoned his individual pursuits in deference to the band.
(b) The Machine worked with Defined Mind on "Shine."
(c) "Shine" is the product of Joe's individual creativity.
(d) Joe has been trying to get out of a machine for 10 years.

Question 3
(a) His music dazzles you.
(b) Joe's national anthem is "Shine."
(c) He created something that sparkles brilliantly.
(d) The song "Shine" is a glorious, brilliant declaration.

Question 4
(a) The career path he chose was not traditional.
(b) He mocked his career path.
(c) Todd Cohen ridiculed Joe's career choice.
(d) His career path was traditional.

Question 5
(a) Joe was caught in a mire when he was young.
(b) He is confused.

PASCARELL'S DEFINED MIND "SHINES"; cont'd.

 (c) His path unclear, he struggled with the confusion of youth.

 (d) When Joe was young, his welter was mired.

Question 6

 (a) Joe moved between jobs while he was finding himself.

 (b) Jobs precluded him from developing his music.

 (c) He aspired to evolve.

 (d) Moving between jobs caused Joe to aspire.

Question 7

 (a) He subjugated himself for a cause.

 (b) His drinking became a problem because he always drank to the dregs.

 (c) Joe found himself in sediment.

 (d) During his period of indecision he wasn't suffering.

Question 8

 (a) Joe did not want to fanatically chase fame and fortune.

 (b) His motivation was to incite.

 (c) He sought fame, but it took time for it to take shape.

 (d) Joe was rabid and self-oriented.

Question 9

 (a) He was the first mechanic to blow up a Porsche.

 (b) Joe was a great mechanic that worked on Porsches.

 (c) Joe was a mechanic and a landscaper at the same time.

 (d) He was a landscaper who blew up Porsches.

Question 10

 (a) Todd brought Joe some lighting fixtures.

(b) Joe was an actuary.

(c) It was dark, and Joe asked Todd for additional illumination.

(d) His motivation was his love of music, and Todd showed him the way.

Question 11

(a) Joe and Todd's band did renovations.

(b) Joe's hiding in the shadows became his trademark.

(c) He didn't seek the limelight, but he was comfortable there.

(d) His isolation caused him to seek the comfort of the spotlight.

Question 12

(a) Joe was immense.

(b) His audience preferred the Grateful Dead.

(c) He was easily distracted on stage.

(d) None of the above.

NINA ZEITLIN
WHY DIDN'T YOU TELL ME

"WDTYM" LISTENING EXCERCISE

Listen to "Why Didn't You Tell Me" all the way through at least once. Then listen to the song again, and in the spaces provided below, list the Word$ that you hear.

NOTES:

_____

_____

"WDYTM" LYRICS

by Nina Zeitlin & Matt Kelly

How come I didn't know you'd be so **sensual**
Why didn't you tell me about your **flagrant** style
Maybe you weren't **cognizant** of anything
How can I make you mine for a while (yeah)

Every single guy that I was with before
Was **crass** and **craven** and insecure
I need a man that knows how to **collaborate**
Instead of someone who just makes me **irate**

Tell me how to **entice** you
I really like you
I have an **addiction** to your **complicit** smile
It's like an **affliction**
With so much **conviction**
I'll tell you a million times that you're mine (yeah)

Sammy thought that he was so **profound**
But he couldn't **assay** the deepest thing around (yeah)
From the **revelation** that I had figured him out
Too **stolid**, **sinister** and on the way out

Tell me how to **entice** you
I really like you
I have a **conjecture** about your **alluring** eyes
It's like an **affliction**
With so much **conviction**
I'll tell you a million times that you're mine (yeah)

(I said) I said
Tell me how to **decoy** you
I really enjoy you
I have an **obsession** with your **comely** smile

"WDYTM" LYRICS cont'd.

It is my mission
My **predisposition**
I have these feelings that I just can't **surmise** (yeah)

How come I didn't know you'd be so **sensual**
Why didn't you tell me about your **flagrant** style
Maybe you weren't **cognizant** of anything
How can I make you mine for a while (yeah)
Mine for a while (yeah), mine for a while (yeah)
How can I make you mine for a while (yeah)

"WDYTM" DICTIONARY

Addiction (n) – dependence; a habitual, compulsive need. **Addict** (n).
> When he was younger he was addicted to sugar.

Affliction (n) – illness; cause of suffering; burden. **Afflicted** (adj).
> Afflicted with arthritis, she found it difficult to walk.

Alluring (v) – appealing, tempting. **Allure** (n).
> He found her distinctive attitude alluring, and asked her to join him for dinner.

Assay (v) – test, analyze, evaluate, determine.
> It was necessary to assay the bracelet to determine its gold content.

Cognizant (adj) – aware of; to know of something. Antonym: ignorant (adj).
> His mirrors were not adjusted properly, so he was not cognizant that he had hit the cones during his driving test.

Comely (adj) – attractive, agreeable. Antonym: homely (adj).
> She was quite comely, and he noticed her the moment she swept into the room.

Complicit (adj) – involvement in, complacent regarding, or ignoring the progress of, activity that is improper. **Complicity** (n).

She worked at the store and turned the alarm off for her partners, so she was arrested for her complicity in the burglary.

Conjecture (v) – opine, guess, contemplate. Antonym: know (v).

We don't know what caused the accident, we can only conjecture.

Conviction (n) – 1. strongly opinion or belief. Antonym: vacillation (n).

It is his conviction that that murderers should face the death penalty.

Conviction (n) – 2. a judgment that one is guilty of a crime. **Convict** (v). Antonym: acquittal (n).

If he is convicted of murder he may face the death penalty.

Crass (adj) – tactless, rude, gross, unrefined, blundering. Antonym: refined (adj).

She was jealous that he had a girlfriend, so she made crass remarks about her to his friends.

Craven (adj) – cowardly. Antonym: brave (adj).

The Private was too craven to face the enemy and rescue his Sergeant.

Decoy (v) – 1. to bait; to lure.

They used a girl hitchhiker as a decoy to get him to stop.

Decoy (n) – 2. bait; a lure.

Duck hunters are well known for using decoys.

Entice (v) – persuade, draw, invite.

To entice urban workers to leave the city, suburban employers are offering them higher salaries.

"WDYTM" DICTIONARY cont'd.

Collaborate (v) – cooperate; work together.

She's heard that Jay-Z and Beyonce will collaborate on their upcoming albums.

Flagrant (adj) – conspicuous, blatant, brazen. Antonym: modest (adj).

He believes that many television shows flagrantly promote violence.

Irate (adj) – angry, incensed, enraged. Antonym: calm (adj).

He worked as a customer service representative and hated when irate customers called to complain.

Obsession (n) – mania, fixation, compulsion; thinking about something or someone constantly. **Obsess** (v).

He was obsessed with cars and owned more than fifty classics.

Predisposition (n) – inclination, leaning, proclivity, propensity; prone to behave or respond in a given manner. **Predispose** (v).

She's never on time; her predisposition is to be late.

Profound (adj) – 1. deep, thoughtful. Antonym: inane (adj).

Steven Hawking, the world's smartest man, has had profound insights into the origins of the universe.

Profound (adj) – 2. to have a significant effect. Antonym: irrelevant (adj).

The internet has had a profound effect on the music industry.

Revelation (n) – disclosure, discovery, insight; to make something known. **Reveal** (v). Antonym: obscure (v).

The media made shocking revelations about former President Bill Clinton's affair.

Sensual (adj) – pleasing to the senses.

Graceful and lissome, the model was noted for her sensual style.

Sinister (adj) – threatening, evil, creepy.
Foreboding and sinister, Dracula is a classic horror figure.

Stolid (adj) – dull, impassive, boring. Antonym: stimulating (adj).
Fitting the stereotype, his accounting professor is a straight-laced, stolid guy.

Surmise (v) – deduce, estimate, infer, gather; figure out.
I surmised how big the parking spot was by comparing it to the car that was next to it.

NOTES:

"WDYTM" SYNONYM MATCHING

Match the following Word$ with their synonyms. Note the letter of the matching synonym in the space adjacent to the word.

	Vocabulary Words	**Synonyms**
1.	_____ Addiction	(a) appealing
2.	_____ Affliction	(b) lure
3.	_____ Alluring	(c) propensity
4.	_____ Assay	(d) deduce
5.	_____ Cognizant	(e) dependence
6.	_____ Collaborate	(f) opine
7.	_____ Comely	(g) persuade
8.	_____ Complicit	(h) cowardly
9.	_____ Conjecture	(i) illness
10.	_____ Conviction	(j) aware
11.	_____ Crass	(k) blatant
12.	_____ Craven	(l) evil
13.	_____ Decoy	(m) evaluate
14.	_____ Entice	(n) complacent
15.	_____ Flagrant	(o) belief
16.	_____ Irate	(p) disclosure
17.	_____ Obsession	(q) attractive
18.	_____ Predisposition	(r) deep
19.	_____ Profound	(s) pleasing
20.	_____ Revelation	(t) angry
21.	_____ Sensual	(u) rude
22.	_____ Sinister	(v) fixation
23.	_____ Stolid	(w) dull
24.	_____ Surmise	(x) cooperate

"WDYTM" SENTENCE COMPLETION

Using a form or tense of the Word$ in the Bank, find the words which best complete the sentences below.

WORD BANK				
Addiction	Affliction	Alluring	Assay	Cognizant
Collaborate	Comely	Complicit	Conjecture	Conviction
Crass	Craven	Decoy	Entice	Flagrant
Irate	Obsession	Predisposition	Profound	Revelation
Sensual	Sinister	Stolid	Surmise	

1. The beautiful Corvette was a _____ to lure customers into the used car lot.

2. Her argument with the store manager caused the woman to become _____.

3. The owner tried to _____ the star player to join the team by offering him a large salary.

4. Looking to incite the players on the home team, the runner said something _____ about the first baseman's wife.

5. In an earlier era, it was common for people to refer to an attractive woman as being _____.

6. The insurance adjuster was very _____ and serious about her work.

7. Stalkers are _____ with the celebrities they follow.

8. It is my personal _____ that Tibet should be free.

9. I found her perfume very _____.

81

"WDYTM" SENTENCE COMPLETION cont'd.

10. Initially, she couldn't figure out how to answer the question, but then she had a _____ and solved it right away.

11. She is _____ to cigarettes and wants to smoke all the time.

12. Given the clues, the police _____ who was responsible for the robbery.

13. Lack of shelter is one of the many _____ of the homeless.

14. Movie villains are always hatching some _____ plot to take over the world.

15. He always gives in because he's _____ to trying to make others happy.

16. The United States is hoping more countries will _____ to rebuild Iraq.

17. The lab needed to _____ the water for pollutants.

18. The defense had suppressed some evidence, so the jury was not _____ of the full facts of the case.

19. The player was thrown out of the game because of the _____ foul he committed.

20. Eating chocolate is a _____ pleasure.

21. There has been a lot of _____ in the media about who will win the election.

22. Abandoning friends in the face of trouble is a _____ act.

23. He was fired for his _____ in the office scandal.

24. The Greek scholar Socrates is considered one of history's most _____ thinkers.

NOTES:

"WDYTM" CROSSWORD PUZZLE

Use the synonyms provided in the clues to identify the Word$ that complete the crossword puzzle on the following page. The numbers run top-to-bottom and left-to-right.

Across

1. Pleasing to the senses
2. Dependence; a habitual, compulsive need
3. Attractive, agreeable
4. Conspicuous, blatant, brazen
5. Inclination, leaning, proclivity, propensity; prone to behave or respond in a given manner
6. To bait; to lure (or) bait, lure
7. Tactless, rude, gross, unrefined, blundering
8. Test, analyze, evaluate, determine
9. Mania, fixation, compulsion
10. Dull, impassive, boring
11. Opine, guess, contemplate
12. Cowardly
13. Illness; cause of suffering; burden
14. Deduce, estimate, infer, gather; figure out

Down

1. Aware of; to know of something
2. Persuade, draw, invite
3. Involvement in, complacent regarding, or ignoring the progress of, activity that is improper.
4. Deep, thoughtful (or) to have a significant effect
5. Cooperate; work together
6. Angry, incensed, enraged
7. Appealing, tempting
8. Disclosure, discovery, insight
9. Threatening, evil, creepy
10. Strongly opinion or belief (or) a judgment that one is guilty of a crime

"WDYTM" CROSSWORD PUZZLE

"WDYTM" SYNONYM SENTENCES

In the following sentences, use correct forms or tenses of the Word$ in the Bank to match the underlined synonyms, and write the correct word in the space provided below each sentence.

Word Bank				
Addiction	Affliction	Alluring	Assay	Cognizant
Collaborate	Comely	Complicit	Conjecture	Conviction
Crass	Craven	Decoy	Entice	Flagrant
Irate	Obsession	Predisposition	Profound	Revelation
Sensual	Sinister	Stolid	Surmise	

1. Saving yourself when others are in danger is <u>cowardly</u>.

   _____

2. The two companies will <u>cooperate</u> to make the project work.

   _____

3. The appraiser will <u>determine</u> the antique's value.

   _____

4. It is my <u>belief</u> that all people deserve proper health care.

   _____

5. He used his charm to <u>persuade</u> her to go out with him.

   _____

6. She is <u>prone</u> to getting sea sick very easily.

   _____

7. Her perfume had an <u>appealing</u> scent.

   _____

8. Loud and obnoxious, he often makes <u>rude</u> remarks.
   _____

9. When she saw that she had received a parking ticket, she became <u>angry</u>.
   _____

10. Unable to control himself, he finally accepted that he was <u>dependent</u>.
    _____

11. Without sufficient information, we can only <u>guess</u> what the results will be.
    _____

12. The guard who opened the lock for the burglars was <u>involved</u> in the crime.
    _____

13. The celebrity's two-day marriage was a <u>blatant</u> attempt to gain publicity.
    _____

14. In her day, Jacqueline Kennedy was quite <u>attractive</u>.
    _____

15. She was <u>aware</u> of the implication of her actions.
    _____

16. During the spring, many people are <u>burdened</u> by allergies.
    _____

17. He isn't flashy at all; he's just a straightforward, <u>boring</u> kind of guy.
    _____

18. Silk is renown for its supple, smooth, <u>pleasing</u> texture.
    _____

19. Electrical appliances have had a <u>significant</u> impact on the way we live.
    _____

"WDYTM" SYNONYM SENTENCES cont'd.

20. By examining the rings of a tree stump, we can <u>deduce</u> how old the tree was when it was cut down.

   _____

21. Socks were a <u>compulsion</u> of his, and he had hundreds of pairs in every color, pattern and size.

   _____

22. The shocking <u>discovery</u> of criminal acts within the department caused a lot of disruption within the community.

   _____

23. In a "bait & switch" scam, an unscrupulous business will try to sell customers an inferior product, but use a better product as a <u>lure</u>.

   _____

24. In video clips, Osama bin Laden reveals a <u>creepy</u> smile when he discusses the attack on the World Trade Center.

   _____

"WHY DIDN'T YOU TELL ME" THIS WAS TOUGH?

- Rebecca Osleeb & Keith London

NYC – Nina Zeitlin, a powerful and soulful singer, had only been in New York a few months when she began collaborating with Defined Mind. Enticed by the unusual idea of writing music that didn't assume that listeners were thick, Nina joined the project without being fully cognizant of the demands of the process.

Initially, she began brainstorming ideas for "Why Didn't You Tell Me" and wound up with little to show for it. Then, as an experiment, Nina left empty spaces in places where she surmised she might want to put Word$. Once the song started to take shape, she went back and began to fill them in with words that corresponded with the rest of the piece. She found that the editing process preoccupied a lot of her time, however, in the end she felt that she had accomplished her goal of creating a song that her audiences would find alluring.

In "Why Didn't You Tell Me" Nina describes a sensual, comely love interest to whom she is addicted due to his "complicit smile" and "flagrant style." And, in describing her efforts to entice him, she figuratively contemplates the use of a decoy. Consequently, I asked Nina if she was writing about someone she once had an obsession with herself, to which she replied, "No, I focused on this theme because I believe that it is something that all people can relate to."

Nina also wanted to convey the qualities of a person that she conjectures might make someone irate. She did so by assigning sinister characteristics to Sammy, her song's imaginary subject. Shallow and given to self-aggrandizement, she tells us that Sammy lacks the capacity to assay even the simplest of subjects. Her narrator informs the listener of her revelation that he is too stolid and sinister to hold her interest. Ultimately Nina contrasts the traits she admired in one young man with the crass and craven qualities of another.

We wrapped up the interview by asking Nina if she had any other comments. Taking a moment to discuss her own convictions, she remarked that good tracks don't need to be brainless, a condition that afflicts most of today's music. It isn't necessary for every musician to write something profound, but people are predisposed to remember things that they hear in songs, a fact that commercials take advantage of. So, she figured why not give it a shot, and try to turn the tide.

> Now, refer to the article you've just read to select the statements that best describe the authors' remarks. Circle the letter that corresponds to the correct answer.

"WDYTM" THIS WAS TOUGH? cont'd.

Question 1

(a) Nina began working with Defined Mind shortly after coming to NYC.

(b) She works with the City of New York.

(c) Collaborating with Defined Mind made Nina soulful.

(d) None of the above.

Question 2

(a) She recognized that writing for this format would be a challenge.

(b) Nina is attracted to tools.

(c) "Why Didn't You Tell Me" is about Nina being mislead.

(d) Nina didn't know what she was getting into.

Question 3

(a) Nina was accustomed to writing for brains.

(b) She was interested in writing in a new idiom.

(c) She complained that this would be too difficult.

(d) Nina is cognizant of difficult procedures.

Question 4

(a) She had a brainstorm.

(b) Nina likes to hunt ducks using decoys.

(c) She was inspired to write the song and complete it afterward.

(d) None of the above.

Question 5

(a) Nina likes to wear masks to hide her feelings.

(b) To gain her love interest's attention she contemplates the use of a lure.

(c) She is addicted to dentistry and outrageous styles.

(d) Nina contemplates writing a poem to her crush to tell him how she feels.

Question 6

(a) Nina appreciates her crush's knowing, sly smile and confident demeanor.

(b) She becomes angry because his smile and style is much nicer than hers.

(c) She admires Sammy for his good looks and style, but doesn't like him.

(d) Nina is sensual and comely.

Question 7

(a) The editing process was fast and efficient.

(b) She corresponded with others who write for Defined Mind.

(c) Nina wrote the song by allotting her time.

(d) Editing the song took a great deal of time.

Question 8

(a) Nina believes that she wrote a great song.

(b) She wants to attract someone utilizing music.

(c) Her audiences are attracted to her.

(d) She created a song that is difficult to find.

Question 9

(a) In "Why Didn't You Tell Me" Nina says that she's addicted to love.

(b) Her love interest doesn't smile and has no style.

(c) Nina wrote about a comely, outgoing young man.

(d) She is a sensual person with an attractive appearance.

Question 10

(a) Sammy is an example of a wonderful man.

(b) Sammy exists as a subject in this song to convey unattractive qualities.

(c) Nina is would like to date Sammy.

(d) Sammy can hold a conversation about any subject.

"WDYTM" THIS WAS TOUGH? cont'd.

Question 11

(a) She wants to write commercials.

(b) She wants to take advantage of commercials.

(c) Nina is afflicted by brainless music.

(d) Nina feels it is easier to remember information from songs.

KEITH MIDDLETON & RODNEY WILLIE
GO!

"GO!" LISTENING EXERCISE

Listen to "Go!" all the way through at least once. Then listen to the song again, and in the spaces provided below, list the Word$ that you hear.

"GO!" LYRICS

by Rodney Willie

Get on your mark (Mark!)
Ready, set, Go!
Get on your mark (Mark!)
Ready, set, Go!
Get on your mark (Mark!)
Ready, set, Go!
I ain't rhymin' to fast
Y'all just listen too slow
(2 times)

Go!
Annihilate 'em with the next flow/
Momentous are my sentences/
Significant for rocking shows/
I'm dropping those (What?! What?!) **labyrinthine** rhyme patterns/
Intricate paradigms that your mind can't **fathom**/
My designs leave 'em **perplexed** and scratching their temples/
Context is **complex**, **antithesis** of simple/
And if you **decipher** my words I give you **credit**/
Very few can see it clearly, so that makes you **esoteric**/
That **merits** you honor/ to **procure** an award/
The highest of **accolades** while a audience applauds/
My **expertise** to bring me everything that money can afford/
Rest **assured**, warlord with a pen for my sword/
See my mind's my Nine, my pen is my Mack Ten/
Use em both when up close and ready for action/
You get blinded by the diamonds shining from light **refraction**/
It's all **inconsequential**, just a minor **distraction**/

Get on your mark (Mark!)
Ready, set, Go!
Get on your mark (Mark!)
Ready, set, Go!

Get on your mark (Mark!)
Ready, set, Go!
I ain't rhymin' to fast
Y'all just listen too slow
(2 times)

I am the **epitome** of everything MCs wanna be/
Revere me/
More important tell people act **accordingly**/
Recording the audio **frequency frequently** leaves/
Lesser MC's **pusillanimous** acting cowardly/
My poetic spirit **borders** on the **pugilistic**/
You need a mouthpiece and a helmet to be safe when you hear it/
So don't get to close (Nooo!!)/
This verbal **virtuoso**/
Will leave you in **vertigo**/
When my voice puts you in choke holds/
Taped up with bandages seeking **punitive** damages/
I got the point of **vantage** on rappers, labels, and managers/
These cats is **amateurs**, **neophytes** against a professional/
So don't feel too bad when you see that it's me that just **bested** you/

Get on your mark (Mark!)
Ready, set, Go!
Get on your mark (Mark!)
Ready, set, Go!
Get on your mark (Mark!)
Ready, set, Go!
I ain't rhymin' to fast
Y'all just listen too slow
(2 times)

On your mark (On your mark)
If you're ready (Get ready)
Get set (Get set)
Here we go! (Here we go!)

"GO!" LYRICS cont'd.

Let's Go!

Get on your mark (Mark!)
Ready, set, Go!
Get on your mark (Mark!)
Ready, set, Go!
Get on your mark (Mark!)
Ready, set, Go!
I ain't rhymin' to fast
Y'all just listen too slow
(2 times)

Ad lib

"GO!" DICTIONARY

Accolades (n), **Accolade** (n) – praise, award; great compliment. Antonym: insult (n).

> Her film started receiving accolades shortly after it premiered, and it ultimately went on to win her an Oscar.

Accordingly (adv) – 1. suitably.

> Wanting to make a good impression on her interview, she dressed accordingly.

Accordingly (adv) – 2. consequently; as a result of.

> His neighbor threatened to sue him, and accordingly, he retained a lawyer.

Amateurs (n), **Amateur** (n) – layperson; one who participates in an activity for recreation. Antonym: professional (n).

> It was his first time surfing, and accordingly, he looked like an amateur.

Annihilate (v) – destroy, kill; idiomatically used to describe superiority in competition.

Our team annihilated the visitors in this past weekend's game.

Antithesis (adj) – opposite, converse. **Antithetical** (adj). Antonym: analogous (adj).

New York City is the antithesis of a small town.

Assured (v), **Assure** (v) – 1. guarantee, promise.

The salesman assured me that I was getting a great deal.

Assured (v) – 2. verify, substantiate; make certain.

I wanted to be assured that I was getting a great deal, so I did some comparison shopping to verify the salesman's claims.

Bested (v), **Best** (v) – beaten, surpassed; to be defeated or outclassed.

Their team had more practice than ours, and consequently, they bested us.

Borders (v), **Border** (v) – 1. to be on the verge of or to approximate something.

His infatuation with grisly video games borders on mental illness.

Borders (n), **Border** (n) – 2. boundary.

The United States and Canada share a border.

Borders (v) – 3. to be physically adjacent to something.

Manhattan and Queens both border the East River.

Complex (adj) – intricate, difficult. Antonym: simple (adj).

Between little black boxes and on-board diagnostic systems, today's cars are far too complex for people to repair on their own.

Context (n) – circumstances; details surrounding a subject. **Contextual** (adj).

On the news his quote seemed harsh; his remark was actually benign, but it had been taken out of context.

"GO!" DICTIONARY cont'd.

Credit (n) – recognition, acknowledgement. Antonym: blame (n).

I wouldn't have been able to write the book without her, so I wanted to give her due credit.

Decipher (v) – decode, grasp; to figure out.

I want to respond to the note she passed me, but I can't because I couldn't decipher her handwriting.

Distraction (n) – disturbance, diversion, interruption. **Distract** (v). Antonym: focus (n).

I can't listen to music while I work because it distracts me.

Epitome (n) – essence, height, archetype, embodiment; perfect example. **Epitomize** (v).

Jacqueline Kennedy epitomized style and grace in the days of Camelot.

Esoteric (adj) – 1. related to knowledge familiar to a small group. Antonym: common (adj).

We both enjoy modern architecture and wound up discussing such esoteric topics as Frank Gehry's latest work.

Esoteric (adj) – 2. perplexing, arcane. Antonym: straightforward (adj).

Their conversation was too esoteric and I couldn't understand anything that they were talking about.

Expertise (n) – knowledge, skill, proficiency. **Expert** (n).

Programming computers requires expertise.

Fathom (v) – comprehend, understand, grasp.

I can't fathom why he thought it would be OK to stay out until sunrise on the night before a college interview.

Frequency (n) – 1. the bandwidth of broadcast radio or television signals.

She wanted to listen to her favorite radio station during our road trip, but we couldn't get that frequency.

Frequency (n) – 2. the pitch or tone of sound waves.

The frequency of the whistle can only be heard by dogs.

Frequency (n) – 3. rate of occurrence or recurrence.

Accidents occur at that intersection with alarming frequency.

Frequently (adv) – regularly, repeatedly, habitually.

He's very absent-minded and he frequently loses his keys.

Inconsequential (adj) – unimportant, minor, trivial. Antonym: important (adj).

Their remarks were completely inconsequential and had no bearing on her decision.

Intricate (adj) – complex, complicated. **Intricacy** (n). Antonym: simple (adj).

Computers are too intricate for most people to repair on their own.

Labyrinthine (adj) – circuitous, convoluted. Antonym: direct (adj).

The narrow, winding streets of Venice are a labyrinthine maze that seems to have been thrown together over the centuries.

Lesser (adj) – smaller; less significant. Antonym: greater (adj).

I don't like either of the candidates very much, and I feel that I'll need to chose between the lesser of two evils.

Merits (v) – 1. to warrant or deserve.

Her bravery merits the highest honor.

Merits (n), **Merit** (n) – 2. benefits, pros. Antonym: disadvantage (n).

She was hired based upon her merits.

"GO!" DICTIONARY cont'd.

Momentous (adj) – important, considerable, historic. Antonym: inconsequential (adj).

> The Apollo 11 moon landing was a momentous accomplishment for mankind.

Neophytes (n), **Neophyte** (n) – beginner, novice. Antonym: veteran (n).

> Everyone starts as a neophyte and builds expertise with practice.

Paradigms (n), **Paradigm** (n) – example, model, standard.

> Julia Child established the paradigm for today's cooking programs.

Perplexed (v), **Perplex** (v) – confuse, confound, befuddle. Antonym: clarify (v).

> We were perplexed by the intricate directions.

Procure (v) – obtain, acquire. Antonym: divest (v).

> She couldn't repair it until she had procured the correct tool.

Pugilistic (adj) – quarrelsome, belligerent; related to boxing. Antonym: conciliatory (adj).

> Embroiled in a heated argument, they each adopted a pugilistic stance as they tried to shout down one another.

Punitive (adj) – corrective, retaliatory; inflicting punishment.

> Since the company refused to make amends for their mistake, she was compelled to take punitive action.

Pusillanimous (adj) – cowardly, craven, timid. Antonym: courageous (adj).

> Pusillanimous in the extreme, the Prince sent others off to wage his battles.

Refraction (n) – the change in direction of light or sound wave as it passes from one material into another. **Refract** (v).

> Although it may look as though your spoon is bending when you place it in a glass of water, it is actually an illusion created by refraction.

Revere (v) – admire, worship. **Reverence** (n). Antonym: revile (v).
Michael Jordon is revered for his skill on the basketball court.

Significant (adj) – meaningful, consequential. Antonym: insignificant (adj).
The school made significant changes to its curriculum to accommodate the new federal regulations.

Vantage (n) – 1. advantage. Antonym: disadvantage (n).
Positioned above the valley, our forces had the invading army at a vantage.

Vantage (n) – 2. perspective.
Positioned above the valley, our forces had an excellent vantage point to observe the invading army's troop movements.

Vertigo (n) – dizziness; confused state of mind.
He had an unbearable fear of heights and was overcome by vertigo whenever he entered a tall building.

Virtuoso (adj) – genius, prodigy; someone with masterful skill in the arts; exhibiting the ability of a virtuoso.
She's been playing the piano since she was a toddler, and now she's a virtuoso who headlines performances around the world.

NOTES:

"GO!" SYNONYM MATCHING

Match the following Word$ with their synonyms. Note the letter of the matching synonym in the space adjacent to the word.

Vocabulary Words	**Synonyms**
1. _____Accolades	(a) decode
2. _____Accordingly	(b) on the verge of
3. _____Amateur	(c) proficiency
4. _____Annihilate	(d) surpassed
5. _____Antithesis	(e) regularly
6. _____Assure	(f) comprehend
7. _____Bested	(g) dizziness
8. _____Borders	(h) disturbance
9. _____Complex	(i) belligerent
10. _____Context	(j) novice
11. _____Credit	(k) trivial
12. _____Decipher	(l) praise
13. _____Distraction	(m) consequently
14. _____Epitome	(n) rate of occurrence
15. _____Esoteric	(o) intricate
16. _____Expertise	(p) layperson
17. _____Fathom	(q) guarantee
18. _____Frequency	(r) essence
19. _____Frequently	(s) opposite
20. _____Inconsequential	(t) recognition
21. _____Intricate	(u) timid
22. _____Labyrinthine	(v) admire
23. _____Lesser	(w) advantage
24. _____Merits	(x) change in direction

Vocabulary Words	Synonyms
25. _____ Momentous	(y) circumstances
26. _____ Neophyte	(z) historic
27. _____ Paradigm	(a1) circuitous
28. _____ Perplex	(a2) meaningful
29. _____ Procure	(a3) prodigy
30. _____ Pugilistic	(a4) arcane
31. _____ Punitive	(a5) to deserve
32. _____ Pusillanimous	(a6) complicated
33. _____ Refraction	(a7) retaliatory
34. _____ Revere	(a8) example
35. _____ Significant	(a9) smaller
36. _____ Vantage	(b1) confuse
37. _____ Vertigo	(b2) destroy
38. _____ Virtuoso	(b3) acquire

NOTES:

_____
_____
_____
_____
_____
_____
_____

"GO!" SENTENCE COMPLETION

Using a form or tense of the Word$ in the Bank, find the words which best complete the sentences below.

WORD BANK				
Accolades	Accordingly	Amateur	Annihilate	Antithesis
Assure	Bested	Borders	Complex	Context
Credit	Decipher	Distraction	Epitome	Esoteric
Expertise	Fathom	Frequency	Frequently	Inconsequential
Intricate	Labyrinthine	Lesser	Merits	Momentous
Neophyte	Paradigm	Perplex	Procure	Pugilistic
Punitive	Pusillanimous	Refraction	Revere	Significant
Vantage	Vertigo	Virtuoso		

1. We have an easy time talking to each other because we're on the same _____.

2. Many academic institutions are working to improve the state of education and are seeking a new _____.

3. He played masterfully and we were treated to a _____ performance.

4. Complex is the _____ of simple.

5. The study's outcome is encouraging and _____ further study.

6. The route we took was _____, and there isn't any way we would be able to get back without better directions.

7. It was a pretty pathetic that they were _____ by one of the worst teams in the league.

8. She's worked in the discipline for many years, and has accumulated

significant _____ on that particular subject.

9. The rollercoaster was too much for him and he was overcome by _____.

10. It looked intimidating, but we _____ him that it was safe.

11. _____ is the antithesis of simple.

12. Our team _____ the competition, and we finished the season undefeated.

13. The chem professor instructed us to behave _____ in the lab, because otherwise, we might blow ourselves to bits.

14. We couldn't _____ why he went to school wearing a pink tutu.

15. During their discussion she convinced him to see the issue from her _____ point.

16. Like everyone else, I started out as a _____, but my expertise grew with training and experience.

17. He gave up his _____ ranking and went pro this season.

18. When I brought up the topic she became _____, but her tone softened as she came to understand my perspective.

19. I find flashing online ads very _____; they make it difficult to read a site's content.

20. She works at a "think-tank" in Washington D.C., and spends her time pondering "buy-side economics" and other _____ subjects.

"GO!" SENTENCE COMPLETION cont'd.

21. Even after hours of interrogation he wouldn't _____ the secret code for his captors.

22. I'll readily acknowledge that it was originally her idea; I have to give _____ where it's due.

23. It is always gratifying to receive _____ and the respect of your peers.

24. His recent unusual behavior _____ on insanity.

25. The new data we received was _____ and did not impact our original findings.

26. Since she didn't have any good options, she was forced to chose between the _____ of two evils.

27. He was _____ by the toy's complicated assembly instructions.

28. The Dali Lama is _____ for his wisdom and spiritual insight.

29. Always ready to come through in the clutch, she _____ grace under pressure.

30. Never _____ , he fought for what was right.

31. A diamond sparkles because light is _____ as it shines through its facets.

32. We need to _____ some additional equipment before we embark on our camping trip.

33. To best understand historical events, it is important that we view them in _____ .

34. I'm _____ preoccupied and forgetful; if my head wasn't attached to my shoulders, I would have already lost it somewhere.

35. Chastising the defendant, the judge awarded the plaintiff $100 million in _____ damages.

36. The findings of the study were _____ and caused us to reconsider our position on the issue.

37. Christening the new ship, the captain remarked, "I would like to say a few words in honor of this _____ occasion."

38. He was perplexed by the toy's _____ assembly instructions.

NOTES:

"GO!" CROSSWORD PUZZLE

Use the synonyms provided in the clues to identify the WordS that complete the crossword puzzle on the following page. The numbers run top-to-bottom and left-to-right.

Across

1. Participates in an activity for recreation
2. Circumstances; details surrounding a subject
3. Unimportant, minor, trivial
4. Beginner, novice
5. On the verge of (or) boundary (or) adjacent
6. Essence, acme, embodiment
7. Comprehend, understand, grasp.
8. Corrective, retaliatory
9. Quarrelsome, belligerent; related to boxing
10. Change in direction of light or sound wave
11. Opposite, converse
12. Knowledge, skill, proficiency
13. Smaller; less significant
14. Suitably (or) consequently; as a result of
15. Cowardly, craven, timid
16. Confused, confounded, befuddled
17. Admire, worship
18. Genius, prodigy; someone with masterful skill
19. Guaranteed, promised (or) substantiated

Down

1. Destroy, kill; superior in competition
2. Praise, awards; great compliments
3. Circuitous, convoluted
4. Intricate, difficult
5. Known to a small group (or) perplexing, arcane
6. Warrant or deserve (or) benefits, pros
7. Advantage (or) perspective
8. Decode, grasp; to figure out
9. Complex, complicated
10. Obtain, acquire
11. Beaten, surpassed
12. Example, model, standard
13. Regularly, repeatedly, habitually
14. Dizziness; confused state of mind
15. Bandwidth (or) pitch (or) recurrence
16. Important, considerable, historic
17. Meaningful, consequential
18. Recognition, acknowledgement
19. Disturbance, diversion, interruption

"GO!" CROSSWORD PUZZLE

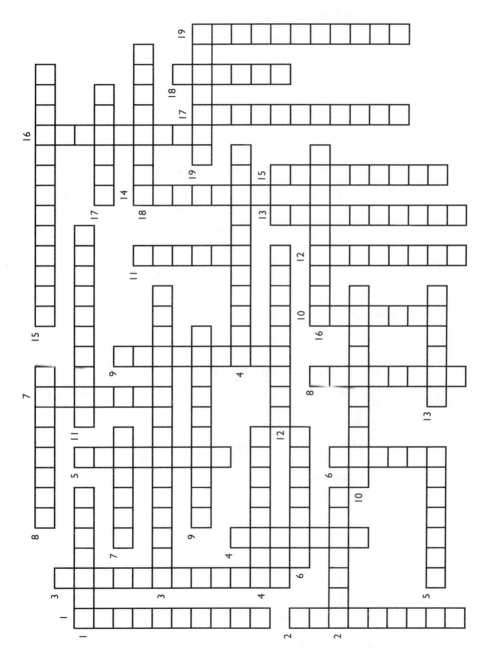

109

"GO!" SYNONYM SENTENCES

In the following sentences, use correct forms or tenses of the Word$ in the Bank to match the underlined synonyms, and write the correct word in the space provided below each sentence.

WORD BANK				
Accolades	Accordingly	Amateur	Annihilate	Antithesis
Assure	Bested	Borders	Complex	Context
Credit	Decipher	Distraction	Epitome	Esoteric
Expertise	Fathom	Frequency	Frequently	Inconsequential
Intricate	Labyrinthine	Lesser	Merits	Momentous
Neophyte	Paradigm	Perplex	Procure	Pugilistic
Punitive	Pusillanimous	Refraction	Revere	Significant
Vantage	Vertigo	Virtuoso		

1. Her reasoning was <u>convoluted</u>, and I still cannot fathom how she arrived at her conclusions.

   _____

2. Even though the theater company is <u>recreational</u>, their production of "Death of a Salesman" was excellent.

   _____

3. Outgoing and friendly, he is the <u>opposite</u> of his curmudgeonly father.

   _____

4. She's in great shape because she exercises <u>regularly</u>.

   _____

5. The defenders <u>destroyed</u> the invading forces as they fought to enter the city.

   _____

6. His partner created a <u>diversion</u> while he absconded with the paintings.

   _____

7. Her physician was concerned about her condition; <u>consequently</u>, he conducted a battery of tests to establish a diagnosis.

   _____

8. He said that although he authored the piece, she deserves much of the <u>recognition</u> for their accomplishment.

   _____

9. He was overcome by <u>dizziness</u> on the Empire State Building's observation deck.

   _____

10. It takes years learn to read and write in Chinese because the language's characters are so <u>intricate</u>.

    _____

11. My dog heard barking on a CD that I was playing, and she stared at the speaker <u>confused</u> as to why she couldn't find the other dogs.

    _____

12. She couldn't possibly <u>comprehend</u> that the dog's barks were recorded and overdubbed into the song I was listening to.

    _____

13. The engineers selected the design based upon its <u>benefits</u>.

    _____

14. The design was well regarded, and it received a variety of <u>compliments</u>.

    _____

15. She <u>beat</u> me in three games out of four.

    _____

16. I <u>promised</u> him that we would arrive at the airport in time to make his flight.

    _____

"GO!" SYNONYM SENTENCES cont'd.

17. In college you have the opportunity to explore <u>arcane</u> subject matter that you wouldn't normally encounter outside of an academic setting.

   _____

18. She was <u>admired</u> for her longstanding role as a the community's spiritual leader and its most determined advocate.

   _____

19. Underhanded and <u>craven</u>, he ratted out his cronies to the feds to save his own skin.

   _____

20. He considers lobbying to be a <u>less significant</u> influence on public policy that it is popularly thought to be.

   _____

21. The completion of the Brooklyn Bridge was a <u>historic</u> event that marked the dawn of a new age in engineering.

   _____

22. She recently earned another belt in karate, but she's still a <u>novice</u> and has a lot of work to do to build her expertise.

   _____

23. She gave a <u>masterful</u> performance at Carnegie Hall and received a standing ovation.

   _____

24. The issue is far more <u>complicated</u> than I had first thought, and I'll need to give it further consideration before I make a decision.

   _____

25. While visiting Rome, I asked our guide to translate a shopkeeper's comments because I couldn't <u>grasp</u> what he was trying to say.

26. I wouldn't call his contributions trivial, but the weren't very <u>meaningful</u> either.

27. I'm not sure how I would have responded to her comments; I imagine it depends on the <u>circumstances</u>.

28. My kid brother's new R/C truck didn't work because the remote control unit was on a different <u>bandwidth</u>.

29. While the article does bring some new information to light, much of it <u>verges</u> on fiction.

30. They couldn't hire her because she did not possess the necessary <u>skill set</u>.

31. When she asked him to turn off his cell phone during the performance he became <u>belligerent</u>.

32. She acquiesced to his requests because they were ultimately to her <u>advantage</u>.

33. The rover sustained a jolt when it landed, but any damage was <u>minimal</u>.

34. Since our neighbors weren't willing to repair the damage they caused, our attorney recommended that we take <u>corrective</u> measures.

"GO!" SYNONYM SENTENCES cont'd.

35. In order to execute the plan in its current form, it will be necessary for us to <u>acquire</u> additional resources.

    _____

36. Both light and sound waves experience <u>a change in direction</u> as they pass though different materials.

    _____

37. General George S. Patton was the <u>embodiment</u> of the war-hardened military man.

    _____

38. In 1954 Steve Allen created the <u>model</u> for the modern talk show.

    _____

RODNEY WILLIE IS READY TO "GO!"

- Keith London

NYC – Rodney Willie, who's known in most contexts as "RW" but credited on DM by his real name, is a lyrical virtuoso who can easily best the most pugilistic MC. Keith Middleton, his musical alter-ego and the epitome of talent and professionalism, is assuredly the antithesis of an amateur and merits his own praise, but upon fathoming the expertise revealed in "Go!" I must give Rodney his due accolades.

As far as I can decipher, his key vantage is that his significant intellect borders on genius. Refracted through his muse, his labyrinthine rhymes put lesser recording artists to shame. His deft use of Word$ annihilates the stereotypes of a hardened street rapper, and he procures an esoteric paradigm unrivaled by any that I have encountered before. Pusillanimous neophytes may be perplexed by the intricacy of his verse, but accordingly, those in the know revere him for the momentous accomplishment that they represent. Any remarks to the contrary are simply punitive.

Complex in the extreme, Rodney's raps frequently bring me to the verge of vertigo when trying to keep up with him in the studio. However, we're always on the same frequency when it comes the qualities that we looking to instill in the tracks, and any distractions ultimately prove to be inconsequential.

> Now, refer to the article you've just read to select the statements that best describe the author's remarks. Circle the letter that corresponds to the correct answer.

Question 1
(a) RW is belligerent, and the name on his DM credit card is "Rodney Willie."
(b) The Table of Contexts credits him as "RW" but DM calls him "Rodney Willie."
(c) Most people call Rodney "RW," but on DM he is credited as "Rodney Willie."
(d) Rodney calls himself "RW," but he asked our staff address him as "Mr. Willie."

Question 2
(a) The author believes that Rodney is a verbal prodigy and a great boxer.
(b) The author regards Rodney as a verbal genius who can surpass even the toughest competitor.
(c) Rodney plays the lyric beautifully, and his best pet pug is named "MC."
(d) Rodney's performance is pure genius, and has been called "The Boxing MC."

Question 3
(a) Keith Middleton, who writes the music, is an outstanding professional who deserves his own accolades.
(b) Keith's converse essence deserves its own guarantees.
(c) Keith, who writes the music to accompany Rodney's lyrics, guarantees that he is a professional.

115

RODNEY WILLIE IS READY TO "GO" cont'd.

(d) Keith Middleton is the epitome of alter-egos, and the author guarantees that he is an amateur.

Question 4

(a) Rodney asked the author to give him the award that he was withholding.

(b) The author couldn't fathom how RW could reveal his expertise to an award.

(c) "Go!" compelled the author to honor Rodney with an award for proficiency.

(d) "Go!" prompted the author to take inventory of Rodney's skill and to complement him.

Question 5

(a) The author is looking to decode Rodney's primary advantage.

(b) The author believes that Rodney's primary advantage is his considerable intellect.

(c) The author his having trouble figuring out how Rodney's point of view influences his work.

(d) The author has been working to determine Rodney's intellectual boundaries.

Question 6

(a) Rodney enjoys embarrassing other performers by using a muse to bend the light in his maze.

(b) Rodney's muse bends sound waves, which results in convoluted rhymes.

(c) Rodney's towering verse are the product of great inspiration, and makes other recording artists look inferior.

(d) Rodney likes to shame other recording artist via his labyrinthine rhymes.

Question 7

(a) The author feels that Rodney's work dispels the notion that artists who rap are incapable of authoring intellectually challenging material.

(b) Rodney destroys stereotypes by acquiring arcane models.

(c) Rodney is a hardened street rapper who said something arcane to the author.

(d) All of the above.

Question 8

(a) Cowardly beginners are confused by Rodney, but those who understand his work worship him.

(b) Timid novices may be befuddled by the complexity of Rodney's work, but appropriately, those who are knowledgeable admire its significance.

(c) Rodney is worshiped and admired by those in-the-know, whereas timid beginners are befuddled by the complexity of his lyrics.

(d) None of the above.

Question 9

(a) Anyone who disagrees with the author will be sued for punitive damages.

(b) Any remarks that conflict with the author's will be punished.

(c) Anyone who disagrees with the author needs to be corrected.

(d) Those who do not believe that Rodney's work is brilliant are just jealous.

Question 10

(a) Rodney enjoys extreme sports that regularly make people dizzy.

(b) Rodney regularly makes his colleagues dizzy in the studio.

(c) The intricacy of Rodney's lyrics regularly makes the author dizzy.

(d) The complexity of Rodney's extremities gives the author vertigo.

Question 11

(a) The author would like Rodney to turn off the radio because it interrupts him.

(b) Despite the quality of the equipment he is using, Rodney cannot find the radio station he and the author both enjoy.

(c) Rodney and the author work together well, and disruptions that might otherwise interfere with their progress prove to be insignificant.

(d) All of the above.

LYLE BEERS & ADRIANNE HECKER
SUPERGIRL

"SUPERGIRL" LISTENING EXERCISE

Listen to "SuperGirl" all the way through at least once. Then listen to the song again, and in the spaces provided below, list the Word$ that you hear.

"SUPERGIRL" LYRICS

by Adrianne Hecker & Lyle Beers

With **candor** we say **pithy** things
We must confess about our **minimal resolve**
Now that the **toxin**'s **seeped** into our veins
Can't **fathom** simple things
This thing's so **infinite**

I come away from the fire a **Phoenix**
Journeying towards the big hot sun

I'm your SuperGirl, **traversing** the **cosmos**
In a super world, uniting the **factions**
SuperGirl, my **declaration**:
Turn in your guns and **manifest** love

Don't **slander**, we've lost no love
Can't **squander** precious time
On things that don't **loom** large
It's so **crucial** to just live **graciously**
Let us **bestow** our gifts
And watch the hate **dissolve**

I've come away from the **mire** a **genius**
Returning now like a **benediction**

I'm your SuperGirl, **traversing** the **cosmos**
In a super world, uniting the **factions**
SuperGirl, my **declaration**:
Turn in your guns and **manifest** love

Our **underlying** spark
Could **dispel** all of the darkness
With **awesome** pride

We'll gently glide through the atmosphere

"SUPERGIRL" LYRICS cont'd.

With **awesome** pride
We'll gently glide through the atmosphere

Quixotic behavior will yet be the savior
Of humanity when it comes undone

I'm your SuperGirl, **traversing** the **cosmos**
In a super world, uniting the **factions**
SuperGirl, my **declaration**:
Turn in your guns and **manifest** love

I'm your SuperGirl, **traversing** the **cosmos**
In a super world, uniting the **factions**
SuperGirl, my **declaration**:
Turn in your guns and **manifest** love

I'm your SuperGirl

"SUPERGIRL" DICTIONARY

Awesome (adj) – great, awe-inspiring, amazing. Antonym: uninspiring (adj).
   The Grand Canyon is an awesome sight.

Benediction (n) – blessing, approval; a prayer asking for help or protection.
Antonym: curse (n).
   The priest ended the service by reciting a benediction.

Bestow (v) – give, confer, grant. Antonym: rescind (v).
   He bestowed his blessing upon his daughter's engagement.

Candor (n) – honesty, frankness, openness. **Candid** (adj), **Candidly** (adv).
Antonym: dishonesty (n)
   Looking for constructive criticism, I appreciated his candor.

Cosmos (n) – outer space; the universe. **Cosmic** (adj). Antonym: atom (n).

The astronomer used a telescope to gaze out into the cosmos.

Crucial (adj) – essential; extremely important or necessary.

She said, "If you want to do well on the exam, it is crucial that you study."

Declaration (n) – statement, announcement; usually regarding a strong belief. **Declare** (v).

He was asked to make a written declaration explaining what he witnessed during the accident.

Dispel (v) – dismiss, eliminate; cause to vanish.

To dispel the rumors of her illness, the politician held a press conference at her gym.

Dissolve (v) – 1. melt. Antonym: solidify (v).

The ice cube dissolved in his freshly brewed coffee.

Dissolve (v) – 2. end, disband. Antonym: initiate (v).

The new military dictator dissolved the country's democratically elected legislature.

Factions (n), **Faction** (n) – group, clique, party; a group within a larger group.

Congress members representing competing interests frequently organize themselves into opposing factions.

Fathom (v) – comprehend, understand, grasp.

I can't fathom why he thought it would be OK to stay out until sunrise on the night before a college interview.

Genius (n) – brilliant; extraordinary intelligence or skill. Antonym: stupidity (n).

She's a genius and finishes her exams in record time.

"SUPERGIRL" DICTIONARY cont'd.

Graciously (adv) – politely; behaving in a courteous manner. **Gracious** (adj).

Giving all of the credit to the team, she graciously accepted the award for MVP.

Infinite (adj) – never-ending, endless, uncountable. **Infinity** (n). Antonym: finite (adj).

As far as we can tell, the cosmos are infinite.

Loom (v) – 1. overhang, appear, project; come into view. Antonym: recede (v).

We came in early from boating yesterday because a storm was looming on the horizon.

Loom (v) – 2. philosophically resonate; have relevance.

Even today, Elvis Presley looms large on the music scene.

Manifest (v) – 1. show; become evident or visible. Antonym: dissipate (v).

Her illness first manifested itself as a high fever.

Manifest (adj) – 2. obvious, apparent. Antonym: subtle (adj).

He didn't know what transgression he committed to prompt her manifest hostility.

Minimal (adj) – the smallest amount or number allowed or possible. **Minimum** (adj). Antonym: Maximum (adj).

The minimal number of credits needed to graduate is forty.

Mire (n) – 1. a bog; gunk, marsh, swamp.

Walking through the swamp, she lost her boot in a mire.

Mire (n) – 2. a difficult situation.

His parents were mired in a messy divorce.

Phoenix (n) – 1. a mythological bird that ignites itself into flames every 500 years, and is born again from its ashes.

The Phoenix rose again, reborn from its ashes.

Phoenix (n) – 2. a term that describes someone who resurrects or redeems themselves in some manner.

Despite having been bankrupt, he rose like a Phoenix to made a great comeback.

Pithy (adj) – terse, concise; to the point. Antonym: rambling (adj).

Her attorney made a pithy remark in response to the plaintiff's comments.

Quixotic (adj) – idealistic but impractical.

The notion that all people will live in peace is nice, but quixotic.

Resolve (v) – 1. solve, decide. **Resolution** (n).

Working together, we can resolve the problem.

Resolve (n) – 2. conviction, determination, tenacity; dedication of purpose. Antonym: indifference (n).

Full of resolve, the stranded mountaineers made their treacherous decent to safety.

Seep (v) – leak, leach, bleed.

The paint seeped out of the can and wound up on everything in the bag.

Slander (n) – insult, malign, defame; make false and malicious statements. Antonym: praise (n/v)

Insisting that he was faithful to his wife, he said the reporter slandered him by writing that he was having an affair.

Squander (v) – waste.

My brother squandered his entire paycheck on a thirty pound stick of gum.

"SUPERGIRL" DICTIONARY cont'd.

Toxin (n) – poison, pollutant, contaminant. **Toxic** (adj).

The industrial plant illegally released toxins that poisoned the local wildlife.

Traversing (v), **Traverse** (v) – cross, travel, navigate; pass through.

Traveling by car, plane, and train, his mom is traversing the globe.

Underlying (adj) – fundamental; describes a principle upon which something is based or is influenced by; primary reason or influence. **Underlie** (v).

Taxes are an underlying issue in the upcoming presidential race.

"SUPERGIRL" SYNONYM MATCHING

Match the following Word$ with their synonyms. Note the letter of the matching synonym in the space adjacent to the word.

	Vocabulary Words	Synonyms
1.	_____ Awesome	(a) endless
2.	_____ Benediction	(b) idealistic
3.	_____ Bestow	(c) show
4.	_____ Candor	(d) marsh
5.	_____ Cosmos	(e) conviction
6.	_____ Crucial	(f) waste
7.	_____ Declaration	(g) primary influence
8.	_____ Dispel	(h) leak
9.	_____ Dissolve	(i) defame
10.	_____ Faction	(j) give
11.	_____ Fathom	(k) smallest
12.	_____ Genius	(l) traveling
13.	_____ Gracious	(m) awe-inspiring

	Vocabulary Words	**Synonyms**
14.	_____ Infinite	(n) concise
15.	_____ Loom	(o) blessing
16.	_____ Manifest	(p) understand
17.	_____ Minimal	(q) openness
18.	_____ Mire	(r) essential
19.	_____ Phoenix	(s) redeemed
20.	_____ Pithy	(t) dismiss
21.	_____ Quixotic	(u) disband
22.	_____ Resolve	(v) statement
23.	_____ Seep	(w) outer space
24.	_____ Slander	(x) poison
25.	_____ Squander	(y) group
26.	_____ Toxin	(z) overhang
27.	_____ Traversing	(a1) extraordinary intelligence
28.	_____ Underlying	(a2) polite

"SUPERGIRL" SENTENCE COMPLETION

Using a form or tense of the Word$ in the Bank, find the words which best complete the sentences below.

WORD BANK				
Awesome	Benediction	Bestow	Candor	Cosmos
Crucial	Declaration	Dispel	Dissolve	Factions
Fathom	Genius	Graciously	Infinite	Loom
Manifest	Minimal	Mire	Phoenix	Pithy
Quixotic	Resolve	Seep	Slander	Squander
Toxin	Traversing	Underlying		

"SUPERGIRL" SENTENCE COMPLETION cont'd.

1. The many _____ in the air are said to be the cause for the increase in cases of asthma in children.

2. He sought their approval as though it was a _____.

3. She tried to _____ what caused her mom's angry reaction.

4. Using the microwave to cook takes a _____ amount of effort.

5. After she was offered a satisfactory, but not perfect, job, her dad told her not to _____ a good opportunity.

6. Looking at the stars, the universe appears to go on into _____.

7. The revolt for political reform originally _____ itself as a series of student protests.

8. They had everything ready for our visit to their summer house and were very _____ hosts.

9. To look at the Earth while walking on the moon must be an _____ sight.

10. The stadium proposal was contested by two _____, people who supported its construction and others who were against it.

11. After the last team in the league's lineup was shuffled, it came back like a _____ and went on to win the championship.

12. I could see the tornado _____ on the horizon, so we left the house to look for a safe place.

13. It is _____ to believe that we can eliminate world hunger.

14. The two of them were _____ in a longstanding argument.

15. I wish that they would just sit down, talk it out, and _____ it.

16. The winner voluntarily submitted herself to a physical to _____ any allegations that she was using anything to enhance her performance.

17. At the start of the initiation ceremony the new inductees made a _____ of faith to the secret society.

18. Occasionally, I gaze at the night sky, and stare into the _____.

19. Oil _____ from the tank, contaminating the surrounding soil.

20. He was always respected for his _____, even though sometimes he was brutally honest.

21. The complexity of Mozart's musical composition is evidence of his _____.

22. Following the writer's claim that she was a criminal, she sued him for _____.

23. Place the pill on your tongue and let it _____.

24. The Purple Heart is a medal _____ on soldiers for suffering injuries in combat.

25. She apologized for her _____ response to my naive question.

26. It is _____ that you to follow the medication's directions.

27. Lewis and Clarke are famous for _____ the Louisiana Purchase.

28. She disagreed with him because she thought his _____ assumptions were wrong.

"SUPERGIRL" CROSSWORD PUZZLE

Use the synonyms provided in the clues to identify the words that complete the crossword puzzle on the following page. The numbers run top-to-bottom and left-to-right.

Across
1. Blessing, approval
2. Group, clique, party
3. Statement, announcement
4. Poison, pollutant, contaminant
5. Terse, concise; to the point
6. Fundamental
7. Essential; extremely important or necessary
8. Crossing, traveling, navigating; pass through
9. Solve, decide (or) conviction, determination, tenacity
10. The smallest amount or number allowed
11. Dismiss, eliminate; cause to vanish
12. Comprehend, understand, grasp
13. Waste
14. Honesty, frankness, openness
15. A difficult situation (or) a bog; gunk, marsh, swamp

Down
1. Never-ending, endless, uncountable
2. Leak, leach, bleed
3. Idealistic but impractical
4. Outer space; the universe
5. Politely; behaving in a courteous manner
6. Overhang, appear, project; come into view
7. Brilliant; extraordinary intelligence or skill
8. Give, confer, grant
9. Obvious, apparent
10. Insult, malign, defame
11. Great, awe-inspiring, amazing
12. Melt (or) end, disband
13. Mythological bird (or) one who resurrects or redeems oneself

Knowledge is a State of Mind™

"SUPERGIRL" CROSSWORD PUZZLE

129

"SUPERGIRL" SYNONYM SENTENCES

In the following sentences, use correct forms or tenses of the Word$ in the Bank to match the underlined synonyms, and write the correct word in the space provided below each sentence.

WORD BANK				
Awesome	Benediction	Bestow	Candor	Cosmos
Crucial	Declaration	Dispel	Dissolve	Factions
Fathom	Genius	Graciously	Infinite	Loom
Manifest	Minimal	Mire	Phoenix	Pithy
Quixotic	Resolve	Seep	Slander	Squander
Toxin	Traversing	Underlying		

1. I can't <u>understand</u> how she could deceive her best friend.

   _____

2. During high tide the harbor is filled with water, but while the tide is out it's a <u>bog</u>.

   _____

3. A few years ago he was down and out, but he worked hard to get his act together, and came back like a <u>mythological bird</u> from the ashes.

   _____

4. Although she was embarrassed to receive the attention of everyone at the event, she was humble and <u>politely</u> accepted the award.

   _____

5. Her aspirations were <u>idealistic</u>, but she persevered and succeeded.

   _____

6. Looking up at night, the cosmos seem to be <u>endless</u>.

   _____

130

7. At their engagement party, her father gave his blessings on them.
   _____

8. If you want to avoid sunburns, it is essential that you wear suntan lotion at the beach.
   _____

9. Architect Frank Gehry's buildings, some of which are constructed with wavy walls and titanium cladding, are regarded as works of pure brilliance.
   _____

10. The smallest amount of pay you can receive in New York is six dollars an hour.
    _____

11. The primary reason that he doesn't go to the movies is that he's afraid of the dark.
    _____

12. Reacting to the negative remarks that their paid spokesman made to the press, the company ended their relationship with him.
    _____

13. The sunrise broke over the horizon like a blessing on the new day.
    _____

14. Having set countless sales records, the Beatles' success still resonates over the music industry, even though they broke up over 30 years ago.
    _____

15. Speaking about poisons that exist in nature, the horticulturist warned us that some wild mushrooms could kill you.
    _____

16. They crossed the mountain range.
    _____

"SUPERGIRL" SYNONYM SENTENCES cont'd.

17. Hoping he would forgive her, she <u>openly</u> told her boyfriend that she had dated another guy.

   _____

18. The new government was in a state of disarray because competing <u>groups</u> were fighting for power.

   _____

19. Looking to end the standoff, the union and corporate officers made a concerted effort to <u>solve</u> their differences.

   _____

20. The hotel room had an <u>amazing</u> view of Central Park.

   _____

21. Genuinely concerned for his estranged sister's welfare, he showed up at the hospital to <u>eliminate</u> the idea that he didn't care.

   _____

22. Whenever I come into large amounts of money, I always seem to <u>waste</u> it.

   _____

23. At the movie premier, the star made a <u>terse</u> remark in response to an interviewer's question about her personal life.

   _____

24. The kids from another clique made <u>malicious</u> comments about my sister.

   _____

25. Bankrupt, addicted, and forsaken by her loved ones, she <u>stated</u> that she would rebuild her life.

   _____

26. The planetarium show made me feel as though I was shooting through the <u>universe</u>.

   _____

27. I cut myself slicing a bagel, and the blood <u>leached</u> through the first bandage I put on.

   _____

28. Finally done with her exams for the year, she showed <u>obvious</u> relief at not having to take any more.

   _____

HECKER & BEERS LAUNCH "SUPERGIRL"

- Keith London & Rebecca Osleeb

NYC – Just before a crucial recording session, we were enjoying some Vietnamese take-out with Adrianne Hecker and Lyle Beers at Native's loft studio, and they graciously agreed to a quick interview while we ate. In town to do the vocal tracks to "SuperGirl," they spoke candidly about their work together and the underlying philosophies that inspired the song.

Given the genius of their compositions, it surprised us to find that the pair have been writing together a minimal amount of time: only one year. And it's awesome that they could manifest such a superlative declaration of resolve with so little prior collaboration. It dispelled our preconception that creative teams need a senescent partnership to produce great work.

Regarding "SuperGirl," its message looms large today given how mired so many factions are in efforts to spread hatred's toxins. Lyle and Adrianne recognize the quixotic nature of hope for universal amity, but they said that it's hard for them to fathom how frequently people squander the peace that they do get.

HECKER & BEERS LAUNCH "SUPERGIRL" cont'd.

Traversing the globe, this political party is slandering that one, one leader is making pithy remarks to another. Adrianne and Lyle wonder when barriers are going to dissolve, and permit settlement to rise like a phoenix. As we wrapped up our conversation and prepared to get to work, I thanked them for bestowing their benediction of reconciliation on us, and as they said, "We can hope..."

Now, refer to the article you've just read to select the statements that best describe the author's remarks. Circle the letter that corresponds to the correct answer.

Question 1

(a) It was crucial that the authors eat Vietnamese take-out.

(b) They were there to accomplish some important work.

(c) Native graciously offered the loft studio for a recording session.

(d) It was important that they ate before the recording session.

Question 2

(a) "SuperGirl" is a candid portrait of Lyle and Adrianne.

(b) The song's inspiring philosophical foundations are honest.

(c) They were in New York to record candid vocal tracks.

(d) The artists openly discussed the ideas behind "SuperGirl."

Question 3

(a) The artists' compositions possess high I.Q.s.

(b) Adrianne and Lyle are geniuses.

(c) Lyle and Adrianne's music is brilliantly written.

(d) The authors were surprised by the artists' intellects.

Question 4

(a) The artists have been working together for only a short time.

(b) Adrianne and Lyle have been a couple for only a short time.

(c) The authors were surprised that they write together only minimally.

(d) Their genius is illustrated by the minimal amount of time they need to write.

Question 5

(a) The artists resolved to manifest a declaration.

(b) The artists create great music despite working together only short time.

(c) The authors enjoy collaborating with superlatives.

(d) With little prior collaboration, the artists and authors declared their resolve.

Question 6

(a) "SuperGirl" echoes the Declaration of Independence.

(b) "SuperGirl" manifests itself as a superlative.

(c) "SuperGirl" is a statement regarding Manifest Destiny.

(d) "SuperGirl" is a great statement of determination.

Question 7

(a) The authors can't spell words related to creative concepts and unusual odors.

(b) They produce great work because they have prior knowledge of how partners should smell.

(c) Originally, the authors thought only older partnerships could create great work.

(d) Creative teams need a good sense of smell in order to produce great work.

Question 8

(a) The song's theme revolves around fractions caught in a sizable pile of muck.

(b) "SuperGirl"'s message is fitting given today's harsh socio-political climate.

(c) "SuperGirl" is a song about a giant weaving in a swamp.

HECKER & BEERS LAUNCH "SUPERGIRL" cont'd.

(d) The message in "SuperGirl" is fitting given many groups' efforts to use poison.

Question 9

(a) Adrianne and Lyle understand that hope for world peace is idealistic.

(b) The artists recognize natural events in the universe that occur quickly.

(c) Lyle and Adrianne know how to recognize Don Quixote.

(d) The artists hope that universal amity is recognized for being quixotically natural.

Question 10

(a) They said that it is hard for to work fathoms below the surface of the ocean.

(b) Lyle and Adrianne feel that people waste their opportunities for quiet.

(c) Adrianne and Lyle cannot fathoming some our frequent squandering.

(d) The artists can't understand why people chose to treat each other so poorly.

Question 11

(a) The artists slander political parties and make terse remarks to world leaders.

(b) Adrianne and Lyle belong to a political party that crosses the globe.

(c) Political parties and world leaders say unflattering things about one another.

(d) They make an observation regarding the excellent state of international relations.

Question 12

(a) The artists contemplate when people will cooperate and allow peace to flourish.

(b) Adrianne and Lyle want superpowers that can dissolve barriers.

(c) They want to acquire a mythical bird that can resurrect itself.

(d) None of the above.

Question 13

(a) Lyle and Adrianne are ordained clergy that can grant blessings.

(b) The authors appreciated Adrianne and Lyle's wishes for world peace.

(c) At the end of their conversation, the artists bestowed a blessing upon the authors.

(d) At the end of their conversation, the authors thanked the artists for their blessings.

KEITH MIDDLETON & RODNEY WILLIE
THE LETTER

"THE LETTER" LISTENING EXERCISE

Listen to "The Letter" all the way through at least once. Then listen to the song again, and in the spaces provided below, list the Word$ that you hear.

"THE LETTER" LYRICS

by Rodney Willie

I wish that we could find a way that we could stay together/
I wanna be with you forever/
Through calm or **tempestuous** weather/(So far away)
Can we go on/ I **surmise** we both know better/
I couldn't let these feelings **fester**/ So I'm writing you this letter

We've been together the **duration** of our high school years/
Quelled all our high school fears/ Cried all our high school tears/
And when our teams played in games we **extolled** them with the loudest cheers/
And when they lost we'd show **disdain** with our other **peers**/
Exacting homework we'd **cogitate** on the answers/
Studied so late we couldn't stay awake the morning after/
Now that it's almost over, I'm more **forlorn** then I've ever been/
I swear I wish we had another year or that school didn't let you in

I wish that we could find a way that we could stay together/
I wanna be with you forever/
Through calm or **tempestuous** weather/(So far away)
Can we go on/ I **surmise** we both know better/
I couldn't let these feelings **fester**/ So I'm writing you this letter

Now I know I seemed **elated**/ When you told me that made it/
I tried to **abstain refrain** from telling you I hate it/
My heart's **debilitated**, don't know if it can handle this/
How **ironic** that you going away to become a **cardiologist**/
Why wasn't I a part of this **colossal** decision?/
Did you not wanna **jeopardize** our last days with fights and **friction**?/
I understand it now but before you leave one thing you must know/
I would've never tried to stop you even though it hurts me so

I'll miss your smile/ I'll miss your walk/
Your **panache** and style/ Our **poignant** talks/
Can't believe your leaving/ Please tell me I'm dreaming/
Come wake me up/ Somebody wake me up

I wish that we could find a way that we could stay together/
I wanna be with you forever/
Through calm or **tempestuous** weather/(So far away)
Can we go on/ I **surmise** we both know better/
I couldn't let these feelings **fester**/ So I'm writing you this letter
(2x)

So far away, so far away/ I **surmise** we both know better...

"THE LETTER" DICTIONARY

Abstain (v) – refrain, desist; give up; do without. Antonym: indulge (v).

The congressmen abstained from voting on a bill that they did not support.

Cardiologist (n) – physician specializing in the heart and cardio-vascular system.

Concerned about his predisposition for heart disease, he saw a cardiologist.

Cogitate (v) – think, consider, reflect, ponder.

It was necessary to cogitate given the issue's complexity and importance.

Colossal (adj) – 1. gigantic, huge, immense; great size. **Colossus** (n). Antonym: miniscule (adj).

One of the 7 wonders of the ancient world, The Colossus of Rhodes was a statue that stood 110 feet tall and took 12 years to complete.

Colossal (adj) – 2. important or great failure Antonym: triumph (adj).

Lasting one season and losing millions of dollars, the XFL was a colossal failure.

Colossal (adj) – 3. important, vital, significant; typically referring to a decision Antonym: inconsequential (adj).

Truman faced a colossal decision of whether or not to use the atom bomb.

Debilitated (v), **Debilitate** (v) – impair, hinder, incapacitate, injure.

He was debilitated by a stroke and now undergoes physical therapy daily.

Disdain (v) – scorn, despise, contempt. Antonym: admire (v).

His ex-girlfriend disdained him.

Duration (n) – period, length; time interval.

The team is toughing it out and digging in for the duration.

Elated (adj) – overjoyed, euphoric, delighted. Antonym: despondent (adj).

She was elated when she found out that she had received a large raise.

Exacting (adj) – 1. demanding, challenging. Antonym: easy (adj).

Medical school is exacting because eventually you'll be making life or death decisions.

Exacting (adj), **Exact** (adj) – 2. precise, correct, accurate. Antonym: imprecise (adj).

It is convenient to use vending machines that can give you exact change.

Exact (v) – 3. take, obtain, demand.

She wanted to exact revenge on the hunter that shot her pet elephant.

Extolled (v), **Extol** (v) – celebrate, praise, commend. Antonym: criticize (v).

The queen's subjects extolled her prosperous reign.

Fester (v) – irritate, aggravate, worsen. Antonym: heal (v).

He said, "You should have a doctor look at that festering boil."

Forlorn (adj) – sad, dejected, lonely, despondent. Antonym: cheerful (adj).

After his girlfriend dumped him he felt abandoned and forlorn.

Friction (n) – 1. resistance, rubbing, abrasion. Antonym: ease (n).

When you apply the brakes in your automobile, pistons compress brake pads against a wheel hub rotor, and the resulting friction slows the car.

Friction (n) – 2. hostility, antagonism, conflict. Antonym: amity (n).

They always disagreed, and whenever they were together there was friction.

Ironic (adj) – paradoxical, incongruous; surprising outcome in light of expected result. Antonym: consistent (adj).

I usually carry an umbrella, and ironically, it rained the day I forgot it at home.

Jeopardize (v) – risk, endanger. **Jeopardy** (n). Antonym: ensure (v).

He didn't want to jeopardize his GPA, so he studied for the final.

"THE LETTER" DICTIONARY cont'd.

Panache (n) – style, élan, confidence, flair. Antonym: inelegance (n).
> He has great panache and always wears the finest suits and handmade shoes.

Peers (n), **Peer** (n) – 1. equal, friend, colleague, contemporary, cohort. Antonyms: superior, inferior (n).
> The legal system entitles one to be judged by a jury of their peers.

Peer (v) – 2. gaze, look intently. Antonym: glance (v).
> She peered into the candy store window, trying to decide what she wanted.

Poignant (adj) – moving, touching, heartbreaking.
> It was a poignant story about a young orphan who is adopted by a loving family.

Quelled (v), **Quell** (v) – 1. suppress, subdue, repress. Antonym: incite (v).
> The National Guard was called in to quell the prison riot.

Quell (v) – 2. allay, alleviate, calm, mitigate. Antonym: terrorize (v).
> It was his first time in a helicopter, so the pilot tried to quell his fear of crashing.

Refrain (v) – 1. abstain; to avoid doing something. Antonym: indulge (v).
> He asked the guy with the cigar, "Would you please refrain from smoking?"

Refrain (v) – 2. chorus; a poetic or musical verse that repeats; idiomatically refers to hearing a repeated excuse.
> Politicians passing the blame has long been a familiar refrain.

Surmise (v) – deduce, estimate, infer, gather; figure out.
> I surmised how big the parking spot was by comparing it to the car adjacent to it.

Tempestuous (adj) – stormy, emotional, passionate. Antonym: calm (v).
> His relationship with his dad is tempestuous and characterized by friction.

"THE LETTER" SYNONYM MATCHING

Match the following Word$ with their synonyms. Note the letter of the matching synonym in the space adjacent to the word.

	Vocabulary Words		Synonyms
1. _____	Abstain	(a)	dejected
2. _____	Cardiologist	(b)	touching
3. _____	Cogitate	(c)	irritate
4. _____	Colossal	(d)	risk
5. _____	Debilitated	(e)	paradoxical
6. _____	Disdain	(f)	suppress
7. _____	Duration	(g)	hostility
8. _____	Elated	(h)	contemporaries
9. _____	Exacting	(i)	do without
10. _____	Extol	(j)	emotional
11. _____	Fester	(k)	ponder
12. _____	Forlorn	(l)	challenging
13. _____	Friction	(m)	time interval
14. _____	Ironic	(n)	incapacitated
15. _____	Jeopardize	(o)	immense
16. _____	Panache	(p)	abstain
17. _____	Peers	(q)	gather
18. _____	Poignant	(r)	heart doctor
19. _____	Quell	(s)	despise
20. _____	Refrain	(t)	style
21. _____	Surmise	(u)	euphoric
22. _____	Tempestuous	(v)	praise

"THE LETTER" SENTENCE COMPLETION

Using a form or tense of the Word$ in the Bank, find the words which best complete the sentences below.

Word Bank				
Abstain	Cardiologist	Cogitate	Colossal	Debilitated
Disdain	Duration	Elated	Exacting	Extolled
Fester	Forlorn	Friction	Ironic	Jeopardize
Panache	Peers	Poignant	Quell	Refrain
Surmise	Tempestuous			

1. Choosing between going away to school or attending college locally and living at home is a _____ decision.

2. "I didn't do it" is a familiar _____ of the guilty.

3. Examining the skid marks, the investigator _____ that the driver did not start braking early enough to avoid the accident.

4. He didn't want to let the problem with sister _____, so he asked her if they could talk it out.

5. I had a terrible case of the flu and I was completely _____.

6. Thousands packed the canyon of lower Broadway to _____ John Glenn upon his return as the first American to orbit the Earth.

7. The Dean made an impassioned plea for cooler heads to prevail as she tried to _____ the student uprising.

8. Those who perished on 9/11 were remembered in a _____ tribute at the site of the World Trade Center.

9. Talented but _____, he could be very engaging, but he could

also be difficult to work with if things didn't go his way.

10. Isn't is _____ that "reality" shows are scripted in editing?

11. Rivals on the court, there was always _____ between them.

12. My dad had a heart attack and now visits the _____ regularly.

13. Sitting in front of their demolished home, they looked _____ but said that they were happy to have survived the hurricane.

14. Since some students are only comfortable talking about their problems with friends, she started a _____ counseling program at her school.

15. She's a vegetarian and _____ from eating meat.

16. He was _____ by his daughter's safe return from her trek through the Himalayas.

17. The art teacher asked his students to draw cartoons for the _____ of the class and to bring in them in the following week.

18. She _____ him because he was an unrepentant chauvinist.

19. Rolls Royce and Jaguar established British marques as the epitome of automotive _____.

20. For centuries philosophers have _____ upon the reason for our existence.

21. If the school doesn't receive additional funding soon, many of its most important programs will be in _____.

22. Detectives need to be tough and _____ to avoid missing clues.

"THE LETTER" CROSSWORD PUZZLE

Use the synonyms provided in the clues to identify the wordS that complete the crossword puzzle on the following page. The numbers run top-to-bottom and left-to-right

Across

1. Equals, friends, colleagues, contemporaries, cohorts
2. Paradoxical, incongruous; surprising outcome in light of expected result
3. Demanding, challenging (or) precise, correct, accurate (or) take, obtain, demand
4. Deduce, estimate, infer, gather; figure out
5. Physician specializing in treatment of the heart and cardio-vascular system
6. Style, élan, confidence, flair
7. Celebrated, praised, exalted, commend
8. Time period
9. Risk, endanger; to make vulnerable
10. Suppressed, subdued, repressed; put down (or) allay, alleviate, calm, mitigate
11. Gigantic, huge, immense; great size (or) great failure (or) important, vital, significant

Down

1. Stormy, emotional, passionate
2. Refrain, desist; give up; do without
3. Abstain; to avoid doing something (or) chorus; a poetic or musical verse that repeats
4. Moving, touching, heartbreaking
5. Scorn, despise, contempt
6. Think, consider, reflect, ponder
7. Irritate, aggravate, worsen
8. Impaired, hindered, incapacitated, injured
9. Resistance, rubbing, abrasion (or) hostility, antagonism, conflict.
10. Sad, dejected, lonely, despondent
11. Overjoyed, euphoric, delighted

Knowledge is a State of Mind™

"THE LETTER" CROSSWORD PUZZLE

147

"THE LETTER" SYNONYM SENTENCES

In the following sentences, use correct forms or tenses of the Word$ in the Bank to match the underlined synonyms, and write the correct word in the space provided below each sentence.

WORD BANK				
Abstain	Cardiologist	Cogitate	Colossal	Debilitated
Disdain	Duration	Elated	Exacting	Extolled
Fester	Forlorn	Friction	Ironic	Jeopardize
Panache	Peers	Poignant	Quell	Refrain
Surmise	Tempestuous			

1. Following a short walk, she said that she was having heart palpitations, and that she better see a <u>doctor</u>.

   _____

2. Before I reach a decision, I will need to <u>think</u> and consider the relevant data carefully.

   _____

3. We stood for the <u>length</u> of their wedding ceremony, and when it was over I couldn't wait to find a couch to crash on.

   _____

4. Thunder scares Dakota, so I tried my best to <u>allay</u> his fear of the storm.

   _____

5. Looking a paw print in on the forest path, the ranger said, "From the size of this impression, we can <u>infer</u> that this mountain lion was about 6 feet long."

   _____

6. It is <u>paradoxical</u> that when she studies exceptionally hard for an exam she'll usually earn a lower grade than when she studies less intensely.

   _____

7. All of these late nights studying are taking a toll on me.

   _____

8. He and his father shared a touching moment when they embraced one another for the first time in ten years.

   _____

9. Her father told her to stop hanging around with the teachers and to spend time with her friends.

   _____

10. While today's movie heroes use brute force to win the day, the leading men of classic movies always succeeded via their wits and style.

    _____

11. He didn't want to endanger his chances of getting a car for graduation, so he made sure that he was always home by curfew.

    _____

12. While putting some new furniture together, I couldn't get one of the nuts to screw onto its bolt, so I put oil on it to reduce the resistance.

    _____

13. Her blister was beginning to get worse, so I told her to go see the nurse.

    _____

14. He was despondent over the loss of his puppy, and we couldn't cheer him up.

    _____

15. However, he was overjoyed when he got home and his mom told him that she had found the puppy hiding in one of the closets.

    _____

16. Our coach praised the benefits of a healthy diet and regular exercise.

    _____

"THE LETTER" SYNONYM SENTENCES cont'd.

17. She also implored us to <u>abstain</u> from smoking.

18. He said that although the project was a <u>total</u> failure, he would get back on his feet and try again.

19. Her relationship with her mom is <u>emotional</u> because they are so much alike.

20. My dad asked my friends to <u>desist</u> from eating all of the chocolate in the house every time they came over.

21. He treats them with <u>contempt</u> whenever they drop by.

22. I think he's mentally <u>impaired</u>; it's only chocolate.

"THE LETTER" EXAMINED

- Keith London

NYC – I've surmised that "The Letter" by Keith Middleton and Rodney Willie, with vocals performed by Avon Marshall, is easily the most poignant track on DM. The story of a forlorn graduate whose girlfriend has gone off to college to become a cardiologist, Avon describes the irony of the elation of love being debilitated by friction.

Their relationship in jeopardy, the graduate cogitates the colossal decision of carrying on for the duration and suffering the toll exacted by his frustration, or to abstain from seeing her any longer. Avon's character seems tempestuous; he extols his love's panache, but cites a refrain familiar to his peers, that without her near, his longing festers and cannot be quelled. And, as much as he disdains saying so, in the end, he believes it best that they part.

> Now, refer to the article you've just read to select the statements that best describe the author's remarks. Circle the letter that corresponds to the correct answer.

Question 1
(a) The author is guessing that "The Letter" is poignant.
(b) After considering the other tracks on DM, the author has deduced that "The Letter" is the most touching of the all of the songs.
(c) Upon his consideration of the songs on DM the author has surmised that the poignant vocals on "The Letter" were preformed by Avon Marshall.
(d) Inferring that "The Letter" was written by Keith Middleton and Rodney Willie, the author surmised that the vocals were performed by Avon Marshall.

Question 2
(a) The graduate is despondent because his girlfriend is becoming a doctor but he isn't.
(b) The girlfriend ditched the graduate because he couldn't get into as good a school as she did.
(c) The graduate is forlorn because his girlfriend went off to school to see a cardiologist.
(d) Avon's graduate is dejected because his love went off to study medicine.

Question 3
(a) The singer describes ironing while his elation is debilitated by friction.
(b) It is paradoxical that the euphoria of love can be impaired by conflict.
(c) It is an unexpected outcome that euphoria can be hindered by abrasion.

"THE LETTER" EXAMINED cont'd.

(d) Avon presents the paradox that an unexpected outcome can be impaired.

Question 4

(a) The couple's love at risk, the graduate ponders his options.

(b) The graduate, being especially bright, has considered how his situation might get him on *Jeopardy!*

(c) The graduate is contemplating how he might jeopardize their relationship.

(d) His girlfriend loves *Jeopardy!*, and he thinks that if he can win, she'll return.

Question 5

(a) The graduate realizes that going on *Jeopardy!* Is a big decision.

(b) The graduate is wondering exactly how long their relationship will be at risk.

(c) The graduate wonders whether or not he can endure the frustration of being separated from his girlfriend.

(d) Driving to see his girlfriend, the graduate wonders how long it will take, and whether or not there will be any tolls that require exact change.

Question 6

(a) Avon's protagonist reflects on the enormity of deciding whether or not to end their relationship.

(b) The protagonist is pondering how long it will be necessary to refrain from seeing his girlfriend.

(c) Avon's character must go without paying exact tolls for the duration of his drive to see his girlfriend.

(d) All of the above.

Question 7

(a) Although he appears emotional, the graduate commends his girlfriend's confidence.

(b) Avon's character is emotional and jealous of his girlfriend's panache.

(c) Extolling élan, Avon's character is overwhelmed with emotion.

(d) The graduate is passionate about his love and praises her flair and sense of style.

Question 8

(a) Citing his girlfriend, the graduate will avoid being with his colleagues.

(b) The graduate repeats some choruses to his friends.

(c) Avon's character repeats a phrase that his contemporaries would understand.

(d) Avon is going to avoid becoming familiar with his cohorts.

Question 9

(a) The graduate's festering cannot be quelled, and he should be seen by a cardiologist right away.

(b) The graduate increasingly misses his girlfriend, and he cannot subdue his longing for her.

(c) The graduate is trying to suppress his longing, but it is becoming irritated.

(d) Avon's character has an irritation that needs to be quelled immediately.

Question 10

(a) In the end, the graduate despises saying, "so."

(b) Although he despises saying so, the graduate believes that the end is the best part.

(c) Avon's character is filled with contempt for his girlfriend.

(d) Although it is a difficult decision, the graduate concludes that he and his girlfriend should break up.

MIA JOHNSON & THE MIA JOHNSON BAND
UPSIDE DOWN

"UPSIDE DOWN" LISTENING EXCERCISE

Listen to "Upside Down" all the way through at least once. Then listen to the song again, and in the spaces provided below, list the Word$ that you hear.

"UPSIDE DOWN" LYRICS

by Mia Johnson

I'll start where I remember
It was dark and I was driving
In my **peripheral** a **glimmer**
Of headlights on my right side

Disconcerting all my insides
An **impact** on me broadside
And it now seems I **reside**

Upside down
Gazing up to see the ground
Upside down
Everything **inverted** all around
Chaos has **incontrovertibly** set in
And my luck has gone **saturnine** on me again

I **incurred** quite a tossing
Overcome by **incredulity**
It took some time after that **jostling**
To regain **equanimity**
After this **calamity**
Occurring with such **celerity**
A **deviant** reality

Upside down
Gazing up to see the ground
Upside down
Everything **inverted** all around
Chaos has **incontrovertibly** set in
And my luck has gone **saturnine** on me again

Despite all of the drama
I was **thaumaturgicaly unscathed**
Looking up now there's a **panorama**
Of **resplendent constellations**
Shining down upon the nations
I have **defied trepidation**
And come out with **jubilation**
Cuz I'm no longer
Upside down
Gazing up to see the ground
Upside down

"UPSIDE DOWN" LYRICS cont'd.

Everything **inverted** all around
Upside down
Upside down

"UPSIDE DOWN" DICTIONARY

Calamity (n) – disaster, catastrophe, tragedy; event that causes suffering.
The local farmers fear a calamity if the river rises above its banks.

Celerity (n) – swiftness or speed of an action.
Jets travel with great celerity, especially when compared to prop driven aircraft.

Chaos (n) – confusion; disorder. **Chaotic** (adj). Antonym: order (n).
The guests couldn't get into the party, the staff was running around trying to find a manager, the DJ didn't show up; it was complete chaos.

Constellations (n), **Constellation** (n) – assemblage; groups of stars that form patterns and have been given names.
In our astronomy class we studied the constellation The Big Dipper.

Defied (v), **Defy** (v) – resist, disregard, challenge; refuse to obey. **Defiance** (n).
I would love to fly like a bird and defy gravity.

Deviant (adj) – abnormal; differing from the norm or from socially accepted standards of behavior. **Deviance** (n). Antonym: normal (adj).
What constitutes deviant behavior varies among cultures, for example here in the U.S. it is illegal to marry a relative, whereas in some societies it is acceptable.

Disconcerting (adj) – disturbing, upsetting, embarrassing. **Disconcert** (v). Antonym: comforting (adj).
She has a disconcerting habit of going back on her word.

Equanimity (n) – composure; the state of being calm, even-tempered, level-headed.

She remained calm and maintained her equanimity when she heard of her husband's accident.

Gazing (v), **Gaze** (v) – stare; fixed attention; to look at something intently.

He enjoys gazing out the window at the city below.

Glimmer (v) – shine, gleam, reflect.

Her car glimmered in the sun after she waxed and polished it.

Impact (n) – 1. crash, collision.

The meteor's impact created a huge crater in the desert.

Impact (n) – 2. influence, impression, effect.

She was a very active volunteer who made a great impact on her community.

Incontrovertibly (adv) – indisputably, unquestionably. **Incontrovertible** (adj). Antonym: disputably (adv).

The video playback incontrovertibly shows that she fouled me.

Incredulity (n) – disbelief, skepticism; not able or wanting to believe something. **Incredulous** (adj). Antonym: conviction (n).

She fought the call and was incredulous, even though the evidence of the foul was on the video playback.

Incurred (v), **Incur** (v) – to bring upon oneself; to sustain an unpleasant outcome; to suffer.

His dad made some stock picks that didn't work out, and he incurred big losses.

Inverted (adj) – upturn; to turn upside down; to reverse the order of two things. **Invert** (v). Antonym: righted (v).

At the air show I watched a stunt plane fly upside down and do an inverted roll.

"UPSIDE DOWN" DICTIONARY cont'd.

Jostling (v), **Jostle** (v) – shove, bump, push. Antonym: coddling (v).

While exiting the arena the singer encountered a crowd of jostling fans.

Jubilation (n) – rejoicing, celebration; an expression of joy. **Jubilant** (adj). Antonym: sadness (n).

The crowd was jubilant when their team won the championship.

Occurring (v), **Occur** (v) – transpire; happen.

The movie we saw last night was about a deli clerk who traveled back in time to prevent a calamity from occurring.

Panorama (n) – vista; an unbroken view of a large area. **Panoramic** (adj).

You can see the panorama of the entire city from the Empire State Building's observation deck.

Peripheral (adj) – tangential, outer, marginal; at the edge. **Periphery** (n). Antonym: central (adj).

During our debate he introduced points that weren't central to the issue, and were only peripherally related.

Reside (v) – to inhabit; to exist in; to live in a given location. **Resident** (n).

I plan to study abroad, and I'd like to reside in London.

Resplendent (adj) – dazzling, stunning, glorious, brilliant. Antonym: dull (adj).

The vintage aircraft's mirror-polished fuselage was resplendent in the bright sunlight.

Saturnine (adj) – melancholy, gloomy, sullen, glum.

She was saturnine over the loss of her grandmother.

Thaumaturgicaly (adv) – magical, miraculously, supernatural; the working of miracles or magic feats. **Thaumaturgy** (n).

In a story I read a knight recited an incantation and thaumaturgicaly defeated the dragon.

Trepidation (n) – fear, anxiety, apprehension. Antonym: confidence (n).

Hoping to be accepted with the early admissions, he opened the envelope from Princeton with great trepidation.

Unscathed (adj) – unharmed, intact; without injury or damage. Antonym: damaged (adj).

Astonishingly, she escaped the car accident unscathed.

NOTES:

"UPSIDE DOWN" SYNONYM MATCHING

Match the following Word$ with their synonyms. Note the letter of the matching synonym in the space adjacent to the word.

Vocabulary Words	**Synonyms**
1. _____ Calamity	(a) abnormal
2. _____ Celerity	(b) stare
3. _____ Chaos	(c) sustain
4. _____ Constellations	(d) bump
5. _____ Defied	(e) live
6. _____ Deviant	(f) disaster
7. _____ Disconcerting	(g) skeptical
8. _____ Equanimity	(h) view
9. _____ Gaze	(i) disregard
10. _____ Glimmer	(j) gloomy
11. _____ Impact	(k) disorder
12. _____ Incontrovertibly	(l) dazzling
13. _____ Incredulous	(m) celebration
14. _____ Incur	(n) disturbing
15. _____ Inverted	(o) speed
16. _____ Jostle	(p) magical
17. _____ Jubilation	(q) upturned
18. _____ Occur	(r) assemblage
19. _____ Panorama	(s) gleam
20. _____ Peripheral	(t) unharmed
21. _____ Reside	(u) anxiety
22. _____ Resplendent	(v) composure
23. _____ Saturnine	(w) outer

Vocabulary Words	Synonyms
24. _____Thaumaturgy	(x) unquestionably
25. _____Trepidation	(y) influence
26. _____Unscathed	(z) transpire

"UPSIDE DOWN" SENTENCE COMPLETION

Using a form or tense of the Word$ in the Bank, find the words which best complete the sentences below.

WORD BANK

Calamity	Celerity	Chaos	Constellations	Defied
Deviant	Disconcerting	Equanimity	Gazing	Glimmer
Impact	Incontrovertibly	Incredulity	Incurred	Inverted
Jostling	Jubilation	Occurring	Panorama	Peripheral
Reside	Resplendent	Saturnine	Thaumaturgy	Trepidation
Unscathed				

1. He _____ the odds and went on to become a champion.

2. At the concert we _____ for position at the foot of the stage.

3. Miraculously, the dog was _____ after being hit by the bike.

4. She often paid her bills after their due date, and _____ many late fees as a result.

5. _____ broke out as the standing-room-only crowd was jostled by the stadium ushers.

6. The company was struck by a series of _____; executive fraud, a massive recall, and a class action suit, all of which led to its bankruptcy.

"UPSIDE DOWN" SENTENCE COMPLETION cont'd.

7. Sitting on a dune above the beach, he _____ out at the ocean and admired the panorama.

8. She's very calm in difficult situations; you have to respect her _____.

9. The crowd was _____ as each massive balloon rose out of the staging area and joined the parade.

10. During the 19th century it was popular to visit circular exhibit halls that displayed _____ paintings of renowned places or events.

11. Crossing the Tappan Zee Bridge on a clear night, you can see the city lights _____ in the distance.

12. Sparkling like a pile of diamonds a hundred miles away, New York is a _____ beacon.

13. Despite the proof, he was _____ and refused to believe that he was raised by wolves.

14. The _____ of the Earth's rotation is 1,070 miles per hour.

15. Humanity's inability to behave humanely is very _____.

16. The _____ "The Big Dipper" is a group of stars that looks like a giant pot in the sky.

17. Their prior partnership was very frustrating, so he approached his new collaboration with the artist with some _____.

18. _____ behavior is not socially acceptable.

19. Her grandparents now _____ in Florida.

20. They were looking for _____ proof of his complicity.

21. A wizard is skilled in _____ .

22. It was awesome; the roller coaster track turned upside down and _____ the cars as we flew into a sharp turn.

23. A stolid woman, she always seems to be wearing a _____ expression on her face.

24. Watching a horror movie in a theater, I was scared senseless when I caught something move quickly through my _____ vision.

25. It doesn't matter how many times I reboot my computer, glitches keep _____ .

26. Meteorites hit the moon regularly, leaving its surface pockmarked with _____ craters.

NOTES:

"UPSIDE DOWN" CROSSWORD PUZZLE

Use the synonyms provided in the clues to identify the words that complete the crossword puzzle on the following page. The numbers run top-to-bottom and left-to-right.

Across

1. Disbelief, skepticism
2. Composure; the state of being calm, even-tempered
3. Rejoicing, celebration, an expression of joy
4. Upturned; to turn upside down
5. Tangential, outer, marginal; at the edge
6. Indisputably, unquestionably
7. Dazzling, stunning, glorious, brilliant
8. Swiftness or speed of an action
9. Magical, miraculous, supernatural
10. Melancholy, gloomy, sullen, glum
11. Unharmed, intact; without injury or damage
12. To inhabit; to exist in; to live in a given location
13. Confusion, disorder
14. Transpire, happen

Down

1. Crash, collision (or) influence, impression, effect
2. Abnormal; differing from accepted behavior
3. Shine, gleam, reflect
4. Resist, disregard, challenge; refuse to obey
5. Assemblages; groups of stars
6. Shove, bump, push
7. Staring; looking at something intently
8. To bring upon oneself; to sustain an unpleasant outcome; to suffer
9. Disaster, catastrophe; an event that causes suffering
10. Fear, anxiety, apprehension
11. Disturbing, upsetting, embarrassing
12. Vista; an unbroken view of a large area

"UPSIDE DOWN" CROSSWORD PUZZLE

165

"UPSIDE DOWN" SYNONYM SENTENCES

In the following sentences, use correct forms or tenses of the Word$ in the Bank to match the underlined synonyms, and write the correct word in the space provided below each sentence.

WORD BANK

Calamity	Celerity	Chaos	Constellations	Defied
Deviant	Disconcerting	Equanimity	Gazing	Glimmer
Impact	Incontrovertibly	Incredulity	Incurred	Inverted
Jostling	Jubilation	Occurring	Panorama	Peripheral
Reside	Resplendent	Saturnine	Thaumaturgy	Trepidation
Unscathed				

1. Her husband better drive with <u>speed</u>, or she'll have the baby in their car.

   _____

2. His <u>sullen</u> gaze lays bare his life's hardships.

   _____

3. Not knowing what to expect, she approached the exam with <u>apprehension</u>.

   _____

4. When World War II ended, <u>celebrating</u> crowds packed Times Square.

   _____

5. For those who reach Mount Everest's summit, it must be sublime to take in the <u>view</u> of the entire world below you.

   _____

6. Remarkably, he was <u>unharmed</u> after falling down the stairs.

   _____

7. The facts prove her statements to be <u>indisputable</u>.

   _____

8. Flying over the shore on a bright summer day, I looked down and saw the beachgoers' sunglasses <u>shine</u> like diamonds scattered across the sand.

   _____

9. Although the Web doesn't appear to have a physical form, it is actually a vast <u>assemblage</u> of interconnected computers.

   _____

10. The protesters <u>challenged</u> the government and staged a sit-in near the capital.

    _____

11. The subway riders <u>bumped</u> one another as they made their way out of the crowded station.

    _____

12. Medieval tales often describe astonishing, <u>supernatural</u> events.

    _____

13. I hate when I bring my car in to be repaired for an intermittent problem, and when I get to the shop, it doesn't <u>happen</u>.

    _____

14. He decided to <u>live</u> in the city because it was close to his job.

    _____

15. Her classic Vette was <u>stunning</u> in bright white livery with blue racing stripes.

    _____

16. Her mom said, "Stop <u>staring</u> out the window and finish your homework!"

    _____

17. We had so much work to do for the fete that we only took care of the essentials; we blew off doing anything that was <u>tangential</u>.

    _____

"UPSIDE DOWN" SYNONYM SENTENCES cont'd.

18. His house was in a state of complete <u>disorder</u> after that party.

    _____

19. It wouldn't have been such a <u>catastrophe</u> if his parents hadn't come back from their vacation early.

    _____

20. It was pretty <u>disturbing</u> to be standing there while they chewed him out.

    _____

21. They were <u>in disbelief</u> that he ignored their instructions not to have anyone over.

    _____

22. I think what they were most upset about was the <u>upside-down</u> ice cream truck in the garage.

    _____

23. This episode is definitely going to have huge <u>effect</u> on his social life for a few months.

    _____

24. His dad, who's pretty melodramatic, yelled, "You have <u>brought upon</u> my wrath!"

    _____

25. I can't believe that he handled it all with such <u>composure</u>.

    _____

26. We don't understand what they're so mad about; it's not like he's <u>abnormal</u> or anything like that.

    _____

MIA JOHNSON GETS INVERTED

- Keith London

Metro Philly – Artists are always looking for stories to write about, but this tale of chaos came looking for Mia Johnson. I'm jubilant that she's here to tell it, because in this one she almost became a permanent resident of Eternal Rest Acres.

Back on a crystal-clear July night, Mia was driving to a late gig when, in her peripheral vision, she spotted a pair of glimmering headlights rushing toward her. Incredulous, she realized that some deviant ran a 'STOP' sign and was about to T-bone her. Despite her trepidation and the disconcerting image of an imminent calamity, she kept her equanimity, thought with celerity, and stood on the gas. Bracing herself for what she knew was about to occur, the other car struck her rear wheel dead-on on the passenger-side, and the impact launched her sideways like a toddler smacking his Hot Wheels with a hockey stick. Flying across the street driver's-door-first, she hit a fire hydrant on the far side of the road, slamming into it with such force that the car flipped. Then, everything, Was still.

Opening her eyes, Mia saw that she was inverted, hanging upside down in her seatbelt. Before she unfastened herself, she ran a mental disaster checklist- Pain? Check. Broken bones? Check. Blood? Double Check. Defying all probability through some thaumaturgical feat, she came through unscathed, and didn't incur a single scratch; just a few bruises. Instead of it being a saturnine moment, it was incontrovertibly one of the best of Mia's life.

She jostled her way out of the seatbelt that saved her life, dropped onto the ceiling, and crawled out through a shattered window. Steeling herself, Mia brought herself to her feet. Confused and startled but intact, she gazed up toward the cosmos, and drank in the resplendent panorama of constellations... safe, and thankful to no longer be "Upside Down."

MIA JOHNSON GETS INVERTED cont'd.

> Now, refer to the article you've just read to select the statements that best describe the author's remarks. Circle the letter that corresponds to the correct answer.

Question 1

(a) Mia was looking for chaos.

(b) Dr. Chaos was looking for Mia.

(c) A catastrophe was going to befall Mia.

(d) Mia was looking for a story to write about.

Question 2

(a) The author was pleased that Mia was going to able to get some rest.

(b) Mia is happy that she'll be able to catch some rest.

(c) The author is elated that Mia became a permanent resident.

(d) The author is very happy that Mia did not pass on.

Question 3

(a) On a beautiful summer evening Mia caught a glimpse of a car that was going to hit her.

(b) The oncoming car's headlights were out.

(c) Mia was late to a gig.

(d) She was late getting to a gig, so despite Mia's poor peripheral vision, she was rushing to get there.

Question 4

(a) Mia couldn't believe it when she realized that a deviant was allowed to drive.

(b) She was in a state of disbelief that some joker just ran a 'STOP' sign, and was about to plow into her.

(c) In a state of disbelief, Mia wondered how the driver of the other car could enjoy a steak while driving.

(d) She could not believe that a law-abiding citizen would pass through a 'STOP' sign.

Question 5

(a) Mia is fearful of disturbing images.

(b) She is nervously apprehensive about disconcerting images.

(c) She was fearful of the impending collision.

(d) Mia has trepidation of disconcerting imminent calamities.

Question 6

(a) Despite her trepidation over the disconcerting image, there was an imminent calamity during which she retained her equanimity for celerity.

(b) Despite her anxiety over the imminent accident, Mia stayed level headed and thought about celery.

(c) In spite of Mia's nervous anxiety regarding the coming collision, she kept her cool, thought with celerity, and stood up in the car.

(d) Despite her fear of the coming collision, she remained level-headed and thought quickly.

Question 7

(a) Mia was wearing braces and she knew that they were going to get hit by the oncoming car.

(b) The oncoming car smashed into her car, throwing it sideways at great speed.

(c) She held herself together, waiting to be struck by a kid with a hockey stick.

(d) The oncoming car smashed into her side, launching the toddler sideways.

Question 8

(a) Her car slid sideways with celerity, smashed into a hydrant, and overturned.

MIA JOHNSON GETS INVERTED cont'd.

    (b) The hydrant flew across the street to flip her car's driver-side door.

    (c) Her drivers-side door flew across the street, smashed into the hydrant and flipped.

    (d) After she slid across the street driver-side-first, the hydrant slammed into the car and flipped it.

Question 9

(a) When Mia opened her eyes she wasn't wearing her seatbelt, but she was upside down.

(b) When Mia opened her eyes, she unfastened herself, and then did a disaster check.

(c) When Mia opened her eyes she was overturned, suspended by her seatbelt.

(d) When Mia opened her eyes, she inverted her mental disaster checklist in her seatbelt.

Question 10

(a) Defying the odds with a magical incantation, she came through unhurt.

(b) Challenging the oncoming car using her supernatural powers, Mia wasn't injured in the crash.

(c) Resisting all probability via some miracle, Mia didn't incur any bruises.

(d) Beating the odds, Mia was miraculously unhurt, incurring only a few bruises.

Question 11

(a) Following the accident Mia was happy.

(b) After the collision, she was melancholy and sullen.

(c) It was indisputably the most saturnine moment of her life.

(d) Mia's young life is incontrovertibly one of the best.

Question 12

(a) Mia hated wearing her seatbelt and pushed her way out of it.

(b) She shoved her way out of her seatbelt and fell onto the ceiling.

(c) She shattered a window struggling to get out of her seatbelt.

(d) The shattered glass broke her seatbelt, dropping her onto the ceiling.

Question 13

(a) Delirious but unscathed, Mia admired the stars shimmering in the night sky.

(b) The accident was caused by her drinking problem; she shouldn't have drank in the constellations.

(c) She is thankful that she no longer needs to drink upside down.

(d) Mia turned into steel, and had to drag herself to her feet.

BLANDING & JACKSON - F.A.M.E. ENT.
MOVE IT

"MOVE IT" LISTENING EXERCISE

Listen to "Move It" all the way through at least once. Then listen to the song again, and in the spaces provided below, list the Word$ that you hear.

"MOVE IT" LYRICS

by Ed Blanding & Troy Jackson with Keith London

Let's see if y'all can **grasp** this clap?
Y'all ready?

We're gonna move it like this
Jump up on it
And clap your hands like this
We're gonna **gambol** like that
Be clear, we here, the party's in the back

I don't wanna **induce** you to do anything you don't wanna do
I'm just that kid that brings **devotion** and a hug or two
I don't wanna commit no **indiscretion**
But like I said I just wanna give you the right **impression**
We can be **symbiotic** if our love is forever
If we **beset** by trouble, we can **resolve** it together
I don't know about **eternity** when starting from scratch
I don't **fret** or pay attention to the **distractions** in my path

That could be our downfall/ What do we need a crowd for
It's just me and you we can paint the town floors
If you're ridin' with me, cool, cause I'm rollin' with you (ok)
Take a pause girl/ Tell me what you wanna do

We're gonna move it like this
Jump up on it and clap your hands like this
We're gonna **gambol** like that
Be clear, we here, the **fete** is in the back
(2x)

Let's go

Y'all **grasp** it yet?
Nah, don't worry
We're gonna move on/ Let's go

The **context** didn't change, but the party's still bumpin'
We in the back with the models, and the convos is comin'
This is a VIP session, you **cavorting** or stallin'
Yo' my money got **clout**, so I ain't got no time for spoilin'
So I **rig** my hat, and brush my shoulders, continue to party
Everything is **euphoric, a**s long as we acting properly
If your friend wants to dance, I can dance with two
We can **frolic** all night, till the party is through

We're gonna move it like this
Jump up on it and clap your hands like this

"MOVE IT" LYRICS cont'd.

We're gonna **gambol** like that
Be clear, we here, the **fete** is in the back
(2x)

We can party tomorrow
You can party tonight
The after party's def
What we doin' tonight
(2x)

We're gonna move it like this
Jump up on it and clap your hands like this
We're gonna **gambol** like that
Be clear, we here, the **fete** is in the back
(2x)

Voice over: "This track is so **sublime**…"

"MOVE IT" DICTIONARY

Beset (v) – overwhelm, inundate, trouble, harass, surround.
> The refugees were best by one catastrophe after another.

Cavorting (v), **Cavort** (v) – jump, horse around, rough-housing; move around in a playful and/or noisy way. Antonym: curtailing (v).
> Wrestling and tackling each other, the children cavorted on the lawn.

Clout (n) – political power; social or financial influence or importance.
> The chairman of the Senate Ethics Committee has enormous clout.

Context (n) – circumstances; details surrounding a subject. **Contextual** (adj).
> On the news her quote seemed harsh; her remark was actually benign, but it had been taken out of context.

Devotion (n), **Devote** (v) – dedication, support, commitment. Antonym: indifference (n).
The volunteer's devotion to helping the homeless is inspiring.

Distraction (n) – disturbance, diversion, interruption. **Distract** (v). Antonym: focus (n).
I can't listen to music while I work because it distracts me.

Eternity (n) – infinity, perpetuity, forever; time without end. **Eternal** (adj).
She said that she would love him for all of eternity and would never leave his side.

Euphoric (adj) – overjoyed, elated, exhilarated; great happiness. **Euphoria** (n). Antonym: miserable (adj).
He was euphoric after she accepted his invitation to the concert.

Fete (n) – party, celebration, carnival.
The student union is throwing a fete for the freshmen.

Fret (v) – worry; to be annoyed or anxious. **Fretful** (adj). Antonym: relax (v).
He spent the day fretting about the argument he had with his boss.

Frolic (v) – play; to behave in a happy or playful manner. Antonym: grieve (v).
The puppies frolicked in the grass.

Gambol (v) – bound, leap, romp. Antonym: crawl (v).
The dancers gamboled across the stage.

Grasp (v) – 1. understand, comprehend. Antonym: misunderstand (v).
The students had a good grasp of some rather difficult material.

Grasp (v) – 2. grab, seize. Antonym: release (v).
Struggling to climb into the helicopter, the stuntman grasped the landing skid.

"MOVE IT" DICTIONARY cont'd.

Impression (n) – 1. perception, feeling, reaction. **Impress** (v).
> He tried to make a good impression on his girlfriend's mom.

Impression (n) – 2. indent, imprint.
> She used her thumb to make an impression in the cookie dough.

Indiscretion (n) – carelessness, tactless; lack of tact or judgment. **Indiscreet** (adj). Antonym: discretion (n).
> The CIA agent that leaked details to the media was fired for his indiscretion.

Induce (v) – persuade, cause; compel using pressure. Antonym: prevent (v).
> She tried to induce her daughter to study for her exams.

Resolve (v) – 1. solve, decide. **Resolution** (n).
> Working together, we can resolve the problem.

Resolve (n) – 2. determination, tenacity. Antonym: indifference (adj).
> Full of resolve, the stranded mountaineers attempted the treacherous decent.

Rig (v) – fix, arrange, prepare, manipulate.
> The competition was rigged by the judges.

Sublime (adj) – awe-inspiring, moving, transcendent, perfect. Antonym: uninspiring (adj).
> More than one wine critic has described a favorite vintage as being sublime.

Symbiotic (adj) – a mutually beneficial, interdependent relationship. Antonym: parasitic (adj).
> In an illustration of the perfect symbiotic relationship, hippos rely on birds to eat flies that would otherwise bite them, and the birds rely on hippos to attract flies, their primary source of food.

"MOVE IT" SYNONYM MATCHING

Match the following Word$ with their synonyms. Note the letter of the matching synonym in the space adjacent to the word.

Vocabulary Words	Synonyms
1. _____ Beset	(a) tactlessness
2. _____ Cavort	(b) bound
3. _____ Clout	(c) elated
4. _____ Context	(d) infinity
5. _____ Devotion	(e) influence
6. _____ Distraction	(f) understand
7. _____ Eternity	(g) pressure
8. _____ Euphoric	(h) inundated
9. _____ Fete	(i) horse around
10. _____ Fret	(j) disturbance
11. _____ Frolic	(k) party
12. _____ Gambol	(l) perception
13. _____ Grasp	(m) mutual benefit
14. _____ Impression	(n) transcendent
15. _____ Indiscretion	(o) circumstances
16. _____ Induce	(p) commitment
17. _____ Resolve	(q) play
18. _____ Rig	(r) worry
19. _____ Sublime	(s) solve
20. _____ Symbiotic	(t) manipulate

NOTES:

_____

_____

"MOVE IT" SENTENCE COMPLETION

Using a form or tense of the Word$ in the Bank, find the words which best complete the sentences below.

WORD BANK

Beset	Cavort	Clout	Context	Devotion
Distraction	Eternity	Euphoric	Fete	Fret
Frolic	Gambol	Grasp	Impression	Indiscretion
Induce	Resolve	Rig	Sublime	Symbiotic

1. She was _____ after finishing the SATs.

2. He couldn't _____ the ideas presented in the article.

3. The neighbor's party was _____ me from my homework.

4. She told him that he needed to _____ the problem today.

5. The _____ to celebrate graduation is being held at my house.

6. He tried to make a good _____ on his girlfriend's parents.

7. In the 1950s Congress investigated game shows that were suspected of being _____.

8. Taken out of _____, the senator's sound-bite made him appear ridiculous.

9. _____ at the fete, the guys tossed their girlfriends in the pool.

10. His bragging went on and on; it lasted for an _____.

11. Puppies like to _____ in the open grass.

12. The protesters _____ her to stop wearing fur by telling her about all of the cute little animals that she would save.

13. Edgar Allen Poe, one of English literature's most renowned authors and a tragic figure, was _____ by turmoil during his life, and died penniless and alone.

14. Following the revelations of his affair with an intern, former President Clinton became known for his _____.

15. The dancers _____ across the stage.

16. The queen is regarded as a political figure, although she has no real political _____.

17. A healthy marriage is a _____ relationship.

18. Man, the beats we heard at the show took you to another place and time; they were _____.

19. I told him, "Don't sit there _____ about Thursday's exam, get off your backside and go study!"

20. Martin Luther King _____ his life to achieving racial equality.

NOTES:

_____

_____

_____

_____

_____

"MOVE IT" CROSSWORD PUZZLE

Use the synonyms provided in the clues to identify the Words that complete the crossword puzzle on the following page. The numbers run top-to-bottom and left-to-right.

Across

1. Solve, decide (or) determination, tenacity
2. Party, celebration, carnival
3. Overjoyed, elated, exhilarated
4. Overwhelm, inundate, trouble
5. Political power; social or financial influence
6. Carelessness; lack of tact or judgment
7. Persuade, cause; compel using pressure
8. Infinity, perpetuity, forever
9. A mutually beneficial, interdependent relationship
10. Understand, comprehend (or) grab, seize

Down

1. Fix, arrange, prepare, manipulate
2. Awe-inspiring, moving, transcendent
3. Jump, horse around, rough-house
4. Dedication, support, commitment
5. Disturbance, diversion, interruption
6. Circumstances; details surrounding a subject
7. Worry; to be annoyed or anxious
8. Perception, feeling, reaction (or) indent, imprint
9. Bound, leap, romp
10. Play; to behave in a happy or playful manner

Knowledge is a State of Mind™

"MOVE IT" CROSSWORD PUZZLE

183

"MOVE IT" SYNONYM SENTENCES

In the following sentences, use correct forms or tenses of the Word$ in the Bank to match the underlined synonyms, and write the correct word in the space provided below each sentence.

Word Bank				
Beset	Cavort	Clout	Context	Devotion
Distraction	Eternity	Euphoric	Fete	Fret
Frolic	Gambol	Grasp	Impression	Indiscretion
Induce	Resolve	Rig	Sublime	Symbiotic

1. The children are <u>playing</u> in the yard.

   _____

2. The street performers <u>leapt</u> across the plaza.

   _____

3. He created a <u>diversion</u> while she slipped out the back door.

   _____

4. My boss says that it doesn't hurt to have friends with <u>influence</u>.

   _____

5. We watched a beautiful sunset the other evening; it was <u>moving</u>.

   _____

6. The kids were <u>rough-housing</u> in the backyard.

   _____

7. He expressed his <u>commitment</u> to his girlfriend by proposing.

   _____

8. Parents often <u>worry</u> about their children.

   _____

9. Although the commercials were only 2 minutes long, it felt as though they went on for an endless amount of time.

   _____

10. Calculus isn't really that hard to comprehend.

    _____

11. After looking at the instructions, I have a pretty good perception of what I need to do.

    _____

12. The two sisters were forced to solve their differences.

    _____

13. He was overjoyed after receiving his acceptance letter to law school.

    _____

14. Urban communities worldwide are overwhelmed by air pollution.

    _____

15. She helped him with his homework, and he helped her with her move; their relationship was mutually beneficial.

    _____

16. If you understand the circumstances in which the article was written, its point is clear.

    _____

17. They persuaded him to do the stunt by offering him a pile of cash.

    _____

18. It is against the law to manipulate the lottery.

    _____

"MOVE IT" SYNONYM SENTENCES cont'd.

19. Dumb criminals tend to be <u>careless</u>, which makes them easy to catch.

   _____

20. The <u>party</u> is at the club on 11th Street and 4th Ave.

   _____

BLANDING & JACKSON "MOVE IT"

- Rebecca Osleeb & Keith London

NYC – Ed Blanding and Troy Jackson of F.A.M.E. Ent. took some time out of their recording schedule to talk with us about their impressive new track "Move It." Sharing a strong symbiotic relationship, Ed wrote most of the lyrics to "Move It" while Troy is responsible for the track's vocal work. Evidently devoted to their audience, all they want to do is to create music that people will enjoy.

However, the guys thought that writing for this album would be easier than it proved to be. Troy remarked, "It took a lot of editing and rigging for us to resolve the problems we confronted while writing this song," and Ed added, "One of the most difficult aspects of creating 'Move It' was finding words that fit within the context of the song, but were also 'Money' words." They didn't fret or let those complications distract them from completing their work, and the guys knew that together they could write a great track that would induce listeners to gambol and cavort to their beats.

We continued our discussion by focusing on the lyrics. Troy and Ed describe "Move It" as a song that should be played at fetes, and it is definitely a track that people can frolic to. Meant to create a euphoric mood, the theme of the song is easily grasped, staged at a party where the song's subject is trying to get to know a young lady. "He's being real with the girl, telling her his feelings," states Ed.

Troy and Ed are determined to gain greater exposure in the music industry, and they trust that they won't become beset by the indiscretions that undermine other young artists in this business. They are hopeful that this experience will give them clout to get more recording opportunities, and as musicians, they aspire to continue turning out sublime beats. Oh, and let's not forget that they'd eventually like to become household names, allowing their tracks to live on for eternity. We have their backs...

> Now, refer to the article you've just read to select the statements that best describe the authors' remarks. Circle the letter that corresponds to the correct answer.

Question 1
(a) Ed and Troy have systematic relationship.
(b) The guys have a mutually beneficial relationship.
(c) "Move It" refers to their management of the recording schedule.
(d) The artists in F.A.M.E. Ent. are concerned about symbiosis.

Question 2
(a) Troy wrote the lyrics and Ed sang.
(b) Ed sang and Troy wrote the lyrics.
(c) They are devoted to enjoying their audience.
(d) It is obvious that they are dedicated to entertaining people.

Question 3
(a) Everyone expects that writing for DM will be difficult.
(b) The guys wanted to prove themselves.
(c) Troy expressed that it took a lot of effort to write the song.
(d) Ed suggested that they rig the Word$.

BLANDING & JACKSON "MOVE IT" cont'd.

Question 4

(a) Ed found it hard to find words that fit the circumstances of the song.

(b) Ed found many good Word$.

(c) "Move It" describes what the artists did to the Word$.

(d) The Word$ were too big to fit into the song.

Question 5

(a) They were very concerned they weren't up to the task.

(b) Diversions interfered with their writing.

(c) Complications distracted them.

(d) They didn't let anything inhibit the progress of their work.

Question 6

(a) Ed and Troy wondered if they could write a song that listeners would enjoy.

(b) They were bounding across the room while they wrote "Move It."

(c) The guys want to gambol and cavort with listeners.

(d) They want to get listeners to dance and party.

Question 7

(a) "Move It' is a song that should be played at feet.

(b) The guys said that "Move It" is a party track, and it fosters an upbeat mood.

(c) Ed and Troy definitely frolic, and they do so at parties.

(d) Frolicking creates euphoria.

Question 8

(a) The song is set on a stage.

(b) The subject is grasping a song.

(c) The theme of "Move It" is easily understood.

(d) Ed is in a state where he tells girls his feelings.

Question 9

(a) Ed and Troy want to get into the music industry.

(b) They are going to suffer from exposure.

(c) The guys are going to expose the music industry.

(d) Troy and Ed are determined to expose themselves to music.

Question 10

(a) The guys are surrounded by the carelessness of other young artists.

(b) Ed and Troy trust that they won't be as careless as other successful artists.

(c) Troy and Ed expect that they won't be harassed.

(d) They trust young artists in the business.

Question 11

(a) The guys want power.

(b) Troy and Ed want more chances to record.

(c) They want the power to record.

(d) Ed and Troy want more opportunities to obtain recordings.

Question 12

(a) As musicians, they hope to keep beating each other.

(b) They want to turn out to be perfect musicians.

(c) As musicians, Troy and Ed perspire.

(d) The guys want to make great music.

Question 13

(a) They only want to hear their music forever.

(b) Ed and Troy want their names on household products.

(c) The guys would like to eventually have names.

(d) They want their tracks to be enjoyed by audiences forever.

NINA ZEITLIN
EPHEMERAL DAYS

"EPHEMERAL DAYS" LISTENING EXERCISE

Listen to "Ephemeral Days" all the way through at least once. Then listen to the song again, and in the spaces provided below, list the Word$ that you hear.

"EPHEMERAL DAYS" LYRICS

by Nina Zeitlin & Matt Kelly

Ephemeral days
Short lived days
In this **enigmatic haze**
I can't even **appraise**

A **cacophony** of feelings
In a **captivating** place
I can't **survey** this city
'Cause I'll be gone without a trace

I had a **vague conception**
Of what I might **perceive**
I knew it'd be **beatific**
Didn't realize I'd never want to leave

Took a plane to Barcelona
Ambled down the streets
The **antiquity intrigued** me
I felt **licentious** as I thought about the people I could meet

Embarking on this **sojourn**
An **odyssey** it would be
Flagrantly elated
Can't **dissuade** me **erroneously**

I had a **vague conception**
Of what I might **perceive**
I knew it'd be **beatific**
Didn't realize I'd never want to leave (yeah)

Surrounded by **novelty**
The **profusion** of what might be
Confounded by **modesty**
And what it could **impart** to me

"EPHEMERAL DAYS" LYRICS cont'd.

The city **endures** forever
But I can't **linger**, I have to **abscond**
I can't **prolong** my time here
So tomorrow I'll be moving on

Ephemeral Days
Short lived days (Hmm)
As I **solemnly** gaze
I know I'll be back someday (yeah)

Ephemeral Days
Yeah

"EPHEMERAL DAYS" DICTIONARY

Abscond (v) – escape, leave; depart secretly.
> They didn't want their wedding to turn into the circus that their parents were planning, so they absconded to Las Vegas to elope.

Ambled (v), **Amble** (v) – stroll, wander, mosey. Antonym: run (v).
> I ambled down the streets of NYC, stopping now and then to window shop.

Antiquity (n) – ancient times, or a relic of ancient times; old age.
> Rome, Italy not only dates to antiquity, but it is also filled with antiquities.

Appraise (v) – evaluate, price, assess, assay. **Appraisal** (n).
> She brought her ring to the jeweler for an appraisal.

Beatific (adj) – good, innocent, virtuous. Antonym: sinister (adj).
> Mother Theresa led a beatific life caring for the impoverished.

Cacophony (n) – noise, din. **Cacophonous** (adj). Antonym: silence (n).
> While we were camping the cacophony of crickets chirping kept us awake.

Captivating (adj) – entrancing, charming, enthralling. **Captivate** (v). Antonym: repellent (adj). Antonym: repellent (adj).

He found the ancient city captivating.

Conception (n) – 1. beginning, outset. **Conceive** (v). Antonym: conclusion (n).

From its conception, all of us recognized that the idea was a stroke of genius.

Conception (n) – 2. idea, notion. **Concept** (n), **Conceive** (v).

Late again, it was obvious that she had no conception of time.

Confounded (v), **Confound** (v) – confuse, puzzle, perplex, baffle. Antonym: clarify (v).

The directions confounded him, so he was unable to use the DVD player.

Dissuade (v) – deter, discourage. Antonym: encourage (v).

Her boss tried to dissuade her from quitting.

Elated (adj) – overjoyed, euphoric, delighted. Antonym: despondent (adj).

She was elated when she found out that she had received a large raise.

Embarking (v), **Embark** (v) – leave, commence; begin a journey or some undertaking; board a boat or airplane.

A frequent literary theme involves characters embarking upon on a journey for one reason or another.

Endures (v), **Endure** (v) – 1. persist; exist for an extended period of time.

Great classical compositions have endured the test of time.

Endures (v), **Endure** (v) – 2. to bear; tolerate.

She said that she couldn't endure another moment of his lunacy, and left him.

Enigmatic (adj) – mysterious, inscrutable; difficult to understand. **Enigma** (n).

Never an easy person to categorize, I always regarded him as enigmatic.

"EPHEMERAL DAYS" DICTIONARY cont'd.

Ephemeral (adj) – short-lived; fleeting, brief.

After saving the baby from the fire he had his "15 minutes of fame," but he knew that all of the attention would be ephemeral.

Erroneously (adv) – incorrectly, mistakenly. **Erroneous** (adj).

The New York Post erroneously reported that Dick Gephardt was the Democratic vice presidential candidate in the 2004 presidential election.

Flagrantly (adv) – conspicuously, blatantly, brazenly. **Flagrant** (adj). Antonym: modest (adj).

He strode down the hall flagrantly flashing his new gold bracelet.

Haze (n) – 1. fog, mist; anything airborne that inhibits one's ability to see. Antonym: clear (adj).

After the brushfire was extinguished a smoky haze lingered in the air for days.

Haze (n) – 2. idiomatically used in reference to memory.

Given that the event occurred over year ago, the witness said that her recollection was hazy.

Impart (v) – tell, grant, reveal, communicate; pass on information.

I enjoy being a mentor and imparting knowledge to other people.

Intrigued (v) – interested, curious. Antonym: disinterested (v).

He was intrigued by their suggestion that they might buy his company.

Licentious (adj) – immoral, lewd, unrestrained. Antonym: modest (adj).

The bouncer kicked him out of the club because of his licentious behavior.

Linger (v) – loiter, persist, hang around.

The cataclysmic events of September 11th 2001 will linger in the minds of Americans forever.

Modesty (n) – reserve, humility, discretion. **Modest** (adj). Antonym: arrogance (n).

> She contributes to many charities, but her modesty precludes her from discussing it.

Novelty (n) – newness, uniqueness. **Novel** (adj).

> Once the novelty of their new toy wore off, the children lost interest in it.

Odyssey (n) – a long, eventful journey.

> The novel I'm reading follows an adopted woman's odyssey to find her biological parents.

Perceive (v) – discern, recognize, notice. **Perception** (n). Antonym: ignore (v).

> Catching a glimpse of the blue car in his rear view mirror again, he perceived that he was being followed.

Profusion (n) – overabundance, surplus, excess, many; large number or amount. Antonym: dearth (n).

> The television station received a profusion of calls about the anchor person's inflammatory remarks.

Prolong (v) – extend, lengthen; draw out; usually associated with time. Antonym: curtail (v).

> We enjoyed our trip to Madrid so much that we decided to stay and prolong it for three more days.

Sojourn (n) – visit; temporary stay.

> Unfortunately I was actually on my way to London on business, so my sojourn in Paris was quite brief.

Solemnly (adv) – seriously, gravely. **Solemn** (adj). Antonym: merrily (adv).

> The news anchor person solemnly described the events that led to the tragic fire.

"EPHEMERAL DAYS" DICTIONARY cont'd.

Survey (v) – review, analyze.

Flying over the remains of the smoldering brushfire, the ranger surveyed the damage to the forest.

Vague (adj) – unclear, indistinct. Antonym: clear (adj).

I have a vague memory of the cousins that I met six years ago.

"EPHEMERAL DAYS" SYNONYM MATCHING

Match the following Word$ with their synonyms. Note the letter of the matching synonym in the space adjacent to the word.

	Vocabulary Words	Synonyms
1.	_____ Abscond	(a) mist
2.	_____ Ambled	(b) newness
3.	_____ Antiquity	(c) unclear
4.	_____ Appraise	(d) reserve
5.	_____ Beatific	(e) escape
6.	_____ Cacophony	(f) visit
7.	_____ Captivating	(g) tell
8.	_____ Conception	(h) begin
9.	_____ Confounded	(i) ancient time
10.	_____ Dissuade	(j) fleeting
11.	_____ Elated	(k) noise
12.	_____ Embark	(l) mysterious
13.	_____ Endure	(m) journey
14.	_____ Enigmatic	(n) wrongly
15.	_____ Ephemeral	(o) strolled
16.	_____ Erroneously	(p) loiter

Vocabulary Words	Synonyms
17. _____ Flagrant	(q) curious
18. _____ Haze	(r) review
19. _____ Impart	(s) overjoyed
20. _____ Intrigued	(t) evaluate
21. _____ Licentious	(u) persist
22. _____ Linger	(v) seriously
23. _____ Modesty	(w) overabundance
24. _____ Novelty	(x) virtuous
25. _____ Odyssey	(y) notion
26. _____ Perceive	(z) discourage
27. _____ Profusion	(a1) extend
28. _____ Prolong	(a2) notice
29. _____ Sojourn	(a3) immoral
30. _____ Solemnly	(a4) entrancing
31. _____ Survey	(a5) blatant
32. _____ Vague	(a6) perplexed

NOTES:

_____

_____

_____

_____

_____

_____

_____

"EPHEMERAL DAYS" SENTENCE COMPLETION

Using a form or tense of the Word$ in the Bank, find the words which best complete the sentences below.

Word Bank

Abscond	Ambled	Antiquity	Appraise	Beatific
Cacophony	Captivating	Conception	Confounded	Dissuade
Elated	Embarking	Endures	Enigmatic	Ephemeral
Erroneously	Flagrantly	Haze	Impart	Intrigued
Licentious	Linger	Modesty	Novelty	Odyssey
Perceive	Profusion	Prolong	Sojourn	Solemnly
Survey	Vague			

1. He had the painting _____ and was surprised to learn that it was very valuable.

2. It is easy to see (and hear) how the _____ of sounds in NYC can overwhelm some people.

3. Pablo Picasso, a painter who often portrayed people's eyes on the same side of their heads, is known for his _____ style.

4. Her _____ smile is angelic.

5. The _____ made it difficult for the driver to see what was ahead.

6. Leaving for their trip, they _____ for the Bahamas from JFK International Airport.

7. We decided to _____ our date by going dancing after we saw the movie.

8. She _____ believed that she would pass English, and she'll be retaking the class during summer school.

9. The professor _____ some of his accumulated wisdom to the class.

10. Telling him that he would wind up flipping burgers, the Principal was determined to _____ my friend from dropping out.

11. After the doctors told her that she had six months to live, she _____ them by overcoming her illness.

12. I _____ down the beach, stopping occasionally to pick up seashells.

13. Sometimes, it's the _____ nature of summer relationships that makes them work.

14. I saw an animated cat and mouse flick that _____ ripped off some classic cartoons.

15. The painting was so beautiful that I couldn't take my eyes off of it; it was _____.

16. Skulking though the alleyway, the jewel thieves _____ with the gems they stole.

17. It is extraordinary that William Shakespeare's works continue to _____ century after century.

18. She was very demure, and her _____ prevented her from talking about her achievements.

19. He had never encountered such a device before and was _____ by its novelty.

"EPHEMERAL DAYS" SENTENCE COMPLETION cont'd.

20. She became totally lost on her way here because the directions weren't complete and were too _____.

21. Recognizing that it was futile to try following the vague directions, she said, "Well, I have no _____ of how to get there."

22. After my friend opened a ketchup bottle by using his belly button, I said, "Well, that was certainly a _____ approach."

23. The readers _____ recited the names of those who lost their lives on 9/11.

24. Before we rented a tent for the party, I went out to _____ the backyard to determine out how it would best fit.

25. It was one of those great ephemeral love affairs, two people meeting one another during a brief _____, enjoying each other's company, and then continuing on their journeys.

26. Las Vegas, which is known as "Sin City," is playing up its _____ image to attract tourists.

27. Opening the stereo cabinet, I found a _____ of wires, and I realized that I had no idea what I was doing.

28. The Pyramids in Giza, Egypt, date to _____, and are thousands of years old

29. Trying to get her laptop fixed, she spoke with four customer service reps, three different technicians, and a software engineer; it was an _____.

30. I may be wrong, but they look like they're up to no good, just _____ in the hallway, furtively looking back and forth.

31. If they're supposed to be in the building, I _____ that they may be waiting for someone to come with the keys to the apartment.

32. She was _____ when she found out that she had won the car.

NOTES:

"EPHEMERAL DAYS" CROSSWORD PUZZLE

Use the synonyms provided in the clues to identify the words that complete the crossword puzzle on the following page. The numbers run top-to-bottom and left-to-right.

Across

1. Confuse, puzzle, perplex
2. Mysterious, inscrutable; difficult to understand
3. Review, analyze
4. A long, eventful journey
5. Serious, grave
6. Deter, discourage
7. Noise, dissonance
8. Tell, grant, communicate; pass on information
9. Distinguish, recognize; take notice
10. Escape, leave; depart secretly
11. Unclear, indistinct
12. Immoral, lewd, unrestrained
13. Persist (or) to bear; tolerate
14. Beginning, outset (or) idea, notion
15. Conspicuous, blatant, brazen
16. Curious about something; interested
17. Evaluate, price, assess, assay

Down

1. Incorrect, mistaken
2. Visit; temporary stay
3. Loiter, persist
4. Leave; begin a journey or some undertaking
5. Entrancing, charming, enthralling
6. Reserve, humility, discretion
7. Stroll, wander, mosey
8. Short-lived; fleeting, brief
9. Fog, mist
10. Newness, uniqueness
11. Ancient times, or a relic of ancient times; old age
12. Overjoyed, euphoric, delighted
13. Extend, lengthen; draw out
14. Good, innocent, virtuous
15. Overabundance, excess, many; large number or amount

"EPHEMERAL DAYS" CROSSWORD PUZZLE

203

"EPHEMERAL DAYS" SYNONYM SENTENCES

In the following sentences, use correct forms or tenses of the Word$ in the Bank to match the underlined synonyms, and write the correct word in the space provided below each sentence.

WORD BANK				
Abscond	Ambled	Antiquity	Appraise	Beatific
Cacophony	Captivating	Conception	Confounded	Dissuade
Elated	Embarking	Endures	Enigmatic	Ephemeral
Erroneously	Flagrantly	Haze	Impart	Intrigued
Licentious	Linger	Modesty	Novelty	Odyssey
Perceive	Profusion	Prolong	Sojourn	Solemnly
Survey	Vague			

1. He wanted to <u>evaluate</u> the situation before deciding what to do.

   _____

2. Despite her great wealth she was a very <u>reserved</u>, understated person.

   _____

3. I haven't lived in Paris for years, but the memories of my time there <u>persist</u>.

   _____

4. Working for over three years to get this company started, it has been an <u>journey</u> to say the least.

   _____

5. At the earliest opportunity, I'm going to take a few days off, and the wife and I are going for a quick <u>visit</u> to South Beach.

   _____

6. She wanted to lay out to tan, but a light <u>fog</u> was blocking the sun.

   _____

7. When he knocked over all of the pots that had been drying, his mom, jarred by the sound of crashing cookware, yelled "What is that noise!?"

   _____

8. Despite his efforts to get her to leave for someplace safe, he couldn't deter her from staying.

   _____

9. We looked at the photo she took of what she told us was the Loch Ness Monster, but all we could make out was the unclear outline of something in the water.

   _____

10. Slipping into the night, the spies escaped with a copy of the secret launch codes.

    _____

11. The burlesque dancers lewdly draped themselves over the show's host.

    _____

12. In a low, serious voice, the doctor informed her that her condition was inoperable.

    _____

13. With roots that reach back thousands of years, the world's major religions all date to ancient times.

    _____

14. I was too excited and couldn't sleep because today we're leaving on our journey.

    _____

15. He's been working on the project for years, but it was originally her idea.

    _____

"EPHEMERAL DAYS" SYNONYM SENTENCES cont'd.

16. After their argument, she <u>mistakenly</u> believed that he would wait for her.

    _____

17. I love to <u>wander</u> through interesting parts of the city that I don't know yet.

    _____

18. Given that his car was gone, I <u>recognized</u> that he had already left.

    _____

19. I was intrigued by the <u>newness</u> of the technology.

    _____

20. The recording star <u>puzzled</u> her critics by becoming more popular than ever.

    _____

21. He was <u>euphoric</u> when he received his acceptance letter from Columbia.

    _____

22. After the tornado she came out of the cellar to <u>review</u> the damage to the house.

    _____

23. On our trek through the Amazon, a native priest <u>revealed</u> his wisdom to us.

    _____

24. Poetry has always been <u>mysterious</u> to her, because she can never figure out what the author is trying to say.

    _____

25. The new technology was <u>interesting</u> and sparked my curiosity.

    _____

26. Lazy summer days are always too <u>fleeting</u>.

    _____

27. I did everything I could to <u>extend</u> my afternoon nap on Sunday, but the din outside kept waking me up.

    _____

28. There is a <u>surplus</u> of diet gimmicks on the market, but that doesn't mean that any of them work.

    _____

29. Dakota is the cutest little kid, and has the most <u>innocent</u> smile.

    _____

30. I urged her to stay inside where it was safe, but she <u>blatantly</u> ignored my advice and walked out into the hurricane.

    _____

31. I always like to <u>hang around</u> after a movie ends to see if the director did anything interesting during the credits.

    _____

32. She was <u>entranced</u> by the film's lush imagery.

    _____

NINA ZEITLIN'S "EPHEMERAL DAYS"

- Rebecca Osleeb & Keith London

NYC – While lingering at Native we had a chance to speak with the beatific Nina Zeitlin, the artist who composed and performs "Ephemeral Days."

Her second track for DM, she conceived the title before she had written the song. The really peculiar part is that it came to Nina just because she was intrigued by the word "ephemeral," which means "fleeting" or "short-lived." Fortuitously, while cruising Europe on vacation, she began to appraise the track's lyrics on her

NINA ZEITLIN'S "EPHEMERAL DAYS" cont'd.

way to Barcelona, Spain, and as a result, the song imparts many of the experiences she had on her odyssey.

Surveying the city, Nina found Barcelona a novel, captivating place, and was in awe at its antiquity. Elated to embark on this sojourn, she was impressed by the flagrant architecture, with which she had a vague familiarity before she arrived. And, accustomed to the bravado of New Yorkers, Nina was confounded by Barcelona's similar profusion of cultures, but struck by the modesty of its inhabitants. Expecting the same dynamic given analogous circumstances, she found the city enigmatic.

Erroneously expecting this trip to be a just another vacation, Nina fell in love with Barcelona as she ambled licentiously through the city's cacophonous streets. Wishing she could have prolonged her journey, her life back home dissuaded her from staying.

Departing was the most solemn aspect of her travels, and despite her desire to remain there, she had to abscond, or as she says, she "might have stayed for good." Barcelona's impact on Nina can't be appraised, but she perceives that however hazy her memories become, they will no doubt, endure.

Now, refer to the article you've just read to select the statements that best describe the authors' remarks. Circle the letter that corresponds to the correct answer.

Question 1

(a) The authors are studio malingerers.

(b) The authors were lingering around Natives.

(c) The authors are recording natives in a studio.

(d) The authors were hanging around the production studio.

Question 2

(a) Nina conceived her second song for DM before she thought of a title.

(b) The title of "Ephemeral Days" is beautifully conceived.

(c) She thought of the title prior to writing the song.

(d) None of the above.

Question 3

(a) Nina likes a word that means "short-lived."

(b) "Ephemeral" is a peculiar word.

(c) "Ephemeral Days" has some peculiar verses.

(d) Peculiar parts came to Nina.

Question 4

(a) She evaluated the lyrics while on a cruise ship to Barcelona, Spain.

(b) Nina was on vacation when she began writing the lyrics.

(c) Her odyssey brought her to forts throughout Europe.

(d) On her way to Barcelona, Nina had many experiences.

Question 5

(a) Ideas and words for the song were written at different times.

(b) Writing "Ephemeral Days" was an odyssey.

(c) She copied parts of "The Odyssey" to write her song.

(d) "Ephemeral Days" is about days being shorter in Barcelona.

Question 6

(a) She found the city magnificent and rich in history.

(b) She was captured in Barcelona while she was measuring it.

(c) Nina found a city book and was struck by its age.

(d) Nina wrote a novel about the city's antiquity.

NINA ZEITLIN'S "EPHEMERAL DAYS" cont'd.

Question 7

(a) Her flagrance was familiar and impressive.

(b) Nina was happy to bark on her sojourn.

(c) She was excited to begin her visit.

(d) She disembarked to find vague architecture.

Question 8

(a) Barcelona's wild architecture was vague, yet familiar to her.

(b) Nina had a modest knowledge of the city's outstanding architecture.

(c) Barcelona, notable for its flagrant architects, is a beautiful city.

(d) Nina was impressed by the flagrant architects she knew.

Question 9

(a) Her New York bravado confounded the city's modest inhabitants.

(b) She was struck by the multiplicity of cultures and the restraint of its citizens.

(c) Accustomed to New Yorkers, she found too many cultures in Barcelona.

(d) New Yorkers' outgoing nature confuses Nina.

Question 10

(a) Nina expected to be mystified by Barcelona's circumstances.

(b) The analogous dynamics of the cities' circumstances were enigmatic.

(c) Compared to New York, she found Barcelona difficult to understand.

(d) Accustomed to New York, the uniformity of Barcelona's cultures mystified her.

Question 11

(a) Nina made a mistake assuming that she would be on vacation.

(b) She wandered through the city looking for trouble.

(c) Barcelona's noisy streets caused her to make errors.

(d) Nina was captivated by Barcelona and savored walking its bustling streets.

Question 12

(a) Nina would have liked to stay in Barcelona, but she needed to get home.

(b) Her friends talked her out of extending her journey.

(c) Barcelona's beauty dissuaded her from prolonging her journey.

(d) Her trip was prolonged by her life back home in New York.

Question 13

(a) She absconded from Barcelona under the solemn cover of night.

(b) Nina was sad to leave Barcelona, but she was compelled to.

(c) The authorities didn't like Nina's lingering, so she had to abscond.

(d) Despite her tendency to linger, her travels were solemn.

Question 14

(a) However perceptive she may be, Nina cannot appraise her impact on Barcelona.

(b) Nina believes that Barcelona will make her memory hazy.

(c) Her enduring memories cannot be appraised because they are hazy.

(d) She expects that she will remember Barcelona for an indefinite period.

JOE PASCARELL & THE MACHINE
SUBLIME

"SUBLIME" LISTENING EXERCISE

Listen to "Sublime" all the way through at least once. Then listen to the song again, and in the spaces provided below, list the Word$ that you hear.

NOTES:

_____

_____

_____

"SUBLIME" LYRICS

by Joe Pascarell

I was **languid** in my **gait**
I was **barren** in my heart
I would **muddle** through the day
Berating everything
Deluded by the **hoax**
Of an **apathetic state**
Then your **iridescent** smile
Took me to a life **sublime**

I'm a **palpitating** mess
When I'm around you
And I'm losing my **finesse**
And I'm **basking** in the glow
Now I **quiver** like a child
Cause I've found you
Vindicate me with your smile
Let it **shimmer** all inside

Now I'm drinking in the **din** of the **random** song of life
As I **scurry** to your home
I can **savor** what's around
And as I **unravel** you
And you **succumb** to me
We can live this **lucid** dream
We can live a life **sublime**

I'm a **palpitating** mess
When I'm around you
And I'm losing my **finesse**
And I'm **basking** in the glow
Now I **quiver** like a child
Cause I've found you
Vindicate me with your smile

"SUBLIME" LYRICS cont'd.

Let it **shimmer** all inside

I'm a **palpitating** mess
When I'm around you
And I'm losing my **finesse**
And I'm **basking** in the glow
Now I **quiver** like a child
Cause I've found you
Vindicate me with your smile
Let it **shimmer** all inside

"SUBLIME" DICTIONARY

Apathetic (adj) – indifferent, uninterested. Antonym: enthusiastic (adj).

You can't be apathetic about going to war.

Barren (adj) – desolate, sterile, unproductive. Antonym: fertile (adj).

Barren and inhospitable, the Sahara Desert's average rainfall is less than 5 inches annually, and daytime temperatures can reach 130 degrees Fahrenheit.

Basking (v), **Bask** (v) – luxuriate, lie, sunbathe; take pleasure in warmth or lying in the sun.

Being cold-blooded, lizards like to bask in the sun.

Berating (v), **Berate** (v) – rebuke, criticize, scold, chastise. Antonym: encourage (v).

She berated him for not making an effort to do a good job.

Deluded (v), **Delude** (v) – deceive, con, mislead.

She's deluding herself if she thinks that she'll get a recording contract, because she's completely tone-deaf.

Din (n) – noise, racket. Antonym: tranquility (n).

When I'm in the city, the din of rumbling trucks and sirens keeps me up at night.

Finesse (n) – skill, poise. Antonym: clumsiness (n).

Placing each part in the tiny case with great care, the watchmaker demonstrated extraordinary finesse when he was repairing my Rolex.

Gait (n) – pace; manner of walking or running.

My father was hurt when he was a child and now walks with an uneven gait.

Hoax (n) – trick, swindle; practical joke.

He was infuriated to discover that his mansion had been burglarized, but then he was relieved to find out that his friends were just playing a hoax.

Iridescent (adj) – glowing, gleaming. **Iridescence** (adj).

Her new cell phone lights up and gives off an iridescent glow when it rings.

Languid (adj) – relaxed, unhurried, lethargic. Antonym: harried (adj).

The audience was bored by the languid pace of the speaker's presentation.

Lucid (adj) – coherent, comprehensible, intelligible; clearly understood. Antonym: incoherent (adj).

After a baseball hit him in the head, the paramedic wanted to make sure that he was lucid.

Muddle (v) – to behave in a confused or disorderly manner; jumbled.

She didn't know her lines in the play and muddled through the performance.

Palpitating (v), **Palpitate** (v) – throb, flutter. **Palpitations** (n).

On our first date I was so nervous my heart was palpitating.

Quiver (v) – tremble, shake.

She was so scared that she began to quiver.

"SUBLIME" DICTIONARY cont'd.

Random (adj) – haphazard; by chance. Antonym: systematic (adj).
He didn't care what color notebook he bought, and just picked one at random.

Savor (v) – relish, appreciate, enjoy.
Prepared by one of the city's finest chefs, she savored every bite of her meal.

Scurry (v) – scamper, dash; move briskly. Antonym: amble (v).
When it was time for his bubble bath he scurried up the stairs to the tub.

Shimmer (v) – twinkle, glint; shine intermittently.
The moonlight shimmered on the surface of the lake.

State (v) – 1. assert; to declare.
She stated that she wasn't going to tolerate his idiocy any longer and left him.

State (n) – 2. condition, circumstances; frame of mind.
He was such a slob, his mom couldn't believe the state of his room.

State (n) – 3. territory, nation, country.
The Secretary of State represents the U.S. in the world forum.

Sublime (adj) – awe-inspiring, perfect, transcendent. Antonym: uninspiring (adj).
The orchestra's performance was the finest I've ever heard; it was sublime.

Succumb (v) – yield, die, submit; give way, give in.
Eve succumbed to the temptation of the forbidden fruit.

Unravel (v) – disentangle, untangle, solve; work loose.
Loosing his supporters one by one, his plan began to unravel.

Vindicate (v) – justify, support, exonerate; clear of blame.
The company's profits vindicated the CEO's unorthodox management style.

"SUBLIME" SYNONYM MATCHING

Match the following Word$ with their synonyms. Note the letter of the matching synonym in the space adjacent to the word.

Vocabulary Words	**Synonyms**
1. _____ Apathetic	(a) twinkle
2. _____ Barren	(b) skill
3. _____ Basking	(c) jumbled
4. _____ Berate	(d) desolate
5. _____ Deluded	(e) relaxed
6. _____ Din	(f) yield
7. _____ Finesse	(g) trick
8. _____ Gait	(h) scold
9. _____ Hoax	(i) disentangle
10. _____ Iridescent	(j) indifferent
11. _____ Languid	(k) coherent
12. _____ Lucid	(l) sunbathing
13. _____ Muddled	(m) scamper
14. _____ Palpitating	(n) perfect
15. _____ Quiver	(o) glow
16. _____ Random	(p) condition
17. _____ Savor	(q) noise
18. _____ Scurry	(r) pace
19. _____ Shimmer	(s) relish
20. _____ State	(t) haphazard
21. _____ Sublime	(u) shake
22. _____ Succumb	(v) deceived
23. _____ Unravel	(w) throbbing
24. _____ Vindicate	(x) exonerate

"SUBLIME" SENTENCE COMPLETION

Using a form or tense of the Word$ in the Bank, find the words which best complete the sentences below.

WORD BANK				
Apathetic	Barren	Basking	Berating	Deluded
Din	Finesse	Gait	Hoax	Iridescent
Languid	Lucid	Muddle	Palpitating	Quiver
Random	Savor	Scurry	Shimmer	State
Sublime	Succumb	Unravel	Vindicate	

1. Looking down at the street from my office window, I watched the people _____ as the rain began to fall.

2. She _____ him for telling her that aliens stole his homework.

3. Questioning him, she thought that his story would _____.

4. Positive that his tale was a _____, she sent him to the principal.

5. Then, all of a sudden, an unusual light with an _____ glow came through the window.

6. We couldn't believe our eyes, but a tall figure that _____ in the light stepped in through the window, and handed the teacher his homework.

7. _____ by the extraordinary events, he came back to the classroom and said, "I told you that aliens stole my homework!"

8. After a great day of swimming and basking in the sun, we ambled down the beach at a _____ pace to head back to our hotel.

9. My grandfather was sent to the hospital with heart _____.

10. The Confederate army _____ to Union forces in March of 1865.

11. When I go to the beach, all I want to do is _____ in the sun.

12. Photographs of Mars depict a _____, rocky landscape.

13. As the bear slowly approached us, we began to _____ with fear.

14. Unable to finish a sentence, it was obvious that her thoughts were _____.

15. After sampling a very fine vintage bottle of wine, the connoisseur remarked, "What a _____ finish."

16. Never having encountered such an extraordinary vintage before, he _____ every drop.

17. His mom said, "He is completely _____ if he expects me to pick up after him for the rest of his life."

18. We cannot become _____ and take democracy for granted.

19. I couldn't keep up with my sister as we walked downtown because she has a much longer _____ than I do.

20. He gave a clear and _____ argument supporting states' rights.

21. The speaker was forced to yell over the _____ of the crowd.

22. After 9/11 it isn't uncommon to be subjected to a _____ search at an airport.

23. But, I'm sad to say, that is today's _____ of affairs.

24. He forgot her name, but handled the situation with such _____ that she was happy to excuse the gaffe.

"SUBLIME" CROSSWORD PUZZLE

Use the synonyms provided in the clues to identify the words that complete the crossword puzzle on the following page. The numbers run top-to-bottom and left-to-right.

Across

1. To behave in a confused or disorderly manner
2. Twinkling, glinting; shining intermittently
3. Rebuke, criticize, scold, chastise
4. Relish, appreciate, enjoy
5. Tremble, shake
6. Relaxed, unhurried, lethargic
7. Yield, die, submit; give way, give in
8. Assert; to declare (or) condition, circumstances; state of mind (or) territory, nation, country
9. Throb, flutter
10. Scamper, dash; move briskly
11. Justify, support, exonerate; clear of blame
12. Glowing, gleaming
13. Trick, swindle; practical joke

Down

1. Coherent, comprehensible, intelligible; clearly understood
2. Luxuriating, lying, sunbathing
3. Awe-inspiring, moving, perfect, transcendent
4. Untangle, disentangle
5. Skill, poise
6. Noise, racket
7. Deceived, con, mislead
8. Indifferent, uninterested
9. Desolate, sterile, unproductive
10. Haphazard, unsystematic; by chance
11. Pace; manner of walking or running

"SUBLIME" CROSSWORD PUZZLE

"SUBLIME" SYNONYM SENTENCES

In the following sentences, use correct forms or tenses of the Word$ in the Bank to match the underlined synonyms, and write the correct word in the space provided below each sentence.

WORD BANK				
Apathetic	Barren	Basking	Berating	Deluded
Din	Finesse	Gait	Hoax	Iridescent
Languid	Lucid	Muddle	Palpitating	Quiver
Random	Savor	Scurry	Shimmer	State
Sublime	Succumb	Unravel	Vindicate	

1. She only slept for a few hours last night and woke up completely <u>confused</u> this morning.

   _____

2. Her beautiful hair <u>glinted</u> in the sunlight.

   _____

3. He found the hose in knots and <u>untangled</u> it so he could to water the plants.

   _____

4. It was an elaborate <u>practical joke</u>, which took months to prepare.

   _____

5. Cold-blooded animals need to <u>lie</u> in the sun to maintain their body temperatures.

   _____

6. Acquitted by the jury, the defendant was <u>exonerated</u>.

   _____

Knowledge is a State of Mind™

7. During hot, humid summer days, I like to keep a relaxed pace.
   _____

8. He lacked skill, but he always got the job done.
   _____

9. Sometimes, given the overwhelming crises here at home, it's hard not to be indifferent about problems elsewhere.
   _____

10. The horse trainer was irate when he found out that the mare he just bought was sterile.
    _____

11. As the Grammy results were read, she shook with anticipation.
    _____

12. Following her fall down the stairs, he asked her how many fingers he was holding up to see if she was coherent.
    _____

13. The mouse dashed across the kitchen floor.
    _____

14. The noise of the traffic kept me awake all night.
    _____

15. There is something transcendent about every morning's sunrise.
    _____

16. I'm always in awe of the sun's glow as it breaches the horizon.
    _____

17. The horse trotted at a moderate pace.
    _____

"SUBLIME" SYNONYM SENTENCES cont'd.

18. To me, events seem pretty <u>haphazard</u>, and good or bad, you never know what's going to happen next.

    _____

19. After he found out that he she conned him, he said "I can't believe that I was so <u>misled</u>!"

    _____

20. My heart was <u>throbbing</u> after the four-mile run.

    _____

21. The teacher <u>rebuked</u> her for coming late to class.

    _____

22. When he awoke in a strange and unfamiliar place, he was in a very confused <u>frame of mind</u>.

    _____

23. Exhausted from battling the disease for years, my grandmother <u>gave in</u> and passed away this morning.

    _____

24. Great achievements are always comprised of small feats, so I <u>relish</u> every accomplishment, no matter how insignificant it might seem.

    _____

THE "SUBLIME" PIECE

- Keith London

NYC - Scurrying into Native's doorway to get in from the rain, I was having heart palpitations from my mad, six-block dash to escape a sudden deluge. It was coming down in buckets. Basking in the reflection of the iridescent bulb overhead, its outline shimmered in the droplets clinging to my coat. There's something sublime about standing just out of the rain and watching New York come to halt as the sky opens up on a summer afternoon.

For a minute, I deluded myself into believing that the downpour was going to end quickly, as I thought of grabbing a quick cup of coffee before I went up to the studio. I succumbed to the fact that that was not going to happen and I headed upstairs. I was lucid, but my pace was languid, and I was feeling pretty apathetic. Everything was cool, but it was just one of those random days when your brain is muddled, and you've lost all of your finesse. Sometimes you think your friends are playing a hoax on you, but unfortunately, that's almost never the case and your day continues to unravel.

But, then again, there are days when your endurance is vindicated. As I exited the elevator and stepped into the loft, I entered a different state. There were some excellent tracks coming out of the studios, and I savored another day among some very talented people making great music. A bit of life returned to my gait, and I quivered for a second when through the din, I heard Adrianne Hecker hit some incredibly high note. I berated myself for letting the rain get the best of me, and then went to kitchen to see if there was any coffee I could make. Of course, the cabinet was barren. Man, I knew I should have grabbed a cup when I was downstairs...

Now, refer to the article you've just read to select the statements that best describe the author's remarks. Circle the letter that corresponds to the correct answer.

Question 1
(a) The article is written from the perspective of a small, scurrying animal.
(b) The author was running to get out of the rain and couldn't catch his breath.
(c) There was a flood in New York that the author was trying to escape.
(d) The author is a jogger who enjoys running in the rain.

THE "SUBLIME" PIECE cont'd.

Question 2

(a) The doorway light cast a glow that twinkled in the rain drops on the author's jacket.

(b) The author wanted to bask in the sun in front of the studio.

(c) Light bulbs were clinging to the author's coat, and were casting a shimmering light in the rain.

(d) The rain drops were reflecting the author's coat while he was basking in the doorway.

Question 3

(a) The author finds perfection standing in the rain on a summer day in New York.

(b) Keith likes to watch for the perfect rain, which can only be spotted from doorways.

(c) The author would like it to rain more often because it brings New York to a standstill.

(d) He savors the odd tranquility that occurs when it rains heavily in New York.

Question 4

(a) Keith is deluding himself that he can go to the studio without coffee.

(b) The author was delusional regarding his ability to stop the rain.

(c) He was kidding himself when he thought that the rain would stop soon.

(d) The author likes to grab coffee, but it needs to be made quickly.

Question 5

(a) He yielded to not getting coffee upstairs.

(b) Keith gave in to the fact that the rain was not going to let up.

(c) The author thought there was coffee upstairs and decided not to bring any.

(d) He died in a coherent, lethargic and indifferent state.

Question 6

(a) The author was coherent, but largely unmotivated.

(b) The rain undermined Keith's mental state, but he could still think clearly.

(c) He was relaxed and understood by those around him, but felt indifferent.

(d) None of the above.

Question 7

(a) It was a haphazard, unusually cold summer day in the city.

(b) Keith had a great deal of poise, and kept it cool, despite his state of confusion.

(c) The author was having one of those days when you can't get it together.

(d) He lives in a state of confusion and does not know when it will happen.

Question 8

(a) His friends were playing a practical joke on him.

(b) Keith thought that his friends were swindling him, and expected that his day would improve.

(c) Keith's friends never play jokes on him, but they would untangle him.

(d) The author was hoping the day would improve, but he didn't expect it to.

Question 9

(a) Keith's fortitude was exonerated by a jury of his peers.

(b) No matter how down you get, if you keep it together, you can come through.

(c) Being vindicated for your endurance occurs only on rare occasions.

(d) All of the above.

Question 10

(a) Once Keith got to the studio, he felt better.

(b) Native's loft studio is a territory independent from the state of New York.

(c) Exiting the elevator and stepping into the loft causes one assert themselves.

(d) Native's loft studio is in a state other than New York.

THE "SUBLIME" PIECE cont'd.

Question 11

(a) There are railway tracks near Native.

(b) Keith enjoys eating around people who write and produce music.

(c) The author appreciates being part of something creative.

(d) He appreciates savoring the talent of excellent tracks.

Question 12

(a) Keith strode into Native, and shook in response to all of the noise there.

(b) Due to the cacophony in the studio, the author trembled as he went to walk back out.

(c) Adrianne Hecker's din in Native's loft studio caused Keith to pace his quivering for a second.

(d) He had more energy, and trembled when he heard a high note over the other music in the studio.

Question 13

(a) The author "kicked himself" for making lousy coffee.

(b) The author chastised himself for letting the rain undermine his mood.

(c) He criticized himself for letting the rain outsmart him.

(d) Keith was irate because he left raindrops in an otherwise empty cabinet.

Question 14

(a) The kitchen cabinet did not contain any coffee.

(b) The author compares the kitchen cabinet to the Sahara Desert.

(c) The kitchen cabinet is sterile.

(d) The author went back downstairs to purchase some coffee.

NINA ZEITLIN
WIDE OPEN SPACES

"WIDE OPEN SPACES" LISTENING EXERCISE

Listen to "Wide Open Spaces" all the way through at least once. Then listen to the song again, and in the spaces provided below, list the Word$ that you hear.

"WIDE OPEN SPACES" LYRICS

by Nina Zeitlin & Mike Pandolfo

I used to love you
I thought you were the **nemesis** of all that is bad
(And) you were **enamored** with me
But now you've changed and we will never (again) have what we (once) had

So I opened my heart to you
Now I open my mind to the free way
Wide open spaces in view
Still a photo of you on the dashboard baby

You can't **abstain** from your **obnoxiousness**
Like a **plague** that's **obtuse** and **obscure**
And you can't **refrain** from your **predilection**
To make me **grave** and **flagging** and **demure**

I hope you **reconcile** your **volatile** behavior
It's like some **contagion**, an **affliction** getting worse
You're a **floundering** mess, filled with **superfluous** distress
I feel **nostalgic** for the man I knew at first

It's **ominous** and **pernicious** to be where I am
(And I) Guess people do change in the end
Every minute with you had felt **effervescent**
Your **conjuration** was a **fallacy**, it was all pretend

You left a **fissure** in my heart, and just a **filament** of my soul
I never thought (that) I could live without you
I put my **credence** in you, **manifesting** hate in me
It's **plausible** that we could see this (or anything) through

I am strong, with more **valor** than you
I've gained **lucidity**
After what you put me through

Now I am strong, but you will never know
'Cause I am gone and it was you that I had to **forgo**

"WIDE OPEN SPACES" DICTIONARY

Abstain (v) – refrain, desist; give up; do without. Antonym: indulge (v).

The congressmen abstained from voting on a bill that they did not support.

Affliction (n) – illness; cause of suffering; burden. **Afflicted** (adj).

Afflicted with arthritis, she found it difficult to walk.

Conjuration (n) – witchcraft; the practice of raising or evoking spirits, demons and storms by means rituals or incantations. **Conjure** (v).

Absorbed in conjuration, the witch chanted an incantation over the boiling cauldron.

Contagion (n) – a source of infection or corruption. Antonym: antibody (n).

The bio-hazard team successfully contained the contagion.

Credence (n) – credibility, weight, acceptance, belief.

I don't place much credence in what most politicians have to say.

Demure (adj) – reserved, decorous, modest; straight-laced. Antonym: flagrant (adj).

This season many retailers are offering more demure styles in order to quell criticism that their clothing lines have been too licentious.

Effervescent (adj) – 1. bubbly, fizzy, sparkling. **Effervescence** (n). Antonym: flat (adj).

Soda and other carbonated beverages are effervescent.

Effervescent (adj) – 2. lively, vibrant, vivacious. Antonym: withdrawn (adj).

Effervescent and personable, she made new friends easily.

"WIDE OPEN SPACES" DICTIONARY cont'd.

Enamored (v) – smitten; in love with; also idiomatically used in reference to appreciation for an object. Antonym: repelled (v).

She was enamored with the dress and bought it immediately.

Fallacy (n) – myth, lie, falsehood; misguided belief. **Fallacious** (adj). Antonym: incoherent (adj).

Following the disaster in Chernobyl, many people came to believe that "safe nuclear power" is a fallacy.

Filament (n) – fiber, thread, strand.

To generate light, an incandescent bulb passes electricity through a wire filament that glows in response to its electrical resistance.

Fissure (n) – crevice, gap, split, fracture.

In May of 2003 "The Old Man of the Mountain," a prominent rock feature on the shoulder of New Hampshire's Profile Mountain, succumbed to fissures that caused it to collapse.

Flagging (adj), **Flag** (adj) – wane, decline, fail, wilt, fade. Antonym: surge (adj).

The color of my old jersey is beginning to flag.

Floundering (adj), **Flounder** (adj) – 1. splash, thrash, struggle.

He didn't know how to swim, so he spent the day floundering in the shallow end of the pool.

Floundering (adj), **Flounder** (adj) – 2. struggle, falter; to succumb to difficulty. Antonym: thrive (adj).

The business had been floundering, but the employees and management banded together to save the company.

Forgo (v) – relinquish, skip ; go without. Antonym: partake (v).

The CEO decided to forgo her salary to cut back on expenses and to save cash.

Grave (adj) – 1. serious, severe, critical. Antonym: trifling (adj).

He cogitated because making the wrong decision could have grave consequences.

Grave (adj) – 2. burial plot.

Over the weekend my family went to the cemetery to visit my grandmother's grave.

Lucidity (n) – clarity, intelligibility; a state of coherence or clear understanding. **Lucid** (adj). Antonym: incoherent (adj).

Assaying the team's loss, the captain gained lucidity when he realized that his showboating kept them from scoring more points.

Manifesting (v) – bringing about; becoming apparent. **Manifest** (adj).

Melting ice fields and rising ocean tides indicate that global warming is manifesting itself most dramatically at the Earth's poles.

Nemesis (n) – arch-enemy, adversary, competitor. Antonym: ally (n).

Baseball fans always look forward to the Boston Red Sox squaring off against their nemesis, the New York Yankees.

Nostalgic (adj) – homesick, reflective, wistful; to think of or long for an earlier, "simpler" period. **Nostalgia** (n). Antonym: unsentimental (adj).

While preparing for his SATs he became nostalgic for third grade, when his biggest problem was deciding what lunchbox he was going to bring to school.

Obnoxiousness (n), **Obnoxious** (adj) – exhibiting insufferable, repugnant behavior.

I wonder if reality show producers actually look for self-absorbed, loud, obnoxious idiots to create drama on their programs?

Obscure (adj) – 1. vague, unclear, incomprehensible. Antonym: apparent (adj).

We missed the turn for his house because the street sign was obscured by trees.

"WIDE OPEN SPACES" DICTIONARY cont'd.

Obscure (adj), **Obscurity** (adj) – 2. little known. Antonym: common (adj).
Sometimes unsigned, obscure, independent recording artists create the most innovative music.

Obtuse (adj) – 1. stupid, thick, dull-witted. Antonym: clever (adj).
I don't mean to be obtuse, but I just don't understand quantum physics.

Obtuse (adj) – 2. an angle between 90 and 180 degrees. Antonym: acute (adj).
An obtuse angle is between 90 and 180 degrees.

Ominous (adj) – foreboding, forbidding, menacing, threatening. Antonym: welcoming (adj).
It was tornado season, and we saw ominous, black clouds hanging low on the horizon.

Pernicious (adj) – evil, malicious, harmful. Antonym: nice (adj).
Many parents regard violent video games as a pernicious influence on children.

Plague (n) – 1. outbreak, pestilence, scourge, blight Antonym: antidote (n).
The Black Plague, which was spread by rat fleas during the 1340s, killed almost one third of the entire population of Europe.

Plague (n) – 2. trouble, pester, bother.
I've been plagued by writer's block, and I haven't been able to finish this book.

Plausible (adj) – believable, credible, possible, likely. Antonym: unlikely (adj).
As far as scientists can tell, a catastrophic meteor impact is the most plausible cause of the onset of the ice age.

Predilection (n) – liking, partiality, penchant, tendency; disposition to.
She has a predilection for sneakers and owns more than 50 pairs.

Reconcile (v) – settle, square; make amends. **Reconciliation** (n). Antonym: divorce (v).

The players union and the team owners met to reconcile their differences so the new season could get underway.

Refrain (v) – 1. abstain; to avoid doing something. Antonym: indulge (v).

The waiter asked the restaurant patron with the cigar, "Sir, would you please refrain from smoking?"

Refrain (v) – 2. chorus; a poetic or musical verse that repeats; idiomatically refers to hearing a repeated excuse.

Politicians passing the blame has long been a familiar refrain.

Superfluous (adj) – extraneous, unnecessary, excess. Antonym: critical (adj).

I can't believe how much superfluous technology auto manufacturers build into today's cars; seriously, does anyone really need a seat that massages your buttocks while you drive?

Valor (n) – bravery, courage, fearlessness. Antonym: critical (adj).

John Wayne once said, "Valor is being scared to death – but saddling up anyway."

Volatile (adj) – unstable, erratic, impulsive, unpredictable. **Volatile** (adj). Antonym: stable (adj).

The Middle East has always been volatile and we can only hope that the region will know peace.

NOTES:

_____

_____

_____

"WIDE OPEN SPACES" SYNONYM MATCHING

Match the following Word$ with their synonyms. Note the letter of the matching synonym in the space adjacent to the word.

Vocabulary Words   **Synonyms**

1. _____Abstain   (a) credible
2. _____Affliction   (b) falsehood
3. _____Conjuration   (c) clarity
4. _____Contagion   (d) arch-enemy
5. _____Credence   (e) falter
6. _____Demure   (f) wane
7. _____Effervescent   (g) wistful
8. _____Enamored   (h) witchcraft
9. _____Fallacy   (i) cause of suffering
10. _____Filament   (j) apparent
11. _____Fissure   (k) serious
12. _____Flag   (l) reserved
13. _____Flounder   (m) outbreak
14. _____Forgo   (n) insufferable
15. _____Grave   (o) evil
16. _____Lucidity   (p) avoid doing
17. _____Manifest   (q) thread
18. _____Nemesis   (r) source of infection
19. _____Nostalgic   (s) partiality
20. _____Obnoxious   (t) relinquish
21. _____Obscure   (u) erratic
22. _____Obtuse   (v) settle
23. _____Ominous   (w) extraneous

Vocabulary Words	Synonyms
24. _____Pernicious	(x) crevice
25. _____Plague	(y) bravery
26. _____Plausible	(z) smitten
27. _____Predilection	(a1) fizzy
28. _____Reconcile	(a2) stupid
29. _____Refrain	(a3) refrain
30. _____Superfluous	(a4) foreboding
31. _____Valor	(a5) credibility
32. _____Volatile	(a6) vague

NOTES:

"WIDE OPEN SPACES" SENTENCE COMPLETION

Using a form or tense of the Word$ in the Bank, find the words which best complete the sentences below.

WORD BANK				
Abstain	Affliction	Conjuration	Contagion	Credence
Demure	Effervescent	Enamored	Fallacy	Filament
Fissure	Flagging	Floundering	Forgo	Grave
Lucidity	Manifesting	Nemesis	Nostalgic	Obnoxiousness
Obscure	Obtuse	Ominous	Pernicious	Plague
Plausible	Predilection	Reconcile	Refrain	Superfluous
Valor	Volatile			

1. The General bestowed a medal on the Private for his _____ in battle.

2. The bird flu virus is a _____ that was thought only to affect chickens and other fowl, but now appears to also be harmful to humans.

3. The Department of Homeland security issued an _____ warning to be on the lookout for 'suspicious activity.'

4. She decided to _____ her bonus, and instead gave it to charity.

5. He was in _____ condition after the accident.

6. She was always loud, crass, and _____.

7. He plays the tenor sax and has a _____ for John Coltrane and jazz from the 1950s.

8. It goes without saying that every super hero needs a _____ to battle.

9. "I'd like to believe that your grandmother ate your homework, but couldn't you at least try to give me a _____ explanation?"

10. Surprisingly, human beings' small toes are _____ and do not help us to stand.

11. Some people are just _____; you can explain something to them a thousand times, but they still don't get it.

12. Although we couldn't stand one another, we sat down face to face, and worked to _____ our differences.

13. Around the holidays I become _____ for the Thanksgiving dinners that we use to have at my grandmother's house.

14. The hurricane first _____ as a tropical storm in the south Caribbean.

15. He was practiced in the art of _____ and referred to himself as a "warlock."

16. Mount St. Helens is a _____, active volcano located 50 miles northeast of Portland, Oregon.

17. After she dumped him for being obnoxious, he made up _____, hurtful claims about his ex.

18. While perusing an _____ journal that was written around 1850, a researcher uncovered new information about Lincoln's hat.

19. Pressure in the volcanic vent decreased after steam was released through a new _____ in the bedrock.

20. Unable to agree on the details of any issue, the peace talks' negotiators are _____ in their effort to reconcile their positions.

"WIDE OPEN SPACES" SENTENCE COMPLETION cont'd.

21. Research shows that children are drinking coffee, but they should _____ from consuming large quantities of caffeine until after the age of 18.

22. In light of the fact that his grandmother likes to eat paper, there might be some _____ to his claim that his she ate his homework.

23. Compelled by an anxious electorate and no employment growth, the candidates have focused on the _____ job market.

24. The United Nations has asked China to _____ from imprisoning human rights activists.

25. Would-be terrorists are _____ airlines with bomb hoaxes and other efforts to disrupt their operations.

26. According to the Center for Disease control, noise-induced hearing loss is currently the most common occupational _____.

27. She recently became _____ with photography, and now she never leaves the house without her camera.

28. Unfortunately, seniors often begin to lose their _____ as they become older and the aging process accelerates.

29. Automotive lighting technology has made significant advances over the past few years, discarding incandescent _____ in favor of electro-reactive gases like xenon.

30. When monks first accidentally created champagne in the 1680s, its _____ was an undesirable trait that was regarded as a sign of poor wine making.

31. Their group was reprimanded for spreading _____, hurtful rumors about other students.

32. Preparing to address the delegates, the keynote speaker adopted a _____, restrained tone of voice and a formal posture.

NOTES:

"WIDE OPEN SPACES" CROSSWORD PUZZLE

Use the synonyms provided in the clues to identify the Words that complete the crossword puzzle on the following page. The numbers run top-to-bottom and left-to-right

Across

1. Bravery, courage, fearlessness
2. Illness; cause of suffering; burden
3. Homesick, reflective, wistful; to think of or long for an earlier, "simpler" period
4. Vague, unclear, incomprehensible (or) little known
5. Arch-enemy, adversary, competitor
6. Clarity, intelligibility; a state of coherence or clear understanding
7. Exhibiting insufferable, repugnant behavior
8. Bubbly, sparkling (or) lively, vivacious
9. Credibility, weight, acceptance, belief
10. Evil, malicious, harmful
11. Waning, declining, failing, wilting, fading
12. Settle, square; make amends
13. Foreboding, forbidding, menacing, threatening
14. Believable, credible, possible, likely
15. Unstable, erratic, impulsive, unpredictable

Down

1. Bringing about; becoming apparent
2. Crevice, gap, split, fracture
3. Extraneous, unnecessary, excess
4. Fiber, thread, strand
5. Refrain, desist; give up; do without
6. Stupid, thick, dull-witted
7. Serious, severe, critical (or) burial plot
8. Relinquish, abstain, refrain, skip; go without
9. Witchcraft; raising spirits via rituals
10. Smitten; in love with
11. A source of infection or corruption
12. Myth, lie, falsehood; misguided belief
13. Struggling, faltering (or) splashing, thrashing
14. Liking, partiality, penchant, tendency
15. Pestilence, scourge (or) trouble, pester
16. Abstain; avoid doing (or) chorus
17. Reserved, decorous, modest; straight-laced

"WIDE OPEN SPACES" CROSSWORD PUZZLE

243

"WIDE OPEN SPACES" SYNONYM SENTENCES

In the following sentences, use correct forms or tenses of the Word$ in the Bank to match the underlined synonyms, and write the correct word in the space provided below each sentence.

WORD BANK

Abstain	Affliction	Conjuration	Contagion	Credence
Demure	Effervescent	Enamored	Fallacy	Filament
Fissure	Flagging	Floundering	Forgo	Grave
Lucidity	Manifesting	Nemesis	Nostalgic	Obnoxious
Obscure	Obtuse	Ominous	Pernicious	Plague
Plausible	Predilection	Reconcile	Refrain	Superfluous
Valor	Volatile			

1. I wish that she would <u>refrain</u> from blowing her nose into her shirt, she's grossing me out.

   _____

2. There isn't a <u>strand</u> of truth to his claim that he's the Queen's mother.

   _____

3. He had a difficult time responding to his opponent's arguments and <u>struggled</u> throughout the debate.

   _____

4. Dr. Evil is Austin Power's <u>arch-enemy</u>.

   _____

5. Given the fact that there are an infinite number of galaxies, it is entirely <u>possible</u> that there is intelligent life somewhere in the universe.

   _____

6. The band's tour was canceled due to <u>waning</u> ticket sales.

   _____

7. She's a pathological liar and I don't put an ounce of belief in anything she has to say.

   _____

8. Don't you hate when you can't get a song's chorus out of your head even though you haven't heard it in three days?

   _____

9. My parents love my current girlfriend, but I think that she's too reserved for my liking.

   _____

10. Recording her expenses when they occur makes it is easier for her to square her checkbook with her bank statements.

    _____

11. The source of infection was traced to a research lab that was active during the cold war.

    _____

12. The event's vivacious host welcomed everyone personally.

    _____

13. The prevalence of brutality and bloodshed on TV has the harmful effect of desensitizing people to violence.

    _____

14. Despite its complexities, she described the process with great clarity, which gave us a better understanding of how it would progress.

    _____

15. It is interesting that even the brightest people will believe almost any falsehood if it is repeated frequently enough.

    _____

"WIDE OPEN SPACES" SYNONYM SENTENCES cont'd.

16. Predicated upon <u>raising spirits</u>, Vodun (aka Voodoo) is a religion that has been practiced in West Africa for over 6,000 years.

   _____

17. Since we don't have the data yet, we'll <u>skip</u> meeting until next week.

   _____

18. An alien seaweed has overwhelmed large areas of the Mediterranean's sea bed, posing a <u>serious</u> threat to its indigenous species.

   _____

19. Recent leading financial indicators have been extremely <u>unpredictable</u>, underscoring the uncertain state of the economy.

   _____

20. I thought that I had made my point clearly, but it seems that he was too <u>thick</u> to grasp it.

   _____

21. Her fiancé is totally <u>insufferable</u>; the first time he came over, he headed straight for the fridge, and then whined that we didn't have any cheese.

   _____

22. She's been <u>troubled</u> by self-doubt, and she just can't seem to shake it.

   _____

23. The <u>illness</u> is weakening his immune system, making him more susceptible to infection.

   _____

24. The city's budget woes are <u>bringing about</u> a new round of service cuts and tax increases.

   _____

25. "Unencumbered by <u>unnecessary</u> posturing, her performance was raw and inspiring."

    _____

26. Away at college, he was swept up by a wave of <u>homesickness</u>, and decided to call some old friends.

    _____

27. Although the score was tied, they won the match due to an <u>little-known</u> technicality.

    _____

28. They're so <u>smitten</u> with one another that the entire world around them could crumble, and they would barely notice.

    _____

29. With an equal number of classes in favor of, or against, the proposed changes, it exposed a <u>split</u> in the student body.

    _____

30. A fearless warrior, Joan of Arc was renown for her faith and <u>courage</u>.

    _____

31. Given the growing deficit and declining tax income, the budget situation appears <u>threatening</u>.

    _____

32. Considering her <u>penchant</u> for yellow, I was surprised that she bought a blue car.

    _____

NINA ZEITLIN LONGS FOR "WIDE OPEN SPACES"

- Keith London

NYC - It is plausible that I've stumbled upon an ominous trend manifesting itself in Nina Zeitlin's work. Perhaps afflicted by some contagion, Nina can't seem to abstain from her predilection for writing nostalgic songs about her nemesis... pernicious men. Now I'm plagued by my efforts to reconcile the volatility of her grave subject matter with the effervescent, and occasionally demure, Nina we know and love.

Perhaps she's enamored with guys who are simply wrong for her, but she can't refrain from dating obnoxious, obtuse, jerks because she's bolstered by valor. They then conjure a seductive web, but it is only a matter of time until fissures appear in their relationship, their mutual attraction flags, and they begin to flounder.

This may be a fallacy, and I don't put a lot of credence in my superfluous conjecturing, but it is always possible that I've found an obscure filament of truth. Then again, maybe I'm flirting with lucidity and I should forgo playing shrink.

Now, refer to the article you've just read to select the statements that best describe the author's remarks. Circle the letter that corresponds to the correct answer.

Question 1

(a) It is possible that the author is clumsy and has fallen on a trend mill.

(b) The author thinks that he may have fallen into a trap that was set in Nina's work.

(c) The author believes that he may have found a foreboding trend in Nina's songs.

(d) It is plausible that the author has identified a singular trend in Nina's songs.

Question 2

(a) Nina has fallen ill and she cannot refrain from waxing nostalgic.

(b) Nina cannot desist from writing songs about being homesick.

(c) Nina can't give up writing songs about "simpler times" and evil men.

(d) Nina seems disposed to writing reflective songs about her bad relationships.

Question 3

(a) Nina wants to be a superhero whose arch-enemies are evil men.

(b) She writes songs about relationships with men who aren't good for her.

(c) Nina's adversaries are malicious men.

(d) She enjoys crime-fighting male villains in her spare time.

Question 4

(a) The author cannot square his image of Nina with her heated lyrics.

(b) Keith's attempts to settle Nina's instability have been troubling.

(c) The author is looking to settle his difficulties with Nina.

(d) Keith is concerned that Nina's erratic behavior might be serious.

Question 5

(a) The subject matter of Nina's songs may be considered grave because she is describing men who are erratic.

(b) The subject matter of Nina's songs may be considered volatile because she is describing men who are pernicious.

(c) The subject matter of Nina's songs may be considered grave because she is describing men who are volatile.

(d) The subject matter of Nina's songs may be considered volatile because she is describing men who are erratic.

NINA ZEITLIN LONGS FOR "WIDE OPEN SPACES" cont'd.

Question 6

(a) The author is concerned that Nina is unstable; sometimes she's serious, sometimes she's bubbly, and at other times she is reserved.

(b) Nina's vibrant, and sometimes decorous, personality belie the resentment captured by her lyrics.

(c) Nina's fizzy, modest, personality belie the volatility captured by her lyrics.

(d) None of the above.

Question 7

(a) It is possible that she is smitten with guys that are wrong for her, but she can't keep herself from dating loutish, stupid idiots.

(b) Perhaps Nina appreciates guys that are wrong for her, but she can't recite the chorus of songs to them because they're thick.

(c) The author conjectures that it is plausible that Nina falls for jerks because she always has an excuse.

(d) Nina is unable to avoid dating dull-witted repugnant louts because she appreciates them for who they are.

Question 8

(a) Nina is courageous to date stupid jerks.

(b) Keith suggests that Nina fearlessly dates louts.

(c) The author poses that Nina's courage encourages her to date jerks.

(d) Nina's valor caused her to start a new extreme sport, "Jerk Dating."

Question 9

(a) Nina's ex boyfriends put on a good face at first, then, once they're dating, problems arise as they begin to reveal their true nature.

(b) The author conjectures that Nina's ex-boyfriends practice witchcraft, and cast spells that split relationships.

(c) The author posits that Nina's jerk ex-boyfriends use incantations to ensnare her, but their enchantments flag over time.

(d) Nina' evil, jerk ex-boyfriend is Spiderman.

Question 10

(a) Her ex-boyfriends offer her the gift of a flag dedicated to her.

(b) Their appreciation for one another wilts, and they begin to thrash.

(c) Their attraction to one another wanes, and they begin to struggle.

(d) To save their relationship the boyfriends take her to Six Flags.

Question 11

(a) The author proposes that he is lying, and that he doesn't believe himself.

(b) Keith suggests that his inferences may be a misguided belief, and that he doesn't put much weight in his theories.

(c) Keith suggests that his inferences stem from a misguided belief of unquestionable credibility.

(d) The article's supposition is a myth that he doesn't regard as acceptable.

Question 12

(a) He may have found a little know thread of truth in his unnecessary lecturing.

(b) The author feels that his extra conjecturing may be a little known thread.

(c) The author's extraneous positing may have found a vague strand.

(d) Keith regards his analysis of Nina's work as extraneous, but he also says that there may be some truth to his inferences.

Question 13

(a) Keith is flirting with a young woman named Lucidity, and should stop.

(b) The author is not a licensed professional trained to deal with issues of lucidity.

(c) The author questions his sanity, and says that he should stop overanalyzing things.

(d) The author is nuts and he should stop pretending to be Sigmund Freud.

COMPLETE CHAPTERS DICTIONARY

Abscond (v) – escape, leave; depart secretly.

They didn't want their wedding to turn into the circus that their parents were planning, so they absconded to Las Vegas to elope.

Abstain (v) – refrain, desist; give up; do without. Antonym: indulge (v).

The congressmen abstained from voting on a bill that they did not support.

Accolades (n), **Accolade** (n) – praise, award; great compliment. Antonym: insult (n).

Her film started receiving accolades shortly after it premiered, and it ultimately went on to win her an Oscar.

Accordingly (adv) – 1. suitably.

Wanting to make a good impression on her interview, she dressed accordingly.

Accordingly (adv) – 2. consequently; as a result of.

His neighbor threatened to sue him, and accordingly, he retained a lawyer.

Acquiesce (v) – assent; agree without protest. Antonym: protest (v), resist (v).

He acquiesced to his boss' demands.

Actuated (v), **Actuate** (v) – motivate; to put into action.

He was actuated by his drive to succeed.

Addiction (n) – dependence; a habitual, compulsive need. **Addict** (n).

When he was younger he was addicted to sugar and constantly ate chocolate.

Affliction (n) – illness; cause of suffering; burden. **Afflicted** (adj).

Afflicted with arthritis, she found it difficult to walk.

Alluring (v) – appealing, tempting. **Allure** (n).

He found her distinctive attitude alluring, and asked her to join him for dinner.

Amateurs (n), **Amateur** (n) – layperson; one who participates in an activity for recreation. Antonym: professional (n).

It was his first time surfing, and accordingly, he looked like an amateur.

Ambled (v), **Amble** (v) – stroll, wander, mosey. Antonym: run (v).

I ambled down the streets of NYC, stopping now and then to window shop.

Amorous (adj) – affectionate; relating to love or romantic desire. Antonym: hateful (adj).

The lovers amorously gazed at one another.

Annihilate (v) – destroy, kill; idiomatically describes superiority in competition.

Our team annihilated the visitors in this past weekend's game.

Antiquity (n) – ancient times, or a relic of ancient times; old age.

Rome, Italy not only dates to antiquity, but it is also filled with antiquities.

Antithesis (adj) – opposite, converse. **Antithetical** (adj). Antonym: analogous (adj).

New York City is the antithesis of a small town.

Apathetic (adj) – indifferent, uninterested. Antonym: enthusiastic (adj). Antonym: invested (adj).

You can't be apathetic about going to war.

Appraise (v) – evaluate, price, assess, assay. **Appraisal** (n).

She brought her ring to the jeweler for an appraisal.

Aroma (n) – fragrant, pleasing scent. **Aromatic** (adj). Antonym: stench (n).

The aroma of her perfume was sweet and exotic.

COMPLETE CHAPTERS DICTIONARY cont'd.

Assay (v) – test, analyze, evaluate, determine.

It was necessary to assay the bracelet to determine its gold content.

Assured (v), **Assure** (v) – 1. guarantee, promise.

The salesman assured me that I was getting a great deal.

Assured (v) – 2. verify, substantiate; make certain.

I wanted to be assured that I was getting a great deal, so I did some comparison shopping to verify the salesman's claims.

Awesome (adj) – great, awe-inspiring, amazing. Antonym: uninspiring (adj).

The Grand Canyon is an awesome sight.

Awkward (adj) – 1. to be uncomfortable in a situation. Antonym: relaxed (adj).

It was awkward to see my best friend at the mall with my older brother.

Awkward (adj) – 2. clumsy; difficult to handle. Antonym: graceful (adj).

The clown's giant shoes caused him to walk awkwardly.

Basking (v), **Bask** (v) – luxuriate, lie, sunbathe; take pleasure in warmth or lying in the sun.

Being cold-blooded, lizards like to bask in the sun.

Barren (adj) – desolate, sterile, unproductive. Antonym: fertile (adj).

Barren and inhospitable, the Sahara Desert's average rainfall is less than 5 inches annually, and daytime temperatures can reach 130 degrees Fahrenheit.

Beatific (adj) – good, innocent, virtuous. Antonym: sinister (adj).

Mother Theresa led a beatific life caring for the impoverished.

Benediction (n) – blessing, approval; a prayer for help. Antonym: curse (n).

The priest ended the service by reciting a benediction.

Berating (v), **Berate** (v) – rebuke, criticize, scold, chastise. Antonym: encourage (v).

She berated him for not making an effort to do a good job.

Beset (v) – overwhelm, inundate, trouble, harass, surround.

The refugees were best by one catastrophe after another.

Bested (v), **Best** (v) – beaten, surpassed; to be defeated or outclassed.

Their team had more practice than ours, and consequently, they bested us.

Bestow (v) – give, confer, grant. Antonym: rescind (v).

He bestowed his blessing upon his daughter's engagement.

Borders (v), **Border** (v) – 1. to be on the verge of or to approximate something.

His infatuation with grisly video games borders on mental illness.

Borders (n), **Border** (n) – 2. boundary.

The United States and Canada share a border.

Borders (v) – 3. to be physically adjacent to something.

Manhattan and Queens both border the East River.

Cacophony (n) – noise, din. **Cacophonous** (adj). Antonym: silence (n).

While we were camping the cacophony of crickets chirping kept us awake.

Calamity (n) – disaster, catastrophe, tragedy; event that causes suffering. Antonym: success (n).

The local farmers fear a calamity if the river rises above its banks.

Candor (n) – honesty, frankness, openness. **Candid** (adj), **Candidly** (adv). Antonym: dishonesty (n)

Looking for constructive criticism, I appreciated his candor.

COMPLETE CHAPTERS DICTIONARY cont'd.

Captivated (v), **Captivate** (v) – entrance, charm, enthrall. Antonym: repel (v).

The audience was captivated by her virtuoso performance.

Captivating (adj) – entrancing, charming, enthralling. **Captivate** (v). Antonym: repellent (adj). Antonym: repellent (adj).

She found the ancient city captivating.

Cardiologist (n) – physician specializing in treatment of the heart and cardio-vascular system.

Concerned about his predisposition for heart disease, he made an appointment to see a cardiologist.

Cavorting (v), **Cavort** (v) – jump, horse around, rough-housing; move around in a playful and/or noisy way. Antonym: curtailing (v).

Wrestling and tackling each other, the children cavorted on the lawn.

Celerity (n) – swiftness or speed of an action.

Modern passenger jets travel with great celerity, especially in comparison to any propeller driven aircraft.

Chaos (n) – confusion; disorder. **Chaotic** (adj). Antonym: order (n).

The guests couldn't get into the party, the staff was running around trying to find a manager, the DJ didn't show up; it was complete chaos.

Clout (n) – political power; social or financial influence or importance.

The chairman of the Senate Ethics Committee has enormous clout.

Cogitate (v) – think, consider, reflect, ponder.

She felt that it was necessary to cogitate given the issue's complexity and importance.

Cognizant (adj) – aware of; to know of something. Antonym: ignorant (adj).

His mirrors were not adjusted properly, so he was not cognizant that he had hit the cones during his driving test.

Collaborate (v) – cooperate; work together.

She's heard that Jay-Z and Beyonce will collaborate on their upcoming albums.

Colossal (adj) – 1. gigantic, huge, immense; great size. **Colossus** (n). Antonym: miniscule (adj).

The Colossus of Rhodes, one of the 7 wonders of the ancient world, was a statue that stood 110 feet tall and took 12 years to complete.

Colossal (adj) – 2. important or great failure Antonym: triumph (adj).

Lasting only one season and losing millions of dollars, the XFL was a colossal failure.

Colossal (adj) – 3. important, vital, significant; typically referring to a decision Antonym: inconsequential (adj).

Contemplating the use of the atom bomb, President Truman faced a colossal decision.

Comely (adj) – attractive, agreeable. Antonym: homely (adj).

She was quite comely, and he noticed her the moment she swept into the room.

Complex (adj) – intricate, difficult. Antonym: simple (adj).

Between little black boxes and on-board diagnostic systems, today's cars are far too complex for people to repair on their own.

Complicit (adj) – involvement in, complacent regarding, or ignoring the progress of, activity that is improper. **Complicity** (n).

She worked at the store and turned the alarm off for her partners, so she was arrested for her complicity in the burglary.

COMPLETE CHAPTERS DICTIONARY cont'd.

Conception (n) – 1. beginning, outset. **Conceive** (v). Antonym: conclusion (n).

From its conception, all of us recognized that the idea was a stroke of genius.

Conception (n) – 2. idea, notion. **Concept** (n), **Conceive** (v).

Late again, it was obvious that he had no conception of time.

Conflagration (n) – inferno, fire.

During the summer, when the weather is hot and dry, the Western U.S. is often beset by a conflagration of brushfires.

Confounded (v), **Confound** (v) – confuse, puzzle, perplex, baffled. Antonym: clarify (v).

The directions confounded her, so she was unable to use the DVD player.

Conjecture (v) – opine, guess, contemplate. Antonym: know (v).

We don't know what caused the accident, we can only conjecture.

Conjuration (n) – witchcraft; the practice of raising or evoking spirits, demons and storms by means rituals or incantations. **Conjure** (v).

Absorbed in conjuration, the witch chanted an incantation over the boiling cauldron.

Consummate (adj) – archetypal, standard, picture-perfect.

A skilled cook and decorator, he is the consummate homemaker.

Constellations (n), **Constellation** (n) – assemblage; groups of stars that form patterns and have been given names.

In our astronomy class we studied the constellation The Big Dipper.

Contagion (n) – a source of infection or corruption. Antonym: antibody (n).

The bio-hazard team successfully contained the contagion.

Context (n) – circumstances; details surrounding a subject. **Contextual** (adj).

On the news her quote seemed harsh; her remark was actually benign, but it had been taken out of context.

Conversely (adv) – in opposition; contrary. **Converse** (adj). Antonym: analogously (adv).

He said that if he passes the final he'd receive a B in Algebra; conversely, if he failed the final he'd receive a D.

Conviction (n) – 1. strongly opinion or belief. Antonym: vacillation (n).

It is his conviction that that murderers should face the death penalty.

Conviction (n) – 2. a judgment that one is guilty of a crime. **Convict** (v). Antonym: acquittal (n).

If he is convicted of murder he may face the death penalty.

Cosmos (n) – outer space; the universe. **Cosmic** (adj). Antonym: atom (n).

The astronomer used a telescope to gaze out into the cosmos.

Crass (adj) – tactless, rude, gross, unrefined, blundering. Antonym: refined (adj).

She was jealous that he had a girlfriend, so she made crass remarks about her to his friends.

Craven (adj) – cowardly. Antonym: brave (adj).

The Private was too craven to face the enemy and rescue his Sergeant.

Credence (n) – credibility, weight, acceptance, belief.

I don't place much credence in what most politicians have to say.

Credit (n) – recognition, acknowledgement. Antonym: blame (n).

I wouldn't have been able to write the book without her, so I wanted to give her due credit.

COMPLETE CHAPTERS DICTIONARY cont'd.

Crucial (adj) – essential; extremely important or necessary.

She said, "If you want to do well on the exam, it is crucial that you study."

Debilitated (v), **Debilitate** (v) – impair, hinder, incapacitate, injure. Antonym: enable (v).

Unfortunately, she was debilitated by a stroke, and now undergoes physical therapy daily.

Decipher (v) – decode, grasp; to figure out.

I want to respond to the note she passed me, but I can't because I couldn't decipher her handwriting.

Declaration (n) – statement, announcement; usually regarding a strong belief. **Declare** (v).

He was asked to make a written declaration explaining what he witnessed during the accident.

Decoy (v) – 1. to bait; to lure.

They used a girl hitchhiker as a decoy to get him to stop.

Decoy (n) – 2. bait; a lure.

Duck hunters are well known for using decoys.

Decree (n) – proclamation, ruling, declaration; an official statement that something must happen.

The king issued a decree stating that his birthday would be a holiday.

Defied (v), **Defy** (v) – resist, disregard, challenge; refuse to obey. **Defiance** (n).

I would love to defy gravity and fly like a bird.

Deleterious (adj) – harmful, damaging. Antonym: helpful (adj).

Smoking is deleterious to your health.

Delirium (n) – confusion, disorientation. Antonym: clarity (n).

She was in a state of delirium after meeting her favorite movie star.

Deluded (v), **Delude** (v) – deceive, con, mislead.

She's deluding herself if she thinks that she'll get a recording contract, because she's completely tone-deaf.

Demure (adj) – reserved, decorous, modest; straight-laced. Antonym: flagrant (adj).

This season many retailers are offering more demure styles in order to quell criticism that their clothing lines have been too licentious.

Deviant (adj) – abnormal; differing from the norm or from socially accepted standards of behavior. **Deviance** (n). Antonym: normal (adj).

What constitutes deviant behavior varies among cultures, for example here in the U.S. it is illegal to marry a relative, whereas in some societies it is acceptable.

Devoid (adj) – lacking, deficient, without. Antonym: plentiful (adj).

Amish homes are devoid of appliances because their faith forbids the use of electricity.

Devotion (n), **Devote** (v) – dedication, support, commitment. Antonym: indifference (n).

The volunteer's devotion to helping the homeless is inspiring.

Din (n) – noise, racket. Antonym: tranquility (n).

When I'm in the city, the din of rumbling trucks and sirens keeps me up at night.

Disconcerting (adj) – disturbing, upsetting, embarrassing. **Disconcert** (v). Antonym: comforting (adj).

She has a disconcerting habit of going back on her word.

COMPLETE CHAPTERS DICTIONARY cont'd.

Disdain (v) – scorn, despise, contempt. Antonym: admire (v).

His ex-girlfriend disdained him.

Dispel (v) – dismiss, eliminate; cause to vanish.

To dispel the rumors of her illness, the politician held a press conference at her gym.

Dissolve (v) – 1. melt. Antonym: solidify (v).

The ice cube dissolved in his freshly brewed coffee.

Dissolve (v) – 2. end, disband. Antonym: initiate (v).

The new military dictator dissolved the country's democratically elected legislature.

Dissuade (v) – deter, discourage. Antonym: encourage (v).

His boss tried to dissuade him from quitting.

Distraction (n) – disturbance, diversion, interruption. **Distract** (v). Antonym: focus (n).

I can't listen to music while I work because it distracts me.

Dregs (n) – sediment, muck, residue, remains, leftovers; what is left behind.

Finishing the entire bottle of chocolate milk, he drank it down to the dregs.

Duration (n) – period, length; time interval.

Although the team hasn't gotten off to a good start this season, they're toughing it out and digging in for the duration.

Ecstasy (n) – rapture, joy, happiness. **Ecstatic** (adj). Antonym: despair (n).

He was ecstatic when he won a trip to the Bahamas.

Effervescent (adj) – 1. bubbly, fizzy, sparkling. **Effervescence** (n). Antonym: flat (adj).

Soda and other carbonated beverages are effervescent.

Effervescent (adj) – 2. lively, vibrant, vivacious. Antonym: withdrawn (adj).

Effervescent and personable, she made new friends easily.

Elated (adj) – overjoyed, euphoric, delighted. Antonym: despondent (adj).

She was elated when she found out that she had received a large raise.

Embarking (v), **Embark** (v) – leave, commence; begin a journey or some undertaking; board a boat or airplane.

A typical literary theme involves characters embarking upon on a journey for one reason or another.

Enamored (v) – smitten; in love with; also idiomatically used in reference to appreciation for an object. Antonym: repelled (v).

Enamored with the dress, she decided to buy it for the prom.

Endures (v), **Endure** (v) – 1. persist; continue to exist for an extended period of time.

A great many classical compositions have endured the test of time.

Endures (v), **Endure** (v) – 2. to bear; tolerate.

After listening to him rant again, she said that she couldn't endure another moment of his lunacy, and she walked out the door.

Enigmatic (adj) – mysterious, inscrutable; difficult to understand. **Enigma** (n).

Never an easy person to categorize, I always regarded her as enigmatic.

Entice (v) – persuade, draw, invite.

To entice urban workers to leave the city, suburban employers are offering them higher salaries.

COMPLETE CHAPTERS DICTIONARY cont'd.

Ephemeral (adj) – short-lived; fleeting, brief.

After saving the baby from the fire he had his "15 minutes of fame," but he knew that all of the attention would be ephemeral.

Epitome (n) – essence, height, archetype, embodiment; perfect example.
Epitomize (v).

Jacqueline Kennedy epitomized style and grace in the days of Camelot.

Equanimity (n) – composure; the state of being calm, even-tempered, level-headed.

She remained calm and maintained her equanimity when she heard of her husband's accident.

Erroneously (adv) – incorrectly, mistakenly. **Erroneous** (adj).

The New York Post erroneously reported that Dick Gephardt was the Democratic vice presidential candidate in the 2004 presidential election.

Esoteric (adj) – 1. known to a small group. Antonym: common (adj).

We both enjoy modern architecture and wound up discussing such esoteric topics as Frank Gehry's latest work.

Esoteric (adj) – 2. perplexing, arcane. Antonym: straightforward (adj).

Their conversation was too esoteric and I couldn't understand anything that they were talking about.

Eternity (n) – infinity, perpetuity, forever; time without end. **Eternal** (adj).

She said that she would love him for all of eternity and would never leave his side.

Euphoric (adj) – overjoyed, elated, exhilarated; great happiness. **Euphoria** (n). Antonym: miserable (adj).

He was euphoric after she accepted his invitation to the concert.

Exact (v) – take, obtain, demand.

She wanted to exact revenge on the hunter that shot her pet elephant.

Exacting (adj) – 1. demanding, challenging. Antonym: easy (adj).

Medical school is exacting because eventually you're likely to be making life or death decisions.

Exacting (adj), **Exact** (adj) – 2. precise, correct, accurate. Antonym: imprecise (adj).

It is convenient to use vending machines that can give you exact change.

Exhilarating (adj) – thrilling, elating. **Exhilarate** (v). Antonym: boring (adj).

Sky diving is exhilarating.

Expertise (n) – knowledge, skill, proficiency. **Expert** (n).

Programming computers requires expertise.

Extolled (v), **Extol** (v) – celebrate, praise, commend. Antonym: criticize (v).

The queen's subjects extolled her prosperous reign.

Factions (n), **Faction** (n) – group, clique, party; a group within a larger group.

Congress members representing competing interests frequently organize themselves into opposing factions.

Fallacy (n) – myth, lie, falsehood; misguided belief. **Fallacious** (adj). Antonym: incoherent (adj).

Following the disaster in Chernobyl, many people came to believe that "safe nuclear power" is a fallacy.

Fathom (v) – comprehend, understand, grasp.

I can't fathom why he thought it would be OK to stay out until sunrise on the night before a college interview.

COMPLETE CHAPTERS DICTIONARY cont'd.

Fester (v) – irritate, aggravate, worsen. Antonym: heal (v).

He said, "You should have a doctor look at that festering boil."

Fete (n) – party, celebration, carnival.

The student union is throwing a fete for the freshmen.

Filament (n) – fiber, thread, strand.

To generate light, an incandescent bulb passes electricity through a wire filament that glows in response to its electrical resistance.

Finesse (n) – skill, poise. Antonym: clumsiness (n).

Placing each part in the tiny case with great care, the watchmaker demonstrated extraordinary finesse when he was repairing my Rolex.

Fissure (n) – crevice, gap, split, fracture.

In May of 2003 "The Old Man of the Mountain," a prominent rock feature on the shoulder of New Hampshire's Profile Mountain, succumbed to fissures that caused it to collapse.

Flagging (adj), **Flag** (adj) – wane, decline, fail, wilt, fade. Antonym: surge (adj).

The color of my old jersey is beginning to flag.

Flagrant (adj) – conspicuous, blatant, brazen. Antonym: modest (adj).

He believes that many television shows flagrantly promote violence.

Flagrantly (adv) – conspicuously, blatantly, brazenly. **Flagrant** (adj). Antonym: modest (adj).

She strode down the hall flagrantly flashing her new gold bracelet.

Floundering (adj), **Flounder** (adj) – 1. splash, thrash, struggle.

He didn't know how to swim, so he spent the day floundering in the shallow end of the pool.

Floundering (adj), **Flounder** (adj) – 2. struggle, falter; to succumb to difficulty. Antonym: thrive (adj).

> The business had been floundering, but the employees and management banded together to save the company.

Fluctuation (n) – flux, variation; to vary irregularly; to rise and fall. Antonym: stability (n).

> Fluctuations in the temperature this summer have made it hard to get to the beach; one day it's hot, the next day you need a sweater.

Follicles (n), **Follicle** (n) – small holes present in skin, the best known are those though which hair grows, "hair follicles."

> He went bald, so he bought a formula that claims to revitalize your hair follicles.

Forgo (v) – relinquish, skip ; go without. Antonym: partake (v).

> The CEO decided to forgo her salary to help cut back on expenses and to save cash.

Forlorn (adj) – sad, dejected, lonely, despondent. Antonym: cheerful (adj).

> After his girlfriend dumped him he felt abandoned and forlorn.

Forsake (v) – abandon, renounce, desert. **Forsaken** (v). Antonym: devote (v).

> Religious leaders ask their followers not to forsake their faith.

Frequency (n) – 1. the bandwidth of broadcast radio or television signals.

> She wanted to listen to her favorite radio station during our road trip, but we couldn't get that frequency.

Frequency (n) – 2. the pitch or tone of sound waves.

> The frequency of the whistle can only be heard by dogs.

COMPLETE CHAPTERS DICTIONARY cont'd.

Frequency (n) – 3. rate of occurrence or recurrence.

Accidents occur at that intersection with alarming frequency.

Frequently (adv) – regularly, repeatedly, habitually.

He's very absent-minded and he frequently loses his keys.

Fret (v) – worry; to be annoyed or anxious. **Fretful** (adj). Antonym: relax (v).

He spent the day fretting about the argument he had with his boss.

Friction (n) – 1. resistance, rubbing, abrasion. Antonym: ease (n).

When you apply the brakes in your automobile, pistons compress brake pads against a wheel hub rotor, and the resulting friction slows the car.

Friction (n) – 2. hostility, antagonism, conflict. Antonym: amity (n).

They always disagreed, and whenever they were together there was friction.

Frigid (adj) – freezing, cold. Antonym: hot (adj).

She resides in Florida during the winter because she dislikes the frigid New York winters.

Frolic (v) – play; to behave in a happy or playful manner. Antonym: grieve (v).

The puppies frolicked in the grass.

Frustrating (v), **Frustrate** (v) – exasperating, vexing, annoying. Antonym: soothing (v).

It's frustrating when I'm hungry and I find a long line at the cafeteria.

Fusion (n) – synthesize; blend or join together. **Fuse** (v). Antonym: separation (n).

She liked his music because he fuses different styles.

Futile (adj) – useless, hopeless, pointless. **Futility** (n). Antonym: useful (adj).

It would be futile to engage Superman in an arm wrestling contest.

Gait (n) – pace; manner of walking or running.
My father was hurt when he was a child and now walks with an uneven gait.

Gambol (v) – bound, leap, romp. Antonym: crawl (v).
The dancers gamboled across the stage.

Gazing (v), **Gaze** (v) – stare; fixed attention; to look at something intently.
He enjoys gazing out the window at the city below.

Genius (n) – brilliant; extraordinary intelligence or skill. Antonym: stupidity (n).
She's a genius and finishes her exams in record time.

Glimmer (v) – shine, gleam, reflect; idiomatically refers to the presence of hope.
Her car glimmered in the sun after she waxed and polished it.

Graciously (adv) – politely; behaving in a courteous manner. **Gracious** (adj).
Giving all of the credit to the team, she graciously accepted the award for MVP.

Grasp (v) – 1. understand, comprehend. Antonym: misunderstand (v).
The students had a good grasp of some rather difficult material.

Grasp (v) – 2. grab, seize. Antonym: release (v).
Struggling to climb back into the helicopter, the stuntman grasped the landing skid.

Grave (adj) – 1. serious, severe, critical. Antonym: trifling (adj).
She cogitated because making the wrong decision could have grave consequences.

Grave (adj) – 2. burial plot.
Over the weekend we went to the cemetery to visit my grandmother's grave.

COMPLETE CHAPTERS DICTIONARY cont'd.

Haze (n) – 1. fog, mist; anything airborne that inhibits one's ability to see. Antonym: clear (adj).

After the brushfire was extinguished a smoky haze lingered in the air for days.

Haze (n) – 2. idiomatically used in reference to memory.

Given that the event occurred over year ago, the witness said that her recollection was hazy.

Hoax (n) – trick, swindle; practical joke.

He was infuriated to discover that his mansion had been burglarized, but then he was relieved to find out that his friends were just playing a hoax.

Ignite (v) – 2. to initiate an angry or controversial situation. Antonym: pacify (v).

Tensions were ignited when the protesters' petition was rejected by the city.

Ignited (v), **Ignite** (v) – 1. light, kindle. Antonym: extinguish (v).

She used a lighter to ignite the firewood.

Illuminate (v) – 1. enlighten, clarify; make something understood. **Illumination** (n). Antonym: obfuscate (v).

His novel illuminates the issues preceding The Civil War.

Illuminate (v) – 2. brighten. **Illumination** (n). Antonym: darken (v).

The footlights illuminated the stage.

Illusion (n) – delusion, chimera; false impression; figment of your imagination. Antonym: reality (n).

When you see a magician saw someone in half it is only an illusion that they've created.

Impact (n) – 1. crash, collision.

The meteor's impact created a huge crater in the desert.

Impact (n) – 2. influence, impression, effect.
She was a very active volunteer who made a great impact on her community.

Impart (v) – tell, grant, reveal, communicate; pass on information.
I enjoy being a mentor and imparting knowledge to other people.

Impression (n) – 1. perception, feeling, reaction. **Impress** (v).
He tried to make a good impression on his girlfriend's mom.

Impression (n) – 2. indent, imprint.
She used her thumb to make an impression in the cookie dough.

Incantation (n) – chant; singing magic spells.
The witch's incantation turned him into a toad.

Incite (v) – compel, spur, impel, provoke, goad; to cause. Antonym: soothe (v).
The jury's controversial verdict incited a riot.

Inconsequential (adj) – unimportant, minor, trivial. Antonym: important (adj).
Their remarks were completely inconsequential and had no bearing on her decision.

Incontrovertibly (adv) – indisputably, unquestionably. **Incontrovertible** (adj). Antonym: disputably (adv).
The video playback incontrovertibly shows that she fouled me.

Incredulity (n) – disbelief, skepticism; not able or wanting to believe something. **Incredulous** (adj). Antonym: conviction (n).
She fought the call and was incredulous, even though the evidence of the foul was on the video playback.

Incurred (v), **Incur** (v) – to bring upon oneself; to sustain an unpleasant outcome; to suffer.

His dad made some stock picks that didn't work out, and he incurred big losses.

Indefatigable (adj) – unrelenting, tireless, determined; never willing to admit defeat.

She is an indefatigable lobbyist for education reform.

Indiscretion (n) – carelessness, tactless; lack of tact or judgment. **Indiscreet** (adj). Antonym: discretion (n).

The CIA agent that leaked details to the media was fired for his indiscretion.

Indisputable (adj) – unquestionable, certain. Antonym: disputable (adj).

The Yankees have indisputably won more championships than any other team in the history of baseball.

Induce (v) – persuade, cause; compel using pressure. Antonym: prevent (v).

She tried to induce her daughter to study for her exams.

Inevitably (adv) – certain, unavoidable. **Inevitable** (adj).

It was inevitable that airlines would lose business after they raised airfares dramatically.

Infatuation (n) – fixation, obsession; an engrossing passion. Antonym: indifference (n).

He was infatuated with her and had pictures of her all over his house.

Infinite (adj) – never-ending, endless, uncountable. **Infinity** (n). Antonym: finite (adj).

As far as we can tell, the cosmos are infinite.

Inimitably (adv) – uniquely, distinctly; not able to be imitated. **Inimitable** (adj). Antonym: commonly (adv).

Snoop Dogg is known for his inimitable style.

Intricate (adj) – complex, complicated. **Intricacy** (n). Antonym: simple (adj).
Computers are too intricate for most people to repair on their own.

Interminable (adj) – endless, incessant. Antonym: finite (adj).
Although the lame movie was short, it seemed interminable to the audience.

Intrigued (v) – interested, curious. Antonym: disinterested (v).
He was intrigued by their suggestion that they might buy his company.

Intuit (v) – perceive, insight, instinct; knowing without logic. **Intuition** (n).
I can usually intuit when someone is not telling me the truth.

Inverted (adj) – upturn; to turn upside down; to reverse the order of two things. **Invert** (v). Antonym: righted (v).
At the air show I watched a stunt plane fly upside down and do an inverted roll.

Invigorating (adj) – revitalizing, energizing. **Invigorate** (v). Antonym: draining (adj).
He was refreshed after he went for an invigorating run in the park.

Irate (adj) – angry, incensed, enraged. Antonym: calm (adj).
He worked as a customer service representative and hated when irate customers called to complain.

Iridescent (adj) – glowing, gleaming. **Iridescence** (adj).
Her new cell phone lights up and gives off an iridescent glow when it rings.

Ironic (adj) – paradoxical, incongruous; surprising outcome in light of expected result. Antonym: consistent (adj).
I usually carry an umbrella, and ironically, it rained the day I forgot it at home.

COMPLETE CHAPTERS DICTIONARY cont'd.

Jeopardize (v) – risk, endanger; to make vulnerable. **Jeopardy** (n). Antonym: ensure (v).

He didn't want to jeopardize his grade point average, so he studied exceptionally hard for the final.

Jostling (v), **Jostle** (v) – shove, bump, push. Antonym: coddling (v).

While exiting the arena the singer encountered a crowd of jostling fans.

Jubilation (n) – rejoicing, celebration; an expression of joy. **Jubilant** (adj). Antonym: sadness (n).

The crowd was jubilant when their team won the championship.

Laboriously (adv) – backbreaking, tedious, grueling; demanding a great deal of work or care. **Laborious** (adj). Antonym: easily (adv).

The designer laboriously hand stitched pearls onto the dress.

Labyrinthine (adj) – circuitous, convoluted. Antonym: direct (adj).

The narrow, winding streets of Venice are a labyrinthine maze that seems to have been thrown together over the centuries.

Languid (adj) – relaxed, unhurried, lethargic. Antonym: harried (adj).

The audience was bored by the languid pace of the speaker's presentation.

Lesser (adj) – smaller; less significant. Antonym: greater (adj).

I don't like either of the candidates very much, and I feel that I'll need to chose between the lesser of two evils.

Licentious (adj) – immoral, lewd, unrestrained. Antonym: modest (adj).

The bouncer kicked him out of the club because of his licentious behavior.

Linger (v) – loiter, persist, hang around.

The events of September 11th will linger in the minds of Americans forever.

Loom (v) – 1. overhang, appear, project; come into view. Antonym: recede (v).

We came in early yesterday because a storm was looming on the horizon.

Loom (v) – 2. philosophically resonate; have relevance.

Even today, Elvis Presley looms large on the music scene.

Lucid (adj) – coherent, comprehensible, intelligible; clearly understood. Antonym: incoherent (adj).

After a baseball hit him in the head, the paramedic wanted to make sure that he was lucid.

Lucidity (n) – clarity, intelligibility; a state of coherence or clear understanding. **Lucid** (adj). Antonym: incoherent (adj).

Assaying the team's loss, the captain gained lucidity when he realized that his showboating kept them from scoring more points.

Lurking (v), **Lurk** (v) – prowl, hide; lie in wait; move about stealthily or undetected. Antonym: parade (v).

He was seen lurking around the parking lot before the truck was stolen.

Manifest (v) – 1. show; become evident or visible. Antonym: dissipate (v).

Her illness first manifested itself as a high fever.

Manifest (adj) – 2. obvious, apparent. Antonym: subtle (adj).

He didn't know what transgression he committed to prompt her manifest hostility.

Manifesting (v) – bringing about; becoming apparent. **Manifest** (adj).

Melting ice fields and rising ocean tides indicate that global warming is manifesting itself most dramatically at the Earth's poles.

COMPLETE CHAPTERS DICTIONARY cont'd.

Marquee (n) – canopy above an entrance; a roof like shelter above a theater entrance.

When it began to rain she ran for shelter under the theater marquee.

Martyr (n) – one who is subjugated; one who endures pain or suffers voluntarily typically to incite change. Antonym: oppressor (n).

She fought for women's rights all of her life and died a martyr for the cause.

Merits (v) – 1. to warrant or deserve.

Her bravery merits the highest honor.

Merits (n), **Merit** (n) – 2. benefits, pros. Antonym: disadvantage (n).

The design was selected based upon its merits.

Minimal (adj) – the smallest amount or number allowed or possible. **Minimum** (adj). Antonym: Maximum (adj).

The minimal number of credits needed to graduate is forty.

Mire (n) – 1. a bog; gunk, marsh, swamp.

Walking through the swamp, she lost her boot in a mire.

Mire (n) – 2. a difficult situation.

His parents were mired in a messy divorce.

Mired (adj) – 1. caught up; in a difficult situation.

She was mired in the conflict between her parents.

Mired (adj) – 2. trapped by a thick substance. **Mire** (n). Antonym: free (adj).

His shoes became mired in the mud.

Modesty (n) – reserve, humility, discretion, diffidence. **Modest** (adj). Antonym: arrogance (n).

She contributes to many charities, but her modesty precludes her from discussing it.

Momentous (adj) – important, considerable, historic. Antonym: inconsequential (adj).

The moon landing was a momentous accomplishment for mankind.

Monotony (n) – repetitiveness, sameness. **Monotonous** (adj). Antonym: variety (n)

Sometimes the monotony of long drives makes me tired.

Muddle (v) – to behave in a confused or disorderly manner; jumbled.

She didn't know her lines in the play and muddled through the performance.

Nemesis (n) – arch-enemy, adversary, competitor. Antonym: ally (n).

Baseball fans always look forward to the Boston Red Sox squaring off against their nemesis, the New York Yankees.

Neophytes (n), **Neophyte** (n) – beginner, novice. Antonym: veteran (n).

Everyone starts as a neophyte and builds expertise with practice.

Nostalgic (adj) – homesick, reflective, wistful; to think of or long for an earlier, "simpler" period. **Nostalgia** (n). Antonym: unsentimental (adj).

While preparing for his SATs he became nostalgic for third grade, when his biggest problem was deciding what lunchbox he was going to bring to school.

Novelty (n) – newness, uniqueness. **Novel** (adj).

The novelty of their new goldfish wore off, so the children lost interest in it.

Obnoxiousness (n), **Obnoxious** (adj) – exhibiting insufferable, repugnant behavior.

I wonder if reality show producers actually look for self-absorbed, loud, obnoxious idiots to create drama on their programs?

COMPLETE CHAPTERS DICTIONARY cont'd.

Obscure (adj) – 1. vague, unclear, incomprehensible. Antonym: apparent (adj).
We missed the turn for his house because the street sign was obscured by trees.

Obscure (adj), **Obscurity** (adj) – 2. little known. Antonym: common (adj).
Sometimes unsigned, obscure, independent recording artists create the most innovative music.

Obsession (n) – mania, fixation, compulsion; thinking about something or someone constantly. **Obsess** (v).
He was obsessed with cars and owned more than fifty classics.

Obtuse (adj) – 1. stupid, thick, dull-witted. Antonym: clever (adj).
I don't mean to be obtuse, but I just don't understand quantum physics.

Obtuse (adj) – 2. an angle between 90 and 180 degrees. Antonym: acute (adj).
An obtuse angle is between 90 and 180 degrees.

Occurring (v), **Occur** (v) – transpire; happen.
The movie we saw last night was about a deli clerk who traveled back in time to prevent a calamity from occurring.

Odyssey (n) – a long, eventful journey.
The novel I am reading follows one man's odyssey to find his biological parents.

Ominous (adj) – foreboding, forbidding, menacing, threatening. Antonym: welcoming (adj).
It was tornado season, and we saw ominous, black clouds low on the horizon.

Palpitating (v), **Palpitate** (v) – throb, flutter. **Palpitations** (n).
On our first date I was so nervous my heart was palpitating.

Panache (n) – style, élan, confidence, flair. Antonym: inelegance (n).

He has tremendous panache and always wears the finest suits, handmade shoes and magnificent silk ties.

Panorama (n) – vista; an unbroken view of a large area. **Panoramic** (adj).

You can see the panorama of the entire city from the Empire State Building's observation deck.

Paradigms (n), **Paradigm** (n) – example, model, standard.

Julia Child established the paradigm for today's cooking programs.

Peer (v) – 2. gaze, look intently. Antonym: glance (v).

He peered into the candy store window, trying to decide what he wanted.

Peers (n), **Peer** (n) – 1. equal, friend, colleague, contemporary, cohort. Antonyms: superior, inferior (n).

The legal system entitles one to be judged by a jury of their peers.

Perceive (v) – distinguish, recognize; take notice. **Perception** (n). Antonym: ignore (v).

Catching a glimpse of the blue car in his rear view mirror again, he perceived that he was being followed.

Peripheral (adj) – tangential, outer, marginal; at the edge. **Periphery** (n). Antonym: central (adj).

During our debate he introduced points that weren't central to the issue, and were only peripherally related.

Pernicious (adj) – evil, malicious, harmful. Antonym: nice (adj).

Many parents regard violent video games as a pernicious influence on children.

Perplexed (v), **Perplex** (v) – confuse, confound, befuddle. Antonym: clarify (v).

We were perplexed by the intricate directions.

COMPLETE CHAPTERS DICTIONARY cont'd.

Perpetuate (v) – preserve, continue, maintain; make something last. **Perpetual** (adj). Antonym: terminate (v).

The local preservation society is working to perpetuate the community's history.

Perusing (v), **Peruse** (v) – scrutinize, examine; read with care. Antonym: skim (v).

She spends her entire Sunday perusing the newspaper for interesting articles.

Phoenix (n) – 1. a mythological bird that ignites itself into flames every 500 years, and is born again from its ashes.

The Phoenix rose again, reborn from its ashes.

Phoenix (n) – 2. a term that describes someone who resurrects or redeems themselves in some manner.

Despite having been bankrupt, he rose like a Phoenix to made a great comeback.

Pithy (adj) – terse, concise; to the point. Antonym: rambling (adj).

Her attorney made a pithy remark in response to the plaintiff's comments.

Plague (n) – 1. outbreak, pestilence, scourge, blight Antonym: antidote (n).

The Black Plague, which was spread by rat fleas during the 1340s, killed almost one third of the entire population of Europe.

Plague (n) – 2. trouble, pester, bother.

Lately I've been plagued by writer's block, and I can't finish writing my book.

Plausible (adj), **Plausibility** (adj) – believable, credible, possible, likely. Antonym: unlikely (adj).

In light of the fact that the universe is comprised of millions of galaxies, it is entirely plausible that intelligent life exists somewhere out there.

Poignant (adj) – moving, touching, heartbreaking.

It was a poignant story about a young orphan who is adopted by a loving family.

Predilection (n) – liking, partiality, penchant, tendency; disposition to.

She has a predilection for sneakers and owns more than 50 pairs.

Predisposition (n) – inclination, leaning, proclivity, propensity; prone to behave or respond in a given manner. **Predispose** (v).

She's never on time; her predisposition is to be late.

Procure (v) – obtain, acquire. Antonym: divest (v).

She couldn't repair it until she had procured the correct tool.

Profound (adj) – 1. deep, thoughtful. Antonym: inane (adj).

Steven Hawking, the world's smartest man, has had profound insights into the origins of the universe.

Profound (adj) – 2. to have a significant effect. Antonym: irrelevant (adj).

The internet has had a profound effect on the music industry.

Profusion (n) – overabundance, excess, surplus, many; large amount. Antonym: dearth (n).

International copyright laws are being revised to stem the profusion of counterfeit goods.

Prolong (v) – extend, lengthen; draw out; usually associated with time. Antonym: curtail (v).

We enjoyed our trip to Spain so much that we decided to prolong our stay for an additional three days.

Propagate (v) – reproduce, spread. Antonym: confine (v).

Scientists working with endangered giant pandas are encouraging them to breed in order to propagate the species.

Proximity (n) – nearness, closeness, immediacy. Antonym: distance (n).

We can walk to the movie theater because of its close proximity to the house.

COMPLETE CHAPTERS DICTIONARY cont'd.

Pugilistic (adj) – quarrelsome, belligerent; related to boxing. Antonym: conciliatory (adj).

Embroiled in a heated argument, they each adopted a pugilistic stance as they tried to shout down one another.

Punitive (adj) – corrective, retaliatory; inflicting punishment.

Since the company refused to make amends for their mistake, she was compelled to take punitive action.

Pursuing (v), **Pursue** (v) – follow, chase; to go after something.

He is pursuing a career in acting.

Pusillanimous (adj) – cowardly, craven, timid. Antonym: courageous (adj).

Pusillanimous in the extreme, the Prince sent others off to wage his battles.

Quelled (v), **Quell** (v) – 1. suppress, subdue, repress; put down. Antonym: incite (v).

The National Guard was called in to quell the prison riot.

Quell (v) – 2. allay, alleviate, calm, mitigate. Antonym: terrorize (v).

It was his first time in a helicopter and he had heard that they had a poor safety record, so the pilot tried to quell his fear of crashing.

Quiver (v) – tremble, shake.

She was so scared that she began to quiver.

Quixotic (adj) – idealistic but impractical.

The notion that all people will live in peace is nice, but quixotic.

Rabid (adj) – 1. extreme, fanatical. Antonym: casual (adj).

He was a rabid Yankees fan, and never missed a game.

Rabid (adj) – 2. a state of infection with rabies. Antonym: healthy (adj).

The dog that bit her was rabid, so she needed a tetanus shot.

Random (adj) – haphazard; by chance. Antonym: systematic (adj).

He didn't care what color notebook he bought, and just picked one at random.

Razing (v), **Raze** (v) – level, burn, devastate, destroy; tear down. Antonym: build (v).

The conflagration razed the town.

Reconcile (v) – settle, square; make amends. **Reconciliation** (n). Antonym: divorce (v).

The players union and the team owners met to reconcile their differences so the new season could get underway.

Rectify (v) – repair, fix; to correct or resolve a problem.

When the blackout occurred the power plant's staff met to determine how they would rectify it.

Refraction (n) – the change in direction of light or sound wave as it passes from one material into another. **Refract** (v).

Although it may look as though your spoon is bending when you place it in a glass of water, it is actually an illusion created by refraction.

Refrain (v) – 1. abstain; to avoid doing something. Antonym: indulge (v).

The waiter asked the restaurant patron with the cigar, "Sir, would you please refrain from smoking?"

Refrain (v) – 2. chorus; a poetic or musical verse that repeats; idiomatically refers to hearing a repeated excuse.

Politicians passing the blame has long been a familiar refrain.

COMPLETE CHAPTERS DICTIONARY cont'd.

Remedy (n) – cure, medicine.

The best remedy for a broken heart is to find solace in your friends.

Renovate (v) – refurbish, restore. **Renovation** (n). Antonym: demolish (v).

They decided to renovate the hundred-year-old house rather than demolish it.

Reside (v) – to inhabit; to exist in; to live in a given location. **Resident** (n).

I plan to study abroad, and I'd like to reside in London.

Resolve (v) – 1. solve, decide. **Resolution** (n).

Working together, we can resolve the problem.

Resolve (n) – 2. conviction, determination, tenacity; dedication of purpose. Antonym: indifference (n).

Full of resolve, the stranded mountaineers attempted the treacherous decent.

Resplendent (adj) – dazzling, stunning, glorious, brilliant. Antonym: dull (adj).

The vintage aircraft's mirror-polished fuselage was resplendent in the sunlight.

Reticence (n) – reluctance, unwillingness; inclination to silence. **Reticent** (adj). Antonym: willingness (n).

Being very shy, she was reticent to participate in the class discussion.

Revelation (n) – disclosure, discovery, insight; to make something known. **Reveal** (v). Antonym: obscure (v).

The media made shocking revelations about former President Bill Clinton's affair.

Revere (v) – admire, worship. **Reverence** (n). Antonym: revile (v).

Michael Jordon is revered for his skill on the basketball court.

Rig (v) – fix, arrange, prepare, manipulate.

The competition was rigged by the judges.

Saturnine (adj) – melancholy, gloomy, sullen, glum.
She was saturnine over the loss of her grandmother.

Savor (v) – relish, appreciate, enjoy.
Prepared by one of the city's finest chefs, she savored every bite of her meal.

Scoff (v) – mock, ridicule; make fun of. Antonym: encourage (v).
The critics scoffed at the comic's attempt to play a dramatic role.

Scurry (v) – scamper, dash; move briskly. Antonym: amble (v).
When she told the child it was time for his bubble bath, he scurried up the steps and jumped into the tub.

Seclusion (n) – isolation, privacy, solitude. Antonym: company (n).
Whenever he was depressed he avoided his friends and went into seclusion.

Sedentary (adj) – inactive. Antonym: active (adj).
His doctor told him to stop being sedentary, get off of the couch, and join a gym.

Seep (v) – leak, leach, bleed.
The paint seeped out of the can and wound up on everything in the bag.

Senescent (adj) – aging; decaying over time. Antonym: youthful (adj).
The twelve-year-old dog was senescent.

Sensual (adj) – pleasing to the senses.
Graceful and lissome, the model was noted for her sensual style.

Shimmer (v) – twinkle, glint; shine intermittently.
The moonlight shimmered on the surface of the lake.

Shroud (n) – 1. blanket, veil, cover; a draped material that envelops an object.
At the funeral the widow wore a shroud that veiled her face.

COMPLETE CHAPTERS DICTIONARY cont'd.

Shroud (v) – 2. hide, cover; shield from view. Antonym: uncover (v).

The leaves shrouded the driveway, making it difficult see the garage.

Significant (adj) – meaningful, consequential. Antonym: insignificant (adj).

The school made significant changes to its curriculum to accommodate the new federal regulations.

Sinister (adj) – threatening, evil, creepy.

Foreboding and sinister, Dracula is a classic horror figure.

Situation (n) – predicament, circumstances; a state of affairs.

Prior to arresting the protester, the police officer assessed the situation.

Skulking (v), **Skulk** (v) – creep, loiter, sneak; to move furtively or secretly.

The spy skulked through the city's streets hoping he wouldn't be detected.

Slander (n) – insult, malign, defame; make false and malicious statements. Antonym: praise (n/v)

Insisting that he was faithful to his wife, he said the reporter slandered him by writing that he was having an affair.

Sojourn (n) – visit; temporary stay.

My sojourn in Paris was only one day because I was on my way to London.

Solace (n) – comfort, support. Antonym: distress (n).

After her husband left her she found solace in writing.

Solemnly (adv) – seriously, gravely. **Solemn** (adj). Antonym: merrily (adv).

The news anchor solemnly described the events that led to the tragic fire.

Squander (v) – waste.

My brother squandered his entire paycheck on a thirty pound stick of gum.

State (v) – 1. assert; to declare.
She stated that she wasn't going to tolerate his idiocy any longer and left him.

State (n) – 2. condition, circumstances; frame of mind.
He was such a slob, his mom couldn't believe the state of his room.

State (n) – 3. territory, nation, country.
The Secretary of State represents the U.S. in the world forum.

Stimulating (adj) – inspiring; thought provoking. **Stimulate** (v). Antonym: boring (adj).
She found their conversation about the upcoming election stimulating.

Stolid (adj) – dull, impassive, boring. Antonym: stimulating (adj).
Fitting the stereotype, his accounting professor is a straight-laced, stolid guy.

Sublime (adj) – awe-inspiring, moving, perfect, transcendent. Antonym: uninspiring (adj).
The orchestra's performance was the finest I've ever heard; it was sublime.

Succumb (v) – yield, die, submit; give way, give in.
Eve succumbed to the temptation of the forbidden fruit.

Superfluous (adj) – extraneous, unnecessary, excess. Antonym: critical (adj).
Auto manufacturers are building superfluous technology into today's cars; does anyone really need a seat that massages your buttocks while you drive?

Surmise (v) – deduce, estimate, infer, gather; figure out.
I surmised how big the parking spot was by comparing it to the car next to it.

Survey (v) – review, analyze.
Flying over the brushfire, the ranger surveyed the damage to the forest.

COMPLETE CHAPTERS DICTIONARY cont'd.

Symbiotic (adj) – a mutually beneficial, interdependent relationship. Antonym: parasitic (adj).

> In an illustration of the perfect symbiotic relationship, hippos rely on birds to eat flies that would otherwise bite them, and the birds rely on hippos to attract flies, their primary source of food.

Synchronously (adv) – simultaneously, concurrently. **Synchronous** (adj). Antonym: sequentially (adv).

> My favorite TV shows are aired synchronously, which forces me to miss one.

Tempestuous (adj) – stormy, emotional, passionate. Antonym: calm (v).

> His relationship with his dad is tempestuous and characterized by friction.

Thaumaturgicaly (adv) – magical, miraculously, supernatural; the working of miracles or magic feats. **Thaumaturgy** (n).

> The knight recited an incantation and thaumaturgicaly defeated the dragon.

Tortuous (adj) – 1. arduous, trying, difficult. Antonym: easy (adj).

> Immigrants find that applying for a green card is a tortuous process.

Tortuous (adj) – 2. characterized by curves. Antonym: straight (adj).

> The winding mountain pass was tortuous.

Toxin (n) – poison, pollutant, contaminant. **Toxic** (adj).

> The industrial plant illegally released toxins that poisoned the local wildlife.

Tranquility (n) – peaceful, calm. **Tranquil** (adj). Antonym: chaos (n).

> Dotted with tranquil lakes, the Adirondacks are a great place to spend the summer.

Traversing (v), **Traverse** (v) – cross, travel, navigate; pass through.

> Traveling by car, plane, and train, his mom is traversing the globe.

Tundra (n) – rolling, treeless plain in the North American arctic and Siberia.
My parents went to Alaska to watch caribou roaming the tundra.

Trepidation (n) – fear, anxiety, apprehension. Antonym: confidence (n).
Hoping to be accepted with the early admissions, he opened the envelope from Princeton with great trepidation.

Underlying (adj) – fundamental; describes a principle upon which something is based or is influenced by; primary reason or influence. **Underlie** (v).
Taxes are an underlying issue in the upcoming presidential race.

Ungainly (adj) – awkward, clumsy, ungraceful. Antonym: graceful (adj).
Penguins walk in an ungainly manner on land, however, they swim gracefully through the water.

Uniformity (n) – standardization, regularity, consistency. **Uniform** (adj). Antonym: irregularity (n).
Restaurant chains strive to maintain the uniformity of their food at all of their locations.

Union (n) – combination, amalgamation, merger. Antonym: separation (n).
At my aunt's wedding the Justice of the Peace asked, "Is there anyone who objects to this union?"

Unravel (v) – disentangle, untangle, solve; work loose.
Loosing his supporters one by one, his plan began to unravel.

Unscathed (adj) – unharmed, intact; without injury or damage. Antonym: damaged (adj).
Astonishingly, she escaped the car accident unscathed.

COMPLETE CHAPTERS DICTIONARY cont'd.

Vacillation (n) – indecision, uncertainty; inability to decide. **Vacillate** (v). Antonym: decision (n).

They couldn't decide and vacillated between getting a cat or a dog.

Valor (n) – bravery, courage, fearlessness. Antonym: critical (adj).

John Wayne said, "Valor is being scared to death – but saddling up anyway."

Vantage (n) – 1. advantage. Antonym: disadvantage (n).

Positioned above the valley, our forces had the invading army at a vantage.

Vantage (n) – 2. perspective.

Positioned above the valley, our forces had an excellent vantage point to observe the invading army's troop movements.

Vague (adj) – unclear, indistinct. Antonym: clear (adj).

I have a vague memory of the cousins that I met six years ago.

Vertigo (n) – dizziness; confused state of mind.

He has a fear of heights and is overcome by vertigo when he enters tall buildings.

Vindicate (v) – justify, support, exonerate; clear of blame.

The company's higher profits vindicated the CEO's unorthodox style.

Virtuoso (adj) – genius, prodigy; someone with masterful skill in the arts; exhibiting the ability of a virtuoso.

She's been playing the piano since she was a toddler, and now she's a virtuoso who headlines performances around the world.

Volatile (adj) – unstable, erratic, impulsive, unpredictable. **Volatile** (adj). Antonym: stable (adj).

The Middle East has always been volatile and has rarely known peace.

Wavering (v), **Waver** (v) – hesitate, hesitancy, fickle; inability to decide or focus. Antonym: deciding (v).

The mayor rebuked wavering council members for failing to support him.

Welter (n) – turmoil; bewildering jumble; a confused mass. Antonym: order (n).

A welter of decade-old newspapers is piled in the garage

End of Combined Chapters Dictionary

COMBINED CHAPTERS EXERCISES

In this section Word$ and exercises from each chapter are combined. If you get hung up on something, the Complete Chapters Dictionary should help out.

COMBO SYNONYM MATCHING

Match the following Word$ with their synonyms. Note the letter of the matching synonym in the space adjacent to the word.

SET #1

Vocabulary Words	Synonyms
1. _____Accolades	(a) speed
2. _____Actuate	(b) disbelief
3. _____Beset	(c) lacking
4. _____Bested	(d) overwhelm
5. _____Candor	(e) shine
6. _____Celerity	(f) enlighten
7. _____Decree	(g) blatant
8. _____Devoid	(h) understand
9. _____Entice	(i) falsehood
10. _____Epitome	(j) beaten
11. _____Fallacy	(k) risk
12. _____Flagrant	(l) state
13. _____Glimmer	(m) honesty
14. _____Grasp	(n) award
15. _____Hoax	(o) lewd
16. _____Illuminate	(p) persuade
17. _____Incredulity	(q) motivate
18. _____Jeopardize	(r) trick
19. _____Licentious	(s) archetype

SET #2 | **Vocabulary Words** | **Synonyms**

1. _____ Laborious   (a) discovery
2. _____ Labyrinthine   (b) abstain
3. _____ Monotony   (c) relish
4. _____ Muddle   (d) tangential
5. _____ Nemesis   (e) fanatical
6. _____ Obtuse   (f) suppress
7. _____ Panache   (g) change in direction
8. _____ Peripheral   (h) jumbled
9. _____ Punitive   (i) repetitiveness
10. _____ Quell   (j) apprehension
11. _____ Rabid   (k) arch-enemy
12. _____ Refraction   (l) awkward
13. _____ Refrain   (m) style
14. _____ Revelation   (n) turmoil
15. _____ Savor   (o) retaliatory
16. _____ Seclusion   (p) prodigy
17. _____ Squander   (q) indistinct
18. _____ Surmise   (r) convoluted
19. _____ Tortuous   (s) combination
20. _____ Trepidation   (t) deduce
21. _____ Ungainly   (u) backbreaking
22. _____ Union   (v) arduous
23. _____ Vague   (w) waste
24. _____ Virtuoso   (x) hesitate
25. _____ Welter   (y) solitude
26. _____ Waver   (z) dull-witted

SET #3>

Defined Mind

SET #3   **Vocabulary Words**   **Synonyms**

1. _____Abscond   (a) din
2. _____Abstain   (b) poise
3. _____Bask   (c) destroy
4. _____Cacophony   (d) escape
5. _____Complicit   (e) evil
6. _____Demure   (f) persist
7. _____Effervescent   (g) manipulate
8. _____Finesse   (h) do without
9. _____Gracious   (i) unstable
10. _____Haze   (j) decorous
11. _____Impart   (k) simultaneously
12. _____Linger   (l) fog
13. _____Manifest   (m) aging
14. _____Novelty   (n) vivacious
15. _____Ominous   (o) primary influence
16. _____Pernicious   (p) polite
17. _____Procure   (q) peaceful
18. _____Raze   (r) sunbathe
19. _____Rig   (s) poison
20. _____Senescent   (t) apparent
21. _____Synchronously   (u) perspective
22. _____Toxin   (v) newness
23. _____Tranquil   (w) obtain
24. _____Underlying   (x) forbidding
25. _____Vantage   (y) communicate
26. _____Volatile   (z) involved

COMBO SENTENCE COMPLETION

Using the Word$ in the Bank, find the words which best complete the sentences below.

WORD BANK				
Annihilated	Appraised	Cavorting	Colossal	Contagion
Crucial	Decoy	Deleterious	Deluded	Dispel
Dissuade	Embarked	Equanimity	Extol	Forsake
Futile	Indiscretions	Intuit	Jostled	Looming
Lucid	Martyr	Merits	Obsessed	Odyssey
Pithy	Poignant	Pugilistic	Propagating	Pursuing
Resplendent	Sedentary	Skulked	Profusion	Survey
Symbiotic				

1. _____ at the fete, the guys tossed their girlfriends in the pool.

2. A healthy marriage is a _____ relationship.

3. He had the painting _____ and was surprised to learn that it was very valuable.

4. They _____ for the Bahamas from JFK International Airport.

5. Telling him that he would wind up flipping burgers, the Principal was determined to _____ my friend from dropping out.

6. Following the revelations of his affair with an intern, former President Clinton became known for his _____.

7. At the concert we _____ for position at the foot of the stage.

8. She's very calm in difficult situations; you have to respect her _____.

9. Sparkling like a pile of diamonds a hundred miles away, New York is a _____ beacon.

COMBO SENTENCE COMPLETION cont'd.

10. He is following his dream by _____ a career in law.

11. The presidential candidates are _____ their ideas by making speeches throughout the country.

12. He was a total couch potato who had a _____ lifestyle

13. The demonstrator was overrun by government forces and died a _____ for his cause.

14. I would never _____ my family.

15. He was so embarrassed after pouring a drink down the front of his pants that he _____ away from the party.

16. Stalkers are _____ with the celebrities they follow.

17. The beautiful Corvette was a _____ to lure customers into the used car lot.

18. The study's outcome is encouraging and _____ further study.

19. Our team _____ the competition, and we finished the season undefeated.

20. When I brought up the topic she became _____ , but her tone softened as she came to understand my perspective.

21. I could see the tornado _____ on the horizon, so we left the house to look for a safe place.

22. The winner voluntarily submitted herself to a physical to _____ any allegations that she was using anything to enhance her performance.

23. It is _____ that you to follow the directions on the medication's label.

24. She apologized for her _____ response to my naive question.

25. Choosing between going away to school or attending college locally and living at home is a _____ decision.

26. Thousands packed the canyon of lower Broadway to _____ John Glenn upon his return as the first American to orbit the Earth.

27. Those who perished on 9/11 were remembered in a _____ tribute at the site of the World Trade Center.

28. She could _____ that I was worried about my upcoming exam.

29. Given the fact that she can't sing, it is _____ for her to try out for "American Idol."

30. Feeding a dog chocolate can be _____ to its health.

31. Working for over three years to get this company started, it has been an _____ to say the least.

32. There is a _____ of diet gimmicks on the market, but that doesn't mean that any of them work.

33. The bird flu virus is a _____ that was thought only to affect chickens and other fowl, but now appears to also be harmful to humans.

34. After the tornado she came out of the cellar to _____ the damage to the house.

35. He delivered a clear and _____ argument supporting states' rights.

36. His mom said, "He is completely _____ if he expects me to pick up after him for the rest of his life."

NOTES:

COMBO CROSSWORD PUZZLE

Use the synonyms provided in the clues to identify the words that complete the crossword puzzle on the following page. The numbers run top-to-bottom and left-to-right.

Across

1. Fog, mist (or) refers to memory
2. Beginner, novice
3. Idealistic but impractical
4. Opposite, converse
5. Indecision, uncertainty; inability to decide
6. Melancholy, gloomy, sullen, glum
7. Disturbing, upsetting
8. Stormy, emotional, passionate
9. Assent; agree without protest
10. Awe-inspiring, moving, perfect, transcendent
11. Comfort, support
12. Bring about settlement; make amends
13. Malign, defame; false/malicious statements
14. Haphazard; by chance
15. Entrance, charm, enthrall
16. Pace; manner of walking or running
17. Vague, incomprehensible (or) little known
18. Repair, fix; to correct or resolve a problem
19. In a difficult situation (or) trapped in muck

Down

1. Example, model, standard
2. Justify, support, exonerate; clear of blame
3. Known to a small group (or) perplexing, arcane
4. Confuse, confound, befuddle
5. Cross, travel, navigate; pass through
6. Relaxed, unhurried, lethargic
7. Angry, incensed, enraged
8. Scrutinize, examine; to read with care
9. Unharmed, intact; without injury or damage
10. Assert (or) condition (or) territory
11. Yield, die, submit; give way, give in
12. Dull, impassive, boring
13. Persist for an extended period (or) bear, tolerate
14. Suppress, repress; put down (or) allay, calm
15. Fragrant, pleasing scent
16. Deep, thoughtful (or) have a significant effect
17. Aware of; to know of something
18. Standardization, regularity, consistency
19. Compel, spur, impel, provoke, goad; to cause

COMBO CROSSWORD PUZZLE

299

COMBO SYNONYM SENTENCES

In the following sentences, use correct forms or tenses of the Word$ in the Bank to match the underlined synonyms, and write the correct word in the space provided below each sentence.

WORD BANK				
Afflicted	Apathetic	Borders	Calamity	Clout
Comely	Confounded	Conversely	Cosmos	Decipher
Debilitated	Din	Dregs	Duration	Ephemeral
Factions	Fathom	Flagging	Fluctuate	Forlorn
Fret	Induced	Incontrovertible	Interminable	Intriguing
Jubilant	Lesser	Perpetual	Plausible	Predilection
Renovate	Scoffed	Sinister	Situation	Superfluous
Wavered				

1. Considering her <u>penchant</u> for yellow, I was surprised that she bought a blue car.

   _____

2. "Unencumbered by <u>extraneous</u> posturing, her performance was raw and inspiring."

   _____

3. The band's tour was canceled due to the <u>waning</u> demand for tickets.

   _____

4. Given the fact that there are an infinite number of galaxies, it is entirely <u>possible</u> that there is intelligent life somewhere in the universe.

   _____

5. The <u>noise</u> of the traffic kept me awake all night.

   _____

300

6. Sometimes, given the overwhelming crises here at home, it's hard not to be indifferent about problems elsewhere.

   _____

7. The new technology was interesting and sparked my curiosity.

   _____

8. Lazy summer days are always too fleeting.

   _____

9. The recording star baffled her critics by becoming more popular than ever.

   _____

10. My boss says that it doesn't hurt to have friends with influence.

    _____

11. Parents often worry about their children.

    _____

12. They persuaded him to do the stunt by offering him a pile of cash.

    _____

13. Although my workout is only an hour long, it seems endless.

    _____

14. They were the consummate odd couple; she was outgoing, and in contrast, he was very shy.

    _____

15. The predicament she found herself in was unsettling.

    _____

16. My dad gets totally furious if I eat in front of the TV; I think he's mentally impaired.

    _____

COMBO SYNONYM SENTENCES cont'd.

17. We stood for the <u>length</u> of their wedding ceremony, and when it was over I couldn't wait to find a couch to crash on.

    _____

18. He was <u>sad</u> over the loss of his puppy, and we couldn't cheer him up.

    _____

19. I can't <u>understand</u> how she could deceive her best friend.

    _____

20. The new government was in a state of disarray because competing <u>groups</u> were fighting for power.

    _____

21. The planetarium show made me feel as though I was shooting through the <u>universe</u>.

    _____

22. While the article does bring some new information to light, much of it <u>verges</u> on fiction.

    _____

23. He considers lobbying to be a <u>less significant</u> influence on public policy that it is popularly thought to be.

    _____

24. While visiting Rome, we asked our guide to translate a shopkeeper's comments because we couldn't <u>figure out</u> what he was trying to say.

    _____

25. In video clips, Osama bin Laden reveals a <u>evil</u> smile when he discusses the attack on the World Trade Center.

    _____

26. During the spring, many people are burdened by allergies.
    _____

27. In her day, Jacqueline Kennedy was quite attractive.
    _____

28. We arrived late to the sale, and the earlier shoppers only left behind the leftovers of what the store had offer.
    _____

29. He decided to restore the house.
    _____

30. The girls mocked his attempt to join the field hockey team.
    _____

31. It wouldn't have been such a disaster if his parents hadn't come back from their vacation early.
    _____

32. The facts prove her statements to be indisputable.
    _____

33. When World War II ended, celebrating crowds packed Times Square.
    _____

34. Stock prices vary day to day.
    _____

35. He hesitated before asking her out on a date.
    _____

36. He was traumatized at the circus when he was a kid, and he now lived in continual fear of little dogs riding bicycles.
    _____

ARTICLE EXCERPTS

The following paragraphs have been selected from articles in the prior chapters. Read each passage, and then select the statements that best describe the author's remarks. Circle the letter that corresponds to the correct answer.

Excerpt 1

NYC - Scurrying into Native's doorway to get in from the rain, I was having heart palpitations from my mad, six-block dash to escape a sudden deluge. It was coming down in buckets. Basking in the reflection of the iridescent bulb overhead, its outline shimmered in the droplets clinging to my coat. There's something sublime about standing just out of the rain and watching New York come to halt as the sky opens up on a summer afternoon.

Question 1

(a) The article is written from the perspective of a small, scurrying animal.

(b) The author was running to get out of the rain and couldn't catch his breath.

(c) There was a flood in New York that the author was trying to escape.

(d) The author is a jogger who enjoys running in the rain.

Question 2

(a) The doorway light cast a glow that twinkled in the rain drops on the author's jacket.

(b) The author wanted to bask in the sun in front of the studio.

(c) Light bulbs were clinging to the author's coat, and were casting a shimmering light in the rain.

(d) The rain drops were reflecting the author's coat while he was basking in the doorway.

Question 3

(a) The author finds perfection standing in the rain on a summer day in New York.

(b) Keith likes to watch for the perfect rain, which can only be spotted from doorways.

(c) The author would like it to rain more often because it brings New York to a standstill.

(d) He savors the odd tranquility that occurs when it rains heavily in New York.

Excerpt 2

As far as I can decipher, his key vantage is that his significant intellect borders on genius. Refracted through Rodney's muse, his labyrinthine rhymes put lesser recording artists to shame. His deft use of Word$ annihilates the stereotypes of a hardened street rapper, and he procures an esoteric paradigm unrivaled by any that I have encountered before. Pusillanimous neophytes may be perplexed by the intricacy of his verse, but accordingly, those in the know revere him for the momentous accomplishment that they represent. Any remarks to the contrary are simply punitive.

Question 4

(a) The author is looking to decode Rodney's primary advantage.

(b) The author believes that Rodney's primary advantage is his intellect.

(c) The author his having trouble figuring out how Rodney's point of view influences his work.

(d) The author has been working to determine Rodney's intellectual boundaries.

Question 5

(a) Rodney enjoys embarrassing other performers by using a muse to bend the light in his maze.

(b) Rodney's muse bends light and sound waves, which ultimately results in convoluted rhymes.

(c) Rodney's towering verse are the product of great inspiration, and makes other recording artists look inferior.

(d) Rodney likes to shame other recording artist via his labyrinthine rhymes.

COMBO CHAPTERS ARTICLE EXCERPTS cont'd.

Question 6

(a) The author feels that Rodney's work dispels the notion that artists who rap are incapable of authoring intellectually challenging material.

(b) Rodney destroys stereotypes by acquiring arcane models.

(c) The author is concerned that Rodney is a hardened street rapper who said something arcane to him.

(d) All of the above.

Question 7

(a) Cowardly beginners are confused by Rodney, but those who understand his work worship him.

(b) Timid novices may be befuddled by the complexity of Rodney's work, but appropriately, those who are knowledgeable admire its significance.

(c) Rodney is worshiped and admired by those in-the-know, whereas timid beginners are befuddled by the complexity of his lyrics.

(d) None of the above.

Question 8

(a) Anyone who disagrees with the author will be sued for punitive damages.

(b) Any remarks that conflict with the author's will be punished.

(c) Anyone who disagrees with the author needs to be corrected.

(d) Those who do not believe that Rodney's work is brilliant are just jealous.

Excerpt 3

Surveying the city, Nina found Barcelona a novel, captivating place, and was in awe at its antiquity. Elated to embark on this sojourn, she was impressed by the flagrant architecture, with which she had a vague familiarity before she arrived. And, accustomed to the bravado of New Yorkers, Nina was confounded by Barcelona's similar profusion of cultures, but struck by the modesty of its inhabitants. Expecting the same dynamic given analogous circumstances, she found the city enigmatic.

Question 9

(a) She found the city magnificent and rich in history.

(b) She was captured in Barcelona while she was measuring it.

(c) Nina found a city book and was struck by its age.

(d) Nina wrote a novel about the city's antiquity.

Question 10

(a) Her flagrance was familiar and impressive.

(b) Nina was happy to bark on her sojourn.

(c) She was excited to begin her visit.

(d) She disembarked to find vague architecture.

Question 11

(a) Barcelona's wild architecture was vague, yet familiar to her.

(b) Nina had a modest knowledge of the city's outstanding architecture.

(c) Barcelona, notable for its flagrant architects, is a beautiful city.

(d) Nina was impressed by the flagrant architects she knew.

Question 12

(a) Her New York bravado confounded the city's modest inhabitants.

(b) She was struck by the multiplicity of cultures and the restraint of its citizens.

(c) Accustomed to New Yorkers, she found too many cultures in Barcelona.

(d) New Yorkers' outgoing nature confuses Nina.

Excerpt 4

In "Why Didn't You Tell Me" Nina describes a sensual, comely love interest to whom she is addicted due to his "complicit smile" and "flagrant style." And, in describing her efforts to entice him, she figuratively contemplates the use of a

COMBO CHAPTERS ARTICLE EXCERPTS cont'd.

decoy. Consequently, I asked Nina if she was writing about someone she once had an obsession with herself, to which she replied, "No, I focused on this theme because I believe that it is something that all people can relate to."

Question 13

(a) Nina likes to wear masks to hide her feelings.

(b) To gain her love interest's attention she contemplates the use of a lure.

(c) She is addicted to dentistry and outrageous styles.

(d) Nina contemplates writing a poem to her crush to tell him how she feels.

Question 14

(a) Nina appreciates her crush's knowing, sly smile and confident demeanor.

(b) She becomes angry because his smile and style is much nicer than hers.

(c) She admires Sammy for his good looks and style, but doesn't like him.

(d) Nina is sensual and comely.

Excerpt 5

Back on a crystal-clear July night, Mia was driving to a late gig when, in her peripheral vision, she spotted a pair of glimmering headlights rushing toward her. Incredulous, she realized that some deviant ran a 'STOP' sign and was about to T-bone her. Despite her trepidation and the disconcerting image of an imminent calamity, she kept her equanimity, thought with celerity, and stood on the gas. Bracing herself for what she knew was about to occur, the other car struck her rear wheel dead-on on the passenger-side, and the impact launched her sideways like a toddler smacking his Hot Wheels with a hockey stick. Flying across the street driver's-door-first, she hit a fire hydrant on the far side of the road, slamming into it with such force that the car flipped. Then, everything, Was still.

Question 15

(a) On a beautiful summer evening Mia saw a car that was going to hit her.

(b) The oncoming car's headlights were out.

(c) Mia was late to a gig.

(d) She was late getting to a gig, so despite Mia's poor peripheral vision, she was rushing to get there.

Question 16

(a) Mia couldn't believe it when she realized that a deviant was allowed to drive.

(b) She was in a state of disbelief that some joker just ran a 'STOP' sign, and was about to plow into her.

(c) In a state of disbelief, Mia wondered how the driver of the other car could enjoy a steak while driving.

(d) She could not believe that a law-abiding citizen would pass through a 'STOP' sign.

Question 17

(a) Mia is fearful of disturbing images.

(b) She is nervously apprehensive about disconcerting images.

(c) She was fearful of the impending collision.

(d) Mia has trepidation of disconcerting imminent calamities.

Question 18

(a) Despite her trepidation over the disconcerting image, there was an imminent calamity during which she retained her equanimity for celerity.

(b) Despite her anxiety over the imminent accident, Mia stayed level headed and thought about celery.

(c) In spite of Mia's nervous anxiety regarding the coming collision, she kept her cool, thought with celerity, and stood up in the car.

(d) Despite her fear of the coming collision, she remained level-headed and thought quickly.

COMBO CHAPTERS ARTICLE EXCERPTS cont'd.

Question 19

(a) Mia was wearing braces and she knew that they were going to get hit by the oncoming car.

(b) The oncoming car smashed into her car, throwing it sideways at great speed.

(c) She held herself together, waiting to be struck by a kid with a hockey stick.

(d) The oncoming car smashed into her passenger side, launching the toddler sideways.

Question 20

(a) Her car slid sideways with celerity, smashed into a hydrant, and overturned.

(b) The hydrant flew across the street to flip her car's driver-side door.

(c) Her drivers-side door flew across the street, smashed into the hydrant and flipped.

(d) After she slid across the street driver-side-first, the hydrant slammed into the car and flipped it.

Excerpt 6

Their music shatters the monotony that saturates the airwaves today, razing the state of uniformity that is so perpetually frustrating. Invigorating and a remedy to rectify the soul, it's impossible for me to be sedentary when I'm listening to their tracks.

Question 21

(a) Keith & Rodney are drenched by sameness.

(b) Keith & Rodney write music that mixes it up.

(c) Keith & Rodney write music that breaks glass.

(d) Keith & Rodney compose music that is on par with other performers you hear on the radio today.

Question 22

(a) The artists' music forges it own path, breaking the typical boundaries present in today's play lists.

(b) The author is exasperated by the artists' music causing fires in places where standardization is the rule.

(c) The artists are continually vexed by devastation caused by today's radios.

(d) Rodney and Keith want to encourage standardization and seek to preserve their exasperation.

Question 23

(a) The author finds the artist's music energizing, and believes that it can be used to cure illnesses.

(b) The author finds the artists energized.

(c) The artists want to remain seated, but the author insists that they get up.

(d) The author finds the artist's music energizing, and regards it as a metaphorical cure for one's state of well being.

Excerpt 7

NYC - It is plausible that I've stumbled upon an ominous trend manifesting itself in Nina Zeitlin's work. Perhaps afflicted by some contagion, Nina can't seem to abstain from her predilection for writing nostalgic songs about her nemesis... pernicious men. Now I'm plagued by my efforts to reconcile the volatility of her grave subject matter with the effervescent, and occasionally demure, Nina we know and love.

Question 24

(a) It is possible that the author is clumsy and has fallen on a trend mill.

(b) The author thinks that he may have fallen into a trap that was set in Nina's work.

(c) The author believes that he may have found a foreboding trend in Nina's songs.

COMBO CHAPTERS ARTICLE EXCERPTS cont'd.

(d) It is plausible that the author has identified a singular trend in Nina's songs.

Question 25

(a) Nina has fallen ill and she cannot refrain from waxing nostalgic.

(b) Nina cannot desist from writing songs about being homesick.

(c) Nina can't give up writing songs about "simpler times" and evil men.

(d) Nina seems disposed to writing reflective songs about her bad relationships.

Question 26

(a) Nina wants to be a superhero whose arch-enemies are evil men.

(b) She writes songs about relationships with men who aren't good for her.

(c) Nina's adversaries are malicious men.

(d) She enjoys crime-fighting male villains in her spare time.

Question 27

(a) The author cannot square his image of Nina with her heated lyrics.

(b) Keith's attempts to settle Nina's instability have been troubling.

(c) The author is looking to settle his difficulties with Nina.

(d) Keith is concerned that Nina's erratic behavior might be serious.

Question 28

(a) The subject matter of Nina's songs may be considered grave because she is describing men who are erratic.

(b) The subject matter of Nina's songs may be considered volatile because she is describing men who are pernicious.

(c) The subject matter of Nina's songs may be considered grave because she is describing men who are volatile.

(d) The subject matter of Nina's songs may be considered volatile because she is describing men who are erratic.

Question 29

(a) The author is concerned that Nina is unstable; sometimes she's serious, sometimes she's bubbly, and at other times she is reserved.

(b) Nina's vibrant, and sometimes decorous, personality belie the resentment captured by her lyrics.

(c) Nina's fizzy, and sometimes modest, personality belie the volatility captured by her lyrics.

(d) None of the above.

Excerpt 8

For her, the worst part is that she intuits that he synchronously cares for her, even though his relationship with her best friend appears to be interminable and senescent. Inevitably, she recognizes that her amorous sentiment cannot be returned, and resigns herself to moving on. Mia turns a fine verse, and despite the tortuous events depicted by the song, she delivers her message with passion instead of despondency.

Question 30

(a) The boyfriend secretly likes her but can't break up with her friend.

(b) "Already Taken" describes a friendship that never ends.

(c) Mia needs to synchronize her watch.

(d) Her best friend has an odd scent.

Question 31

(a) The events discussed in "Already Taken" are readily resolved.

(b) Mia's storytelling reflects vitality rather than sadness.

(c) She's a depressing writer.

(d) Her song causes the listener to turn around.

COMBO CHAPTERS ARTICLE EXCERPTS cont'd.

Excerpt 9

Traversing the globe, this political party is slandering that one, one leader is making pithy remarks to another. Adrianne and Lyle wonder when the barriers people put up are going to dissolve, and permit settlement to rise like a phoenix. As we wrapped up our conversation and prepared to get to work, I thanked them for bestowing their benediction of reconciliation on us, and as they said, "We can hope..."

Question 32

(a) The artists slander political parties and make terse remarks to world leaders.

(b) Adrianne and Lyle belong to a political party that crosses the globe.

(c) Political parties and world leaders malign one another.

(d) They comment on the excellent state of international relations.

Question 33

(a) The artists contemplate when people will cooperate and allow peace to flourish.

(b) Adrianne and Lyle want superpowers that can dissolve barriers.

(c) They want to acquire a mythical bird that can resurrect itself.

(d) None of the above.

Question 34

(a) Lyle and Adrianne are ordained clergy that can grant blessings.

(b) The authors appreciated Adrianne and Lyle's wishes for world peace.

(c) At the end of their conversation, the artists bestowed a blessing upon the authors.

(d) At the end of their conversation, the authors thanked the artists for their blessings.

Excerpt 10

Their relationship in jeopardy, the graduate cogitates the colossal decision of carrying on for the duration and suffering the toll exacted by his frustration, or to abstain from seeing her any longer. Avon's character seems tempestuous; he extols his love's panache, but cites a refrain familiar to his peers, that without her near, his longing festers and cannot be quelled. And, as much as he disdains saying so, in the end, he believes it best that they part.

Question 35

(a) The couple's love at risk, the graduate ponders his options.

(b) The graduate, being especially bright, has considered how his situation might get him on *Jeopardy!*

(c) The graduate is contemplating how he might jeopardize their relationship.

(d) His girlfriend loves *Jeopardy!*, and he thinks that if he can win, she'll return.

Question 36

(a) The graduate realizes that going on *Jeopardy!* Is a big decision.

(b) The graduate is wondering exactly how long their relationship will be at risk.

(c) The graduate wonders whether or not he can endure the frustration of being separated from his girlfriend.

(d) Driving to see his girlfriend, the graduate wonders how long it will take, and whether or not there will be any tolls that require exact change.

Question 37

(a) Avon's protagonist reflects on the enormity of deciding whether or not to end their relationship.

(b) The protagonist wonders how long he will need to refrain from seeing her.

(c) Avon's character must go without paying exact tolls for the duration of his drive to see his girlfriend.

(d) All of the above.

COMBO CHAPTERS ARTICLE EXCERPTS cont'd.

Question 38

(a) Although he's sad, the graduate commends his girlfriend's confidence.

(b) Avon's character is emotional and jealous of his girlfriend's panache.

(c) Extolling élan, Avon's character is overwhelmed with emotion.

(d) He is passionate about his love and praises her flair and sense of style.

Question 39

(a) Citing his girlfriend, the graduate will avoid being with his colleagues.

(b) The graduate repeats some choruses to his friends.

(c) Avon's character repeats a phrase that his cohorts would understand.

(d) Avon is going to avoid becoming familiar with his cohorts.

Question 40

(a) The graduate's festering cannot be quelled, and he should be seen by a cardiologist right away.

(b) The graduate increasingly misses his girlfriend, and he cannot subdue his longing for her.

(c) The graduate is trying to suppress his longing, but it is becoming irritated.

(d) Avon's character has an irritation that needs to be quelled immediately.

Question 41

(a) In the end, the graduate despises saying "so."

(b) Although he despises saying so, the graduate believes that the end is the best part.

(c) Avon's character is filled with contempt for his girlfriend.

(d) Although it is a difficult decision, the graduate concludes that he and his girlfriend should break up.

Excerpt 11

Having started The Machine with Todd Cohen, Joe scoffed at taking on traditional career, but mired in the welter of youth, he vacillated between jobs while his aspirations evolved. He wasn't a martyr or in the dregs, but he wasn't incited by the rabid pursuit of fame and self-orientation that marks many performers, and it took time for his calling to take shape. Alternately a premier auto mechanic (he use to create and work on blown Porsches) and a landscaper, his path couldn't have been less clear. However, fortunately for us, he was still young when his talent made itself apparent to him and others, and people soon sought him out.

Question 42

(a) Joe was caught in a mire when he was young.

(b) He is confused.

(c) His path unclear, he struggled with the confusion of youth.

(d) When Joe was young, his welter was mired.

Question 43

(a) Joe moved between jobs while he was finding himself.

(b) Jobs precluded him from developing his music.

(c) He aspired to evolve.

(d) Moving between jobs caused Joe to aspire.

Question 44

(a) He subjugated himself for a cause.

(b) His drinking became a problem because he always drank to the dregs.

(c) Joe found himself in sediment.

(d) During his period of indecision he wasn't suffering.

Question 45

(a) Joe did not want to fanatically chase fame and fortune.

COMBO CHAPTERS ARTICLE EXCERPTS cont'd.

(b) His motivation was to incite.

(c) He sought fame, but it took time for it to take shape.

(d) Joe was rabid and self-oriented.

Question 46

(a) He was the first mechanic to blow up a Porsche.

(b) Joe was a great mechanic that worked on Porsches.

(c) Joe was a mechanic and a landscaper at the same time.

(d) He was a landscaper who blew up Porsches.

Excerpt 12

However, the guys believed that writing for this album would be easier than it proved to be. Troy remarked, "It took a lot of editing and rigging for us to resolve the problems we confronted while writing this song," and Ed added, "One of the most difficult aspects of creating 'Move It' was finding words that fit within the context of the song, but were also 'Money' words." They didn't fret or let those complications distract them from completing their work, and the guys knew that together they could write a great track that would induce listeners to gambol and cavort to their beats.

Question 47

(a) Everyone expects that writing for DM will be difficult.

(b) The guys wanted to prove themselves.

(c) Troy expressed that it took a lot of effort to write the song.

(d) Ed suggested that they rig the Word$.

Question 48

(a) Ed found it hard to find words that fit the circumstances of the song.

(b) Ed found many good Word$.

(c) "Move It" describes what the artists did to the Word$.

(d) The Word$ were too big to fit into the song.

Question 49

(a) They were very concerned they weren't up to the task.

(b) Diversions interfered with their writing.

(c) Complications distracted them.

(d) They didn't let anything inhibit the progress of their work.

Question 50

(a) Ed and Troy wondered if they could write a song that listeners would enjoy.

(b) They were bounding across the room and messing around while they wrote "Move It."

(c) The guys want to gambol and cavort with listeners.

(d) They want to get listeners to dance and party.

"HOT" – ANSWER KEYS

"HOT" LISTENING EXERCISE ANSWER KEY

Conflagration	Decree	Devoid
Exhilarating	Fluctuation	Follicles
Frigid	Frustrating	Fusion
Ignited	Illusion	Indefatigable
Indisputable	Invigorating	Marquee
Monotony	Perpetuate	Perusing
Profusion	Propagate	Proximity
Pursuing	Raze	Rectify
Remedy	Saturate	Seclusion
Sedentary	Stimulating	Tundra
Ungainly	Uniformity	Union
Vacillate	Wavering	

"HOT" SYNONYM MATCHING ANSWER KEY

	Letter	Vocabulary Word	Synonym
1.	(l)	Conflagration	fire
2.	(y)	Decree	declaration
3.	(a2)	Devoid	lacking
4.	(a1)	Exhilarating	elating
5.	(s)	Fluctuation	variation
6.	(q)	Follicles	holes
7.	(d)	Frigid	cold
8.	(a4)	Frustrating	annoying
9.	(t)	Fusion	join
10.	(g)	Ignited	kindle

	Letter	Vocabulary Word	Synonym
11.	(v)	Illusion	delusion
12.	(u)	Indefatigable	unrelenting
13.	(a5)	indisputable	certain
14.	(x)	Invigorating	revitalizing
15.	(a3)	Marquee	tent
16.	(h)	Monotony	sameness
17.	(f)	Perpetuate	continue
18.	(a6)	Peruse	examine
19.	(m)	Profusion	excess
20.	(b)	Propagate	spread
21.	(a8)	Proximity	nearness
22.	(i)	Pursue	follow
23.	(z)	Raze	level
24.	(p)	Rectify	correct
25.	(a9)	Remedy	cure
26.	(k)	Saturate	soak
27.	(r)	Seclusion	isolation
28.	(o)	Sedentary	inactive
29.	(j)	Stimulate	inspire
30.	(a)	Tundra	arctic plain
31.	(e)	Ungainly	ungraceful
32.	(c)	Uniformity	standardization
33.	(a7)	Union	combination
34.	(w)	Vacillation	indecision
35.	(n)	Waver	hesitate

"HOT" SENTENCE COMPLETION ANSWER KEY

1. During the debate, his opponent found his remarks to be **indisputable**, making it difficult for him to debate against him.

2. He is following his dream by **pursuing** a career in law.

3. An open, rolling plain, there is little vegetation on the **tundra**.

4. Her **follicles** were damaged over the years by the constant dying and straightening of her hair.

5. The **conflagration** that razed the forest is thought to have been started by a cigarette.

6. The presidential candidates are **propagating** their ideas by making speeches throughout the country.

7. She was **frustrated** by her little brother's refusal to move his feet off of her books.

8. My backpack was **ungainly** because it had too much stuff in it.

9. The Olympic torch was **ignited** during the opening ceremony in Athens.

10. The **decree** declared that the country would be handed over to its new government.

11. She enjoys the college classes that she's taking, and she finds them very **stimulating**.

12. Her income is never steady; it usually **fluctuates** between $40,000 and $100,000 a year.

13. It's as though he's an immovable, **sedentary** blob; he's always vegging out in front of the boob tube.

14. We have to get that boy out of the house; he'd find my new morning exercise program **invigorating**.

15. The numbing **monotony** of her life bored her, eventually leading her to quit her job to travel around the world.

16. Working to figure out what was wrong, the technicians were doing everything they could to **rectify** the problem.

17. My grandmother believes that the best **remedy** for a cold is homemade chicken soup.

18. His plan to ride a ferret across the country defies logic, and is **devoid** of any sense.

19. She is an **indefatigable** competitor, who gives 100% of herself during every game.

20. In some cultures women are kept in **seclusion** and are rarely seen in public.

21. While I'm editing the book I need to **peruse** the exercises to verify that everything makes sense.

22. Alaska isn't always **frigid**; as a matter of fact, during the summer it can get quite hot.

23. The building's manager decided to replace the **marquee** over the main entrance.

24. The best thing about the location of my office is its **proximity** to my house.

25. The studio released its latest movie and inundated the press with a **profusion** of PR materials.

26. I've heard that hang gliding is **exhilarating**, and that there is no thrill that can compare.

27. At the end of the day I'm tired, and my concentration tends to **waver**.

28. His music is described as a **fusion** of hip hop and alternative styles.

29. The novel 1984 is a cautionary tale that describes the monotony of a society based on **uniformity**.

30. The aim of the preservation society is to **perpetuate** the cultures and traditions of their country.

"HOT" SENTENCE COMPLETION ANSWER KEY cont'd.

31. She is **vacillating** between taking a job that is closer to home and a job that offers more money.

32. The next door neighbors **razed** their house and are building an entirely new one on the same foundation.

33. The massive corporate merger is reported to be a **union** of equals.

34. Mirages are only **illusions** caused by the heat rising off of the desert sand, which distorts the view of the horizon.

35. The tie-dying instructions require you to **saturate** the shirt with water before you place it in the dye.

"HOT" CROSSWORD ANSWERS

Across
1. Ignite
2. Pursue
3. Illusion
4. Indefatigable
5. Uniformity
6. Frigid
7. Profusion
8. Conflagration
9. Vacillate
10. Follicle
11. Perpetuate
12. Invigorate
13. Seclusion
14. Decree
15. Fluctuation
16. Propagate
17. Marquee
18. Remedy

Down
1. Devoid
2. Ungainly
3. Indisputable
4. Raze
5. Fusion
6. Tundra
7. Rectify
8. Frustrating
9. Stimulating
10. Union
11. Exhilarating
12. Proximity
13. Saturate
14. Waver
15. Sedentary
16. Perused
17. Monotony

"HOT" SYNONYM SENTENCES ANSWER KEY

1. Stock prices **fluctuate** day to day.
2. During the long winters the **tundra** is barren and cold.
3. The **conflagration** spread quickly, and thankfully no one was hurt.
4. I enjoy reading the newspaper because I find it **stimulating**.
5. Her mother always said, "**Pursue** your dreams."
6. He **ignited** the campfire with a match.
7. "We will do whatever is necessary to **rectify** the situation."
8. The researcher **perused** the results of the study prior to making any announcements regarding its outcome.
9. She was an **indefatigable** protester against animal testing, and didn't end her boycott until the company agreed to release its monkeys.
10. When he does his homework, he likes to **seclude** himself.
11. She had made her dream come true; her name was in lights on the theater **marquee**.
12. It isn't always easy making choices, and sometimes I **vacillate**.
13. I'm not sure that those dance lessons are helping him out very much; he's still looks pretty **ungainly** when he does his routine.
14. I find it **frustrating** when people jostle me to get into the subway.
15. This summer she has a job in a factory where all she does is put popsicle sticks in molds all day, and she said that the **monotony** is going to drive her crazy.
16. As a result of his **sedentary** lifestyle he was 50 lbs overweight.
17. A native of southern California, he finds Massachusetts **frigid**.
18. The best **remedy** for the flu is to drink lots of fluids and to get some rest.

"HOT" SYNONYM SENTENCES ANSWER KEY cont'd.

19. He **wavered** before asking her out on a date.

20. The community group was the result a **union** of different factions from throughout the area.

21. When manufacturing consumer goods, it is important to have a measure of **uniformity** to ensure that each item produced is the same.

22. Despite the **profusion** of TV channels, I can never find anything to watch.

23. My dad says, "Of course you can't find anything good on, TV is **devoid** of anything intellectually stimulating."

24. Our parents bought our house based on its **proximity** to a good school.

25. He was traumatized at the circus when he was a kid, and he now lived in **perpetual** fear of little dogs riding bicycles.

26. After the hurricane severely damaged the house, we needed to **raze** it, and build a new one.

27. The plaintiff's lawyer stated, "Given the facts of the case, it is **indisputable** that my client is innocent."

28. The special interest group worked to **propagate** rumors about the competing candidate.

29. The sponge won't hold any more liquid, it's **saturated**.

30. We went to an interesting restaurant last night where the cuisine is a **fusion** of Cuban and Chinese foods.

31. Four-foot-three inches tall and ninety pounds, he had no **illusions** that he was going to win a round against the World Heavyweight Champion.

32. My visit to the day spa was **invigorating**.

33. My friend said that bungee jumping in New Zealand was **exhilarating**, although I'm not sure that I'd want to try it.

34. The crazy king issued a **decree** stating that all of the country's citizens were required to wear their socks on the outside of their shoes.

35. If you look closely at your arm, you can see the **follicles** in your skin.

MIDDLETON & WILLIE, TOO "HOT" ANSWERS

Question 1
(b) The author enjoys working with Rodney & Keith.

Question 2
(c) The author is using fire as a metaphor to describe the intensity of the artists' music.

Question 3
(a) The artists combine different musical styles to create a unique sound.

Question 4
(a) Avon is a tireless and inspiring performer.

Question 5
(d) Avon Marshall is a genuinely gifted performer, and he is very comfortable in the studio.

Question 6
(b) Keith & Rodney write music that mixes it up.

Question 7
(a) The artists' music forges it own path, breaking the typical boundaries present in today's play lists.

Question 8
(d) The author finds the artist's music energizing, and regards it as a metaphorical cure for one's state of well being.

Question 9
(b) The artists are making it in the recoding industry and are building their reputations.

MIDDLETON & WILLIE TOO "HOT" ANSWERS cont'd.

Question 10

(a) The author expects the artists to perform publicly, sell their CDs in stores, and to become famous.

Question 11

(c) The artists and author have worked closely, giving the author an appreciation for the artists' combination of talents, and their preparedness for stardom.

Question 12

(b) Rodney and Keith are working hard to achieve stardom.

"ALREADY TAKEN" – ANSWER KEYS

"ALREADY TAKEN" LISTENING EXERCISE ANSWER KEY

Acquiesce	Amorous	Aroma
Awkward	Consummate	Conversely
Deleterious	Delirium	Ecstasy
Enamored	Futile	Incantation
Inevitably	Infatuation	Inimitable
Interminable	Intuit	Laboriously
Proximity	Reticence	Senescent
Shroud	Situation	Synchronously
Tortuous	Tranquility	

"ALREADY TAKEN" SYNONYM MATCHING ANS. KEY

	Letter	Vocabulary Word	Synonym
1.	(g)	Acquiesce	agree
2.	(u)	Amorous	affectionate
3.	(k)	Aroma	pleasing scent
4.	(r)	Awkward	uncomfortable
5.	(n)	Consummate	archetype
6.	(e)	Conversely	contrary
7.	(y)	Deleterious	harmful
8.	(z)	Delirium	disorientation
9.	(j)	Ecstasy	joy
10.	(o)	Enamored	smitten
11.	(x)	Futile	useless
12.	(b)	Incantation	spell
13.	(d)	Inevitably	certain

"ALREADY TAKEN" SYNONYM MATCHING ANSWERS cont'd.

Letter	Vocabulary Word	Synonym
14. (s)	Infatuation	fixation
15. (t)	Inimitable	unique
16. (c)	Interminable	endless
17. (i)	Intuit	perceive
18. (v)	Laboriously	grueling
19. (l)	Proximity	nearness
20. (w)	Reticence	reluctance
21. (q)	Senescent	aging
22. (m)	Shrouded	covered
23. (h)	Situation	predicament
24. (f)	Synchronously	simultaneous
25. (a)	Tortuous	arduous
26. (p)	Tranquility	peaceful

"ALREADY TAKEN" SENTENCE COMPLETION ANS. KEY

1. We live in close **proximity** to our neighbors.

2. Time never stops, and **inevitably** everything changes.

3. She was in a state of **ecstasy** when she was accepted to Yale.

4. In the United States people drive on the right hand side of the road; **conversely** in Britain you would drive on the left hand side.

5. The hikers' route through the mountain pass was **tortuous**.

6. When the boxer regained consciousness after getting knocked out, he awoke in a state of **delirium**.

7. The president of the student government **acquiesced** to the demands of the student body.

8. Professionals working in the fashion industry strive to create their own **inimitable** style.

9. His father's stories about his childhood were **interminable**.

10. Given the fact that she can't sing, it's **futile** for her to try out for "American Idol," unless she wants to be on the "blooper" reel!

11. The hood of the explorer's parka **shrouded** her face.

12. My mother became **enamored** with my father the first time she saw him.

13. I love the **tranquility** of the ocean when the weather is calm.

14. She could **intuit** that I was worried about my upcoming exam.

15. Feeding a dog chocolate can be **deleterious** to its health.

16. She was **infatuated** with the her favorite band, and she listened to their CD constantly.

17. The **aroma** of freshly baked pastries filled the air.

18. She created an awkward **situation** by asking me to help her cheat on the test.

19. It was **awkward** for me to see my dad dating after my parents got divorced.

20. The witches chanted an **incantation** around a boiling potion.

21. Always the **consummate** professional, she managed the meeting flawlessly.

22. After the banquet, he **laboriously** washed every dish by hand.

23. She was **reticent** to speak in front of the class.

24. On some SUVs the front wheels move **synchronously** with the back wheels.

25. The fourteen-year-old cat is **senescent**.

26. The two lovers gazed at one another **amorously**.

"ALREADY TAKEN" CROSSWORD ANSWERS

Down
1. aroma
2. intuit
3. futile
4. interminable
5. deleterious
6. infatuation
7. inimitably
8. conversely
9. situation
10. enamored
11. synchronously
12. tortuous

Across
1. amorous
2. reticence
3. consummate
4. incantation
5. delirium
6. proximity
7. awkward
8. tranquility
9. senescent
10. ecstasy
11. laboriously
12. inevitably
13. acquiesce
14. shroud

"ALREADY TAKEN" SYNONYM SENTENCES ANS. KEY

1. The bakery was filled with the **aroma** of fresh bread.
2. If you don't have a CD player it's **futile** to try to listen to a CD.
3. She discovered an **amorous** love letter in her locker.
4. The sorceress' **incantation** made him fall in love with a chicken.
5. Her style is **inimitable**.
6. The **situation** she found herself in was unsettling.
7. When two things occur at the same time they happen **synchronously**.
8. She was **ecstatic** when she found out that she had won the Nobel Prize.
9. Although she didn't tell him, he could **intuit** when she was mad at him.
10. Although my workout is only an hour long, it seems **interminable**.
11. I am **infatuated** with romantic novels.
12. He **acquiesced** to their demands.

13. I am not **enamored** with BMW's new designs.

14. Polished and poised, she was the **consummate** professional.

15. They were the consummate odd couple; she was outgoing, and **conversely**, he was very shy.

16. The bus was in such **proximity** to my car that it almost hit us.

17. After the accident, the driver was in a state of **delirium**.

18. When going on a first date I always feel **awkward**.

19. Shaking a baby can be **deleterious** to the child's health.

20. I enjoy the **tranquility** of a quiet afternoon.

21. It is **inevitable** that children will grow up.

22. The old crumbling building is **senescent**.

23. He was **reticent** to share his opinions with the class.

24. Often, the path to success is **tortuous**.

25. The first snowfall of winter **shrouded** the hills.

26. Writing a novel by hand is a **laborious** task.

FIVE MINUTES WITH MIA JOHNSON ANSWERS

Question 1
(c) After many requests, Mia agreed to do the interview with resignation.

Question 2
(b) Recording a full-length CD is grueling work.

Question 3
(d) Mia has her own unique style.

Question 4
(d) Mia sings about the difficulty of falling for someone who cannot reciprocate.

FIVE MINUTES WITH MIA JOHNSON ANSWERS cont'd.

Question 5

(b) She acknowledges that she can't date her best friend's boyfriend.

Question 6

(c) Her predicament has left her feeling uncomfortable

Question 7

(a) She did not readily discuss whom she may have written the song about.

Question 8

(c) "Already Taken" uses music to give the listener contrasting feelings.

Question 9

(a) "Already Taken" is like a mystical chant that causes the listener to remember.

Question 10

(d) Mia is obsessed with her girlfriend's boyfriend, and the situation is awkward.

Question 11

(a) The boyfriend secretly likes her but can't break up with her friend.

Question 12

(b) Mia's storytelling reflects vitality rather than sadness.

"SHINE" – ANSWER KEYS

"SHINE" LISTENING EXERCISE ANSWER KEY

Actuated	Captivated	Dregs
Forsake	Illuminate	Inciting
Lurking	Martyr	Mired
Rabid	Renovate	Resplendent
Scoff	Seclusion	Skulking
Solace	Vacillation	Welter

"SHINE" SYNONYM MATCHING ANSWER KEY

	Letter	Vocabulary Word	Synonym
1.	(o)	Actuate	motivate
2.	(m)	Captivate	charmed
3.	(b)	Dregs	sediment
4.	(a)	Forsake	abandon
5.	(l)	Illuminate	clarify
6.	(p)	Incite	goad
7.	(e)	Lurk	lie-in-wait
8.	(r)	Martyred	subjugated
9.	(h)	Mired	caught up
10.	(n)	Rabid	fanatical
11.	(i)	Renovate	refurbish
12.	(f)	Resplendent	dazzling
13.	(q)	Scoff	mock
14.	(d)	Seclusion	isolation
15.	(j)	Skulk	sneak

"SHINE" SYNONYM MATCHING ANSWER KEY cont'd.

Letter	Vocabulary Word	Synonym
16. (c)	Solace	comfort
17. (g)	Vacillation	indecision
18. (k)	Welter	confusion

"SHINE" SENTENCE COMPLETION ANSWER KEY

1. Her children gave her **solace** after her husband's death.

2. The demonstrator was overrun by government forces and died a **martyr** for his cause.

3. Paparazzi often **lurk** in the bushes around celebrities' homes, waiting to ambush them.

4. He was so embarrassed after pouring a drink down the front of his pants that he **skulked** away from the party.

5. She was attacked by a bloodthirsty hamster when she was a child, and she's had a **rabid** hatred of them ever since.

6. Critics **scoffed** at Henry Ford's early attempts to build a car.

7. He was fired for **inciting** co-workers to rebel against the new company rules.

8. The story and the beauty of the film **captivated** audiences.

9. She **vacillated** between deciding to go to Florida and going to California.

10. The entire building was **renovated** after asbestos was found in the walls.

11. Their strong commitment to their community **actuated** them to volunteer.

12. I would never **forsake** my family.

13. The queen wore a **resplendent** jewel encrusted gown.

14. Seeking **seclusion**, the reclusive star flew to a private island.

15. At the garage sale there was a **welter** of CDs and cassettes to look through.

16. The diary she left behind **illuminated** her thinking and clarified why she ran off with the guy who runs the deli.

17. As the horse pulled the wagon its wheels became **mired** in the mud.

18. She drank the chocolate milk down to the **dregs**.

"SHINE" CROSSWORD ANSWERS

Down
1. illuminate
2. scoff
3. actuate
4. vacillate
5. welter
6. dregs
7. rabid
8. lurk
9. solace
10. seclusion

Across
1. incite
2. fo'sake
3. captivated
4. mired
5. resplendent
6. skulk
7. martyr
8. renovate

"SHINE" SYNONYM SENTENCES ANSWER KEY

1. He decided to **renovate** the house.

2. Her diamond earrings were **resplendent**.

3. He **vacillated** between having smooth or chunky peanut butter.

4. His blue eyes **captivated** the girls.

5. The girls **scoffed at** his attempt to join the field hockey team.

6. The professor **illuminated** the themes conveyed in Shakespeare' plays.

"SHINE" SYNONYM SENTENCES ANSWER KEY cont'd.

7. The prisoner was placed in **seclusion** after disobeying the warden.
8. I found the cat **lurking** in the bushes, stalking the birds.
9. In an effort to **actuate** the players, the coach gave an impassioned speech at half time.
10. She found **solace** in her friends after losing her job.
11. I've been **mired** in work at the studio.
12. The escaped convict was found **skulking** around the city.
13. The professor's office was a **welter** of books, papers and scientific bric-a-brac.
14. We arrived late to the sale, and the earlier shoppers only left behind the **dregs** of what the store had offer.
15. She is a **rabid** basketball fan.
16. He was **inciting** the crowd to riot.
17. Would you **forsake** your beliefs for money?
18. He went to prison for speaking his mind about the government, and **martyred** himself for his beliefs.

PASCARELL'S DEFINED MIND "SHINE"S ANSWERS

Question 1
(b) His performances have enthralled audiences.

Question 2
(c) "Shine" is the product of Joe's individual creativity.

Question 3
(d) The song "Shine" is a glorious, brilliant declaration.

Question 4

(a) The career path he chose was not traditional.

Question 5

(c) His path unclear, he struggled with the confusion of youth.

Question 6

(a) Joe moved between jobs while he was finding himself.

Question 7

(d) During his period of indecision he wasn't suffering.

Question 8

(a) Joe did not want to fanatically chase fame and fortune.

Question 9

(b) Joe was a great mechanic that worked on Porsches.

Question 10

(d) His motivation was his love of music, and Todd showed him the way.

Question 11

(c) He didn't seek the limelight, but he was comfortable there.

Question 12

(d) None of the above.

"WDYTM" - ANSWER KEYS

"WDYTM" LISTENING ANSWER KEY

Addiction	Affliction	Alluring
Assay	Cognizant	Collaborate
Comely	Complicit	Conjecture
Conviction	Crass	Craven
Decoy	Entice	Flagrant
Irate	Obsession	Predisposition
Profound	Revelation	Sensual
Sinister	Stolid	Surmise

"WDYTM" SYNONYM MATCHING ANSWER KEY

	Letter	Vocabulary Word	Synonym
1.	(e)	Addiction	dependence
2.	(i)	Affliction	illness
3.	(a)	Alluring	appealing
4.	(m)	Assay	evaluate
5.	(j)	Cognizant	aware
6.	(x)	Collaborate	cooperate
7.	(q)	Comely	attractive
8.	(n)	Complicit	complacent
9.	(f)	Conjecture	opine
10.	(o)	Conviction	belief
11.	(u)	Crass	rude
12.	(h)	Craven	cowardly
13.	(b)	Decoy	lure
14.	(g)	Entice	persuade

	Letter	Vocabulary Word	Synonym
15.	(k)	Flagrant	blatant
16.	(t)	Irate	angry
17.	(v)	Obsession	fixation
18.	(c)	Predisposition	propensity
19.	(r)	Profound	deep
20.	(p)	Revelation	disclosure
21.	(s)	Sensual	pleasing
22.	(l)	Sinister	evil
23.	(w)	Stolid	dull
24.	(d)	Surmise	deduce

"WDYTM" SENTENCE COMPLETION ANSWER KEY

1. The beautiful Corvette was a **decoy** to lure customers into the used car lot.

2. Her argument with the store manager caused the woman to become **irate**.

3. The owner tried to **entice** the star player to join the team by offering him a large salary.

4. Looking to incite the players on the home team, the runner said something **crass** about the first baseman's wife.

5. In an earlier era, it was common for people to refer to an attractive woman as being **comely**.

6. The insurance adjuster was very **stolid** and serious about her work.

7. Stalkers are **obsessed** with the celebrities they follow.

8. It is my personal **conviction** that Tibet should be free.

9. I found her perfume very **alluring**.

"WDYTM" SENTENCE COMPLETION ANSWER KEY cont'd.

10. Initially, she couldn't figure out how to answer the question, but then she had a **revelation** and solved it right away.

11. She is **addicted** to cigarettes and wants to smoke all the time.

12. Given the clues, the police **surmised** who was responsible for the robbery.

13. Lack of shelter is one of the many **afflictions** of the homeless.

14. Movie villains are always hatching some **sinister** plot to take over the world.

15. He always gives in because he's **predisposed** to trying to make others happy.

16. The United States is hoping more countries will **collaborate** to rebuild Iraq.

17. The lab needed to **assay** the water for pollutants.

18. The defense had suppressed some evidence, so the jury was not **cognizant** of the full facts of the case.

19. The player was thrown out of the game because of the **flagrant** foul he committed.

20. Eating chocolate is a **sensual** pleasure.

21. There has been a lot of **conjecture** in the media about who will win the election.

22. Abandoning friends in the face of trouble is a **craven** act.

23. He was fired for his **complicity** in the office scandal.

24. The Greek scholar Socrates is considered one of history's most **profound** thinkers.

"WDYTM" CROSSWORD ANSWERS

Down
1. cognizant
2. entice
3. complicit
4. profound
5. collaborate
6. irate
7. alluring
8. revelation
9. sinister
10. conviction

Across
1. sensual
2. addiction
3. comely
4. flagrant
5. predisposition
6. decoy
7. crass
8. assay
9. obsession
10. stolid
11. conjecture
12. craven
13. affliction
14. surmise

"WDYTM" SYNONYM SENTENCES ANSWER KEY

1. Saving yourself when others are in danger is **craven**.
2. The two companies will **collaborate** to make the project work.
3. The appraiser will **assay** the antique's value.
4. It is my **conviction** that all people deserve proper health care.
5. He used his charm to **entice** her to go out with him.
6. She is **predisposed** to getting sea sick very easily.
7. Her perfume had an **alluring** scent.
8. Loud and obnoxious, he often makes **crass** remarks.
9. When she saw that she had received a parking ticket, she became **irate**.
10. Unable to control himself, he finally accepted that he was **addicted**.
11. Without sufficient information, we can only **conjecture** what the results will be.

"WDYTM" SYNONYM SENTENCES ANSWER KEY cont'd.

12. The guard who opened the lock for the burglars was **complicit** in the crime.

13. The celebrity's two-day marriage was a **flagrant** attempt to gain publicity.

14. In her day, Jacqueline Kennedy was quite **comely**.

15. She was **cognizant** of the implication of her actions.

16. During the spring, many people are **afflicted** by allergies.

17. He isn't flashy at all; he's just a straightforward, **stolid** kind of guy.

18. Silk is renown for its supple, smooth, **sensual** texture.

19. Electrical appliances have had a **profound** impact on the way we live.

20. By examining the rings of a tree stump, we can **surmise** how old the tree was when it was cut down.

21. Socks were a **obsession** of his, and he had hundreds of pairs in every color, pattern and size.

22. The shocking **revelation** of criminal acts within the department caused a lot of disruption within the community.

23. In a "bait & switch" scam, an unscrupulous business will try to sell customers an inferior product, but use a better product as a **decoy**.

24. In video clips, Osama bin Laden reveals a **sinister** smile when he discusses the attack on the World Trade Center.

"WDYTM" THIS WOULD BE TOUGH? ANSWERS

Question 1

(a) Nina began working with Defined Mind shortly after coming to NYC.

"WDYTM" THIS WOULD BE TOUGH ANSWERS cont'd.

Question 2
(d) Nina didn't know what she was getting into.

Question 3
(b) She was interested in writing in a new idiom.

Question 4
(c) She was inspired to write the song and complete it afterward.

Question 5
(b) To gain her love interest's attention she contemplates the use of a lure.

Question 6
(a) Nina appreciates her crush's knowing, sly smile and confident demeanor.

Question 7
(d) Editing the song took a great deal of time.

Question 8
(a) Nina believes that she wrote a great song.

Question 9
(c) Nina wrote about a comely, outgoing young man.

Question 10
(b) Sammy exists as a subject in this song to convey unattractive qualities.

Question 11
(d) Nina feels it is easier to remember information from songs.

"GO!" – ANSWER KEYS

"GO!" LISTENING EXCERCISE ANSWER KEY

Accolades	Accordingly	Amateur
Annihilate	Antithesis	Assure
Bested	Borders	Complex
Context	Credit	Decipher
Distraction	Epitome	Esoteric
Expertise	Fathom	Frequency
Frequently	Inconsequential	Intricate
Labyrinthine	Lesser	Merits
Momentous	Neophyte	Paradigm
Perplex	Procure	Pugilistic
Punitive	Pusillanimous	Refraction
Revere	Significant	Vantage
Vertigo	Virtuoso	

"GO!" SYNONYM MATCHING ANSWER KEY

	Letter	Vocabulary Word	Synonym
1.	(l)	Accolades	praise
2.	(m)	Accordingly	consequently
3.	(p)	Amateur	layperson
4.	(b2)	Annihilate	destroy
5.	(s)	Antithesis	opposite
6.	(q)	Assure	guarantee
7.	(d)	Bested	surpassed
8.	(b)	Borders	on the verge of
9.	(o)	Complex	intricate

Letter	Vocabulary Word	Synonym
10. (y)	Context	circumstances
11. (t)	Credit	recognition
12. (a)	Decipher	decode
13. (h)	Distraction	disturbance
14. (r)	Epitome	essence
15. (a4)	Esoteric	arcane
16. (c)	Expertise	proficiency
17. (f)	Fathom	comprehend
18. (n)	Frequency	rate of occurrence
19. (e)	Frequently	regularly
20. (k)	Inconsequential	trivial
21. (a6)	Intricate	complicated
22. (a1)	Labyrinthine	circuitous
23. (a9)	Lesser	smaller
24. (a5)	Merits	to deserve
25. (z)	Momentous	historic
26. (j)	Neophyte	novice
27. (a8)	Paradigm	example
28. (b1)	Perplex	confuse
29. (b3)	Procure	acquire
30. (i)	Pugilistic	belligerent
31. (a7)	Punitive	retaliatory
32. (u)	Pusillanimous	timid
33. (x)	Refraction	change in direction
34. (v)	Revere	admire
35. (a2)	Significant	meaningful
36. (w)	Vantage	advantage

"GO!" SYNONYM MATCHING ANSWER KEY cont'd.

37. (g)   Vertigo   dizziness
38. (a3)   Virtuoso   prodigy

"GO!" SENTENCE COMPLETION ANSWER KEY

1. We have an easy time talking to each other because we're on the same **frequency**.
2. Many academic institutions are working to improve the state of education and are seeking a new **paradigm**.
3. He played masterfully and we were treated to a **virtuoso** performance.
4. Complex is the **antithesis** of simple.
5. The study's outcome is encouraging and **merits** further study.
6. The route we took was **labyrinthine**, and there isn't any way we would be able to get back without better directions.
7. It was a pretty pathetic that they were **bested** by one of the worst teams in the league.
8. She's worked in the discipline for many years, and has accumulated significant **expertise** on that particular subject.
9. The rollercoaster was too much for him and he was overcome by **vertigo**.
10. It looked intimidating, but we **assured** him that it was safe.
11. **Complex** is the antithesis of simple.
12. Our team **annihilated** the competition, and we finished the season undefeated.
13. The chem professor instructed us to behave **accordingly** in the lab, because otherwise, we might blow ourselves to bits.

14. We couldn't **fathom** why he went to school wearing a pink tutu.

15. During their discussion she convinced him to see the issue from her **vantage** point.

16. Like everyone else, I started out as a **neophyte**, but my expertise grew with training and experience.

17. He gave up his **amateur** ranking and went pro this season.

18. When I brought up the topic she became **pugilistic**, but her tone softened as she came to understand my perspective.

19. I find flashing online ads very **distracting**; they make it difficult to read a site's content.

20. She works at a "think-tank" in Washington D.C., and spends her time pondering "buy-side economics" and other **esoteric** subjects.

21. Even after hours of interrogation he wouldn't **decipher** the secret code for his captors.

22. I'll readily acknowledge that it was originally her idea; I have to give **credit** where it's due.

23. It is always gratifying to receive **accolades** and the respect of your peers.

24. His recent unusual behavior **borders** on insanity.

25. The new data we received was **inconsequential** and did not impact our original findings.

26. Since she didn't have any good options, she was forced to chose between the **lesser** of two evils.

27. He was **perplexed** by the toy's complicated assembly instructions.

28. The Dali Lama is **revered** for his wisdom and spiritual insight.

29. Always ready to come through in the clutch, she **epitomized** grace under pressure.

30. Never **pusillanimous**, he fought for what was right.

"GO!" SENTENCE COMPLETION ANSWER KEY cont'd.

31. A diamond sparkles because light is **refracted** as it shines through its facets.

32. We need to **procure** some additional equipment before we embark on our camping trip.

33. To best understand historical events, it is important that we view them in **context**.

34. I'm **frequently** preoccupied and forgetful; if my head wasn't attached to my shoulders, I would have already lost it somewhere.

35. Chastising the defendant, the judge awarded the plaintiff $100 million in **punitive** damages.

36. The findings of the study were **significant** and caused us to reconsider our position on the issue.

37. Christening the new ship, the captain said, "I would like to say a few words in honor of this **momentous** occasion."

38. He was perplexed by the toy's **intricate** assembly instructions.

"GO!" CROSSWORD ANSWERS

Across
1. amateur
2. context
3. inconsequential
4. neophyte
5. borders
6. epitome
7. fathom
8. punitive
9. pugilistic
10. refraction
11. antithesis
12. expertise
13. lesser
14. accordingly
15. pusillanimous
16. perplexed
17. revere
18. virtuoso
19. assured

Down
1. annihilate
2. accolades
3. labyrinthine
4. complex
5. esoteric
6. merits
7. vantage
8. decipher
9. intricate
10. procure
11. bested
12. paradigm
13. frequently
14. vertigo
15. frequency
16. momentous
17. significant
18. credit
19. distraction

"GO!" SYNONYM SENTENCES ANSWER KEY

1. Her reasoning was **labyrinthine**, and I still cannot fathom how she arrived at her conclusions.

2. Even though the theater company is **amateur**, their production of "Death of a Salesman" was excellent.

3. Outgoing and friendly, he is the **antithesis** of his curmudgeonly father.

4. She's in great shape because she exercises **frequently**.

5. The defenders **annihilated** the invading forces as they fought to enter the city.

6. His partner created a **distraction** while he absconded with the paintings.

7. Her physician was concerned about her condition; **accordingly**, he conducted a battery of tests to establish a diagnosis.

8. He said that although he authored the piece, she deserves much of the **credit** for their accomplishment.

9. He was overcome by **vertigo** on the Empire State Building's observation deck.

10. It takes years to learn to read and write in Chinese because the language's characters are so **complex**.

11. My dog heard barking on a CD that I was playing, and she stared at the speaker **perplexed** as to why she couldn't find the other dogs.

12. She couldn't possibly **fathom** that the dogs' barks were recorded and overdubbed into the song I was listening to.

13. The engineers selected the design based upon its **merits**.

14. The design was well regarded, and it received a variety of **accolades**.

15. She **bested** me in three games out of four.

"GO!" SENTENCE COMPLETION ANSWER KEY cont'd.

16. I **assured** him that we would arrive at the airport in time to make his flight.

17. In college you have the opportunity to explore **esoteric** subject matter that you wouldn't normally encounter outside of an academic setting.

18. She was **revered** for her longstanding role as a the community's spiritual leader and its most determined advocate.

19. Underhanded and **pusillanimous**, he ratted out his cronies to the feds to save his own skin.

20. He considers lobbying to be a **lesser** influence on public policy that it is popularly thought to be.

21. The completion of the Brooklyn Bridge was a **momentous** event that marked the dawn of a new age in engineering.

22. She recently earned another belt in karate, but she's still a **neophyte** and has a lot of work to do to build her expertise.

23. She gave a **virtuoso** performance at Carnegie Hall and received a standing ovation.

24. The issue is far more **intricate** than I had first thought, and I'll need to give it further consideration before I make a decision.

25. While visiting Rome, we asked our guide to translate a shopkeeper's comments because we couldn't **decipher** what he was trying to say.

26. I wouldn't call his contributions trivial, but the weren't very **significant** either.

27. I'm not sure how I would have responded to her comments; I imagine it depends on the **context**.

28. My kid brother's new R/C truck didn't work because the remote control unit was on a different **frequency**.

29. While the article does bring some new information to light, much of it **borders** on fiction.

30. They couldn't hire her because she did not possess the necessary **expertise**.

31. When she asked him to turn off his cell phone during the performance he became **pugilistic**.

32. She acquiesced to his requests because they were ultimately to her **vantage**.

33. The rover sustained a jolt when it landed, but any damage was **inconsequential**.

34. Since our neighbors weren't willing to repair the damage they caused, our attorney recommended that we take **punitive** measures.

35. In order to execute the plan in its current form it will be necessary for us to **procure** additional resources.

36. Both light and sound waves experience **refraction** as they pass though different materials.

37. General George S. Patton was the **epitome** of the war-hardened military man.

38. In 1954 Steve Allen created the **paradigm** for the modern talk show.

RODNEY WILLIE IS READY TO "GO!" ANSWERS

Question 1
(c) Most people call Rodney "RW," but on DM he is credited as "Rodney Willie."

Question 2
(b) The author regards Rodney as a verbal genius who can surpass even the toughest competitor.

RODNEY WILLIE IS READY TO "GO!" ANSWERS cont'd.

Question 3
(a) Keith Middleton, who writes the music, is an outstanding professional who deserves his own accolades.

Question 4
(d) "Go!" prompted the author to take inventory of Rodney's skill and to complement him.

Question 5
(b) The author believes that Rodney's primary advantage is his considerable intellect.

Question 6
(c) Rodney's towering verse are the product of great inspiration, and makes other recording artists look inferior.

Question 7
(a) The author feels that Rodney's work dispels the notion that artists who rap are incapable of authoring intellectually challenging material.

Question 8
(b) Timid novices may be befuddled by the complexity of Rodney's work, but appropriately, those who are knowledgeable admire its significance.

Question 9
(d) Those who do not believe that Rodney's work is brilliant are just jealous.

Question 10
(c) The intricacy of Rodney's lyrics regularly makes the author dizzy

Question 11
(c) Rodney and the author work together well, and disruptions that might otherwise interfere with their progress prove to be insignificant.

"SUPERGIRL" -- ANSWER KEYS

"SUPERGIRL" LISTENING EXERCISE ANSWER KEY

Awesome	Benediction	Bestow
Candor	Cosmos	Crucial
Declaration	Dispel	Dissolve
Factions	Fathom	Genius
Graciously	Intricate	Loom
Manifest	Minimal	Mire
Phoenix	Pithy	Quixotic
Resolve	Seep	Slander
Squander	Toxin's	Traversing
Underlying		

"SUPERGIRL SYNONYM MATCHING ANSWER KEY

	Letter	Vocabulary Word	Synonym
1.	(m)	Awesome	awe-inspiring
2.	(o)	Benediction	blessing
3.	(j)	Bestow	give
4.	(q)	Candor	openness
5.	(w)	Cosmos	outer space
6.	(r)	Crucial	essential
7.	(v)	Declaration	statement
8.	(t)	Dispel	dismiss
9.	(u)	Dissolved	disband
10.	(y)	Faction	group
11.	(p)	Fathom	understand
12.	(a1)	Genius	extraordinary intelligence

"SUPERGIRL" SYNONYM MATCHING ANSWER KEY cont'd.

	Letter	Vocabulary Word	Synonym
13.	(a2)	Gracious	polite
14.	(a)	infinite	endless
15.	(z)	Loom	overhang
16.	(c)	Manifest	show
17.	(k)	Minimal	smallest
18.	(d)	Mire	marsh
19.	(s)	Phoenix	redeemed
20.	(n)	Pithy	concise
21.	(b)	Quixotic	idealistic
22.	(e)	Resolve	conviction
23.	(h)	Seep	leak
24.	(i)	Slander	defame
25.	(f)	Squander	waste
26.	(x)	Toxin	poison
27.	(l)	Traversing	traveling
28.	(g)	Underlying	primary influence

"SUPERGIRL" SENTENCE COMPLETION ANSWER KEY

1. The many **toxins** in the air are said to be the cause for the increase in cases of asthma in children.

2. He sought their approval as though it was a **benediction**.

3. She tried to **fathom** what caused her mom's angry reaction.

4. Using the microwave to cook takes a **minimal** amount of effort.

5. After she was offered a satisfactory, but not perfect, job, her dad told her not to **squander** a good opportunity.

6. Looking at the stars, the universe appears to go on into **infinity**.
7. The revolt for political reform originally **manifested** itself as a series of student protests.
8. They had everything ready for our visit to their summer house and were very **gracious** hosts.
9. To look at the Earth while walking on the moon must be an **awesome** sight.
10. The stadium proposal was contested by two **factions**, people who supported its construction and others who were against it.
11. After the last team in the league's lineup was shuffled, it came back like a **phoenix** and went on to win the championship.
12. I could see the tornado **looming** on the horizon, so we left the house to look for a safe place.
13. It is **quixotic** to believe that we can eliminate world hunger.
14. The two of them were **mired** in a longstanding argument.
15. I wish that they would just sit down, talk it out, and **resolve** it.
16. The winner voluntarily submitted herself to a physical to **dispel** any allegations that she was using anything to enhance her performance.
17. At the start of the initiation ceremony the new inductees made a **declaration** of faith to the secret society.
18. Occasionally, I gaze at the night sky, and stare into the **cosmos**.
19. Oil **seeped** from the tank, contaminating the surrounding soil.
20. He was always respected for his **candor**, even though sometimes he was brutally honest.
21. The complexity of Mozart's musical composition is evidence of his **genius**.

"SUPERGIRL" SENTENCE COMPLETION ANSWER KEY cont'd.

22. Following the writer's claim that she was a criminal, she sued him for **slander**.

23. Place the pill on your tongue and let it **dissolve**.

24. The Purple Heart is a medal **bestowed** on soldiers for suffering injuries in combat.

25. She apologized for her **pithy** response to my naive question.

26. It is **crucial** that you to follow the medication's directions.

27. Lewis and Clarke are famous for **traversing** the Louisiana Purchase

28. She disagreed with him because she thought his **underlying** assumptions were wrong.

"SUPERGIRL" CROSSWORD ANSWERS

Down
1. infinite
2. seep
3. quixotic
4. cosmos
5. graciously
6. loom
7. genius
8. bestow
9. manifest
10. slander
11. awesome
12. dissolve
13. phoenix

Across
1. benediction
2. faction
3. declaration
4. toxin
5. pithy
6. underlying
7. crucial
8. traversing
9. resolve
10. minimal
11. dispel
12. fathom
13. squander
14. candor
15. mire

"SUPERGIRL" SYNONYM SENTENCES ANSWER KEY

1. I can't **fathom** how she could deceive her best friend.

2. During high tide the harbor is filled with water, but while the tide is out it's a **mire**.

3. A few years ago he was down and out, but he worked hard to get his act together, and came back like a **phoenix** from the ashes.

4. Although she was embarrassed to receive the attention of everyone at the event, she was humble and **graciously** accepted the award.

5. Her aspirations were **quixotic**, but she persevered and succeeded.

6. Looking up at night, the cosmos seem to be **infinite**.

7. At their engagement party, her father **bestowed** his blessings on them.

8. If you want to avoid sunburns, it is **crucial** that you wear suntan lotion at the beach.

9. Architect Frank Gehry's buildings, some of which are constructed with wavy walls and titanium cladding, are regarded as works of pure **genius**.

10. The **minimal** amount of pay you can receive in New York is six dollars an hour.

11. The **underlying** reason that he doesn't go to the movies is that he's afraid of the dark.

12. Reacting to the negative remarks that their paid spokesman made to the press, the company **dissolved** their relationship with him.

13. The sunrise broke over the horizon like a **benediction** on the new day.

14. Having set countless sales records, the Beatles' success still **looms** over the music industry, even though they broke up over 30 years ago.

15. Speaking about **toxins** that exist in nature, the horticulturist warned us that some wild mushrooms could kill you.

16. They **traversed** the mountain range.

17. Hoping he would forgive her, she **candidly** told her boyfriend that she had dated another guy.

18. The new government was in a state of disarray because competing **factions** were fighting for power.

"SUPERGIRL" SYNONYM SENTENCES ANSWER KEY cont'd.

19. Looking to end the standoff, the union and corporate officers made a concerted effort to **resolve** their differences.

20. The hotel room had an **awesome** view of Central Park.

21. Genuinely concerned for his estranged sister's welfare, he showed up at the hospital to **dispel** the idea that he didn't care.

22. Whenever I come into large amounts of money, I always seem to **squander** it.

23. At the movie premier, the star made a **pithy** remark in response to an interviewer's question about her personal life.

24. The kids from another clique made **slanderous** comments about my sister.

25. Bankrupt, addicted, and forsaken by her loved ones, she **declared** that she would rebuild her life.

26. The planetarium show made me feel as though I was shooting through the **cosmos**.

27. I cut myself slicing a bagel, and the blood **seeped** through the first bandage I put on.

28. Finally done with her exams for the year, she showed **manifest** relief at not having to take any more.

HECKER & BEERS LAUNCH "SUPERGIRL" ANSWERS

Question 1
(b) They were there to accomplish some important work.

Question 2
(d) The artists openly discussed the ideas behind "SuperGirl."

Question 3
(c) Lyle and Adrianne's music is brilliantly written.

Question 4

(a) The artists have been working together for only a short time.

Question 5

(b) Lyle and Adrianne create great music despite working together only short time.

Question 6

(d) "SuperGirl" is a great statement of determination.

Question 7

(c) Originally, the authors' thought only older partnerships could create great work.

Question 8

(b) "SuperGirl"'s message is fitting given today's harsh socio-political climate.

Question 9

(a) Adrianne and Lyle understand that hope for world peace is idealistic.

Question 10

(d) The artists can't understand why people chose to treat each other so poorly.

Question 11

(c) Political parties and world leaders say unflattering things about one another.

Question 12

(a) The artists contemplate when people will cooperate and allow peace to flourish.

Question 13

(b) The authors appreciated Adrianne and Lyle's wishes for world peace.

"THE LETTER" – ANSWER KEYS

"THE LETTER" LISTENING EXERCISE ANSWER KEY

Abstain	Cardiologist	Cogitate
Colossal	Debilitated	Disdain
Duration	Elated	Exacting
Extolled	Fester	Forlorn
Friction	Ironic	Jeopardize
Panache	Peers	Poignant
Quell	Refrain	Surmise
Tempestuous		

"THE LETTER" SYNONYM MATCHING ANSWER KEY

	Letter	Vocabulary Word	Synonym
1.	(i)	Abstain	do without
2.	(r)	Cardiologist	heart doctor
3.	(k)	Cogitate	ponder
4.	(o)	Colossal	immense
5.	(n)	Debilitated	incapacitated
6.	(s)	Disdain	despise
7.	(m)	Duration	time interval
8.	(u)	Elated	euphoric
9.	(l)	Exacting	challenging
10.	(v)	Extolled	praise
11.	(c)	Fester	irritate
12.	(a)	Forlorn	dejected
13.	(g)	Friction	hostility
14.	(e)	Ironic	paradoxical

	Letter	Vocabulary Word	Synonym
15.	(d)	Jeopardize	risk
16.	(t)	Panache	style
17.	(h)	Peers	contemporaries
18.	(b)	Poignant	touching
19.	(f)	Quell	suppress
20.	(p)	Refrain	abstain
21.	(q)	Surmise	gather
22.	(j)	Tempestuous	emotional

"THE LETTER" SENTENCE COMPLETION ANSWER KEY

1. Choosing between going away to school or attending college locally and living at home is a **colossal** decision.

2. "I didn't do it" is a familiar **refrain** of the guilty.

3. Examining the skid marks, the investigator **surmised** that the driver did not start braking early enough to avoid the accident.

4. He didn't want to let the problem with sister **fester**, so he asked her if they could talk it out.

5. I had a terrible case of the flu and I was completely **debilitated**.

6. Thousands packed the canyon of lower Broadway to **extol** John Glenn upon his return as the first American to orbit the Earth.

7. The Dean made an impassioned plea for cooler heads to prevail as she tried to **quell** the student uprising.

8. Those who perished on 9/11 were remembered in a **poignant** tribute at the site of the World Trade Center.

9. Talented but **tempestuous**, he could be very engaging, but he could also be difficult to work with if things didn't go his way.

"THE LETTER" SENTENCE COMPLETION ANSWER KEY cont'd.

10. Isn't is **ironic** that "reality" shows are scripted in editing?

11. Rivals on the court, there was always **friction** between them.

12. My dad had a heart attack and now visits the **cardiologist** regularly.

13. Sitting in front of their demolished home, they looked **forlorn** but said that they were happy to have survived the hurricane.

14. Since some students are only comfortable talking about their problems with friends, she started a **peer** counseling program at her school.

15. She's a vegetarian and **abstains** from eating meat.

16. He was **elated** by his daughter's safe return from her trek through the Himalayas.

17. The art teacher asked his students to draw cartoons for the **duration** of the class and to bring in them in the following week.

18. She **disdained** him because he was an unrepentant chauvinist.

19. Rolls Royce and Jaguar established British marques as the epitome of automotive **panache**.

20. For centuries philosophers have **cogitated** upon the reason for our existence.

21. If the school doesn't receive additional funding soon, many of its most important programs will be in **jeopardy**.

22. Detectives need to be tough and **exacting** to avoid missing clues.

"THE LETTER" CROSSWORD ANSWERS

Down
1. tempestuous
2. abstain
3. refrain
4. poignant
5. disdain
6. cogitate
7. fester
8. debilitated
9. friction
10. forlorn
11. elated

Across
1. peers
2. ironic
3. exacting
4. surmise
5. cardiologist
6. panache
7. extolled
8. duration
9. jeopardize
10. quelled
11. colossal

"THE LETTER" SYNONYM SENTENCES ANSWER KEY

1. Following a short walk, she said that she was having heart palpitations, and that she should see a **cardiologist**.

2. Before I reach a decision, I will need to **cogitate** and consider the relevant data carefully.

3. We stood for the **duration** of their wedding ceremony, and when it was over I couldn't wait to find a couch to crash on.

4. Thunder scares Dakota, so I tried my best to **quell** his fear of the storm.

5. Looking a paw print in on the forest path, the ranger said, "From the size of this impression, we can **surmise** that this mountain lion was about 6 feet long."

6. It is **ironic** that when she studies exceptionally hard for an exam she'll usually earn a lower grade than when she studies less intensely.

7. All of these late nights studying are **exacting** a toll on me.

"THE LETTER" SYNONYM SENTENCES ANSWER KEY cont'd.

8. He and his father shared a **poignant** moment when they embraced one another for the first time in ten years.

9. Her father told her to stop hanging around with the teachers and to spend time with her **peers**.

10. While today's movie heroes use brute force to win the day, the leading men of classic movies always succeeded via their wits and **panache**.

11. He didn't want to **jeopardize** his chances of getting a car for graduation, so he made sure that he was always home by curfew.

12. While putting some new furniture together, I couldn't get one of the nuts to screw onto its bolt, so I put oil on it to reduce the **friction**.

13. Her blister was beginning to **fester**, so I told her to go see the nurse.

14. He was **forlorn** over the loss of his puppy, and we couldn't cheer him up.

15. However, he was **elated** when he got home and his mom told him that she had found the puppy hiding in one of the closets.

16. Our coach **extolled** the benefits of a healthy diet and regular exercise.

17. She also implored us to **refrain** from smoking.

18. He said that although the project was a **colossal** failure, he would get back on his feet and try again.

19. Her relationship with her mom is **tempestuous** because they are so much alike.

20. My dad asked my friends to **refrain** from eating all of the chocolate in the house every time they came over.

21. He treats them with **disdain** whenever they drop by.

22. I think he's mentally **debilitated**; it's only chocolate.

"THE LETTER" EXAMINED ANSWERS

Question 1
(b) After considering the other tracks on DM, the author has deduced that "The Letter" is the most touching of the all of the songs.

Question 2
(d) Avon's graduate is dejected because his love went off to study medicine.

Question 3
(b) It is paradoxical that the euphoria of love can be impaired by conflict.

Question 4
(a) The couple's love at risk, the graduate ponders his options.

Question 5
(c) The graduate wonders whether or not he can endure the frustration of being separated from his girlfriend.

Question 6
(a) Avon's protagonist reflects on the enormity of deciding whether or not to end their relationship.

Question 7
(d) The graduate is passionate about his love and praises her flair and sense of style.

Question 8
(c) Avon's character repeats a phrase that his contemporaries would understand.

Question 9
(b) The graduate increasingly misses his girlfriend, and he cannot subdue his longing for her.

Question 10
(d) Although it is a difficult decision, the graduate concludes that he and his girlfriend should break up.

"UPSIDE DOWN" – ANSWER KEYS

"UPSIDE DOWN" LISTENING ANSWER KEY

Calamity	Celerity	Chaos
Constellations	Defied	Deviant
Disconcerting	Equanimity	Gazing
Glimmer	Impact	Incontrovertibly
Incredulity	Incurred	Inverted
Jostling	Jubilation	Occurring
Panorama	Peripheral	Reside
Resplendent	Saturnine	Thaumaturgy
Trepidation	Unscathed	

"UPSIDE DOWN" SYNONYM MATCHING ANSWER KEY

	Letter	Vocabulary Word	Synonym
1.	(f)	Calamity	disaster
2.	(o)	Celerity	speed
3.	(k)	Chaos	disorder
4.	(r)	Constellations	assemblage
5.	(i)	Defied	disregard
6.	(a)	Deviant	abnormal
7.	(n)	Disconcerting	disturbing
8.	(v)	Equanimity	composure
9.	(b)	Gaze	stare
10.	(s)	Glimmer	gleam
11.	(y)	Impact	influence
12.	(x)	Incontrovertibly	unquestionably
13.	(g)	Incredulous	skeptical

	Letter	Vocabulary Word	Synonym
14.	(c)	Incur	sustain
15.	(q)	Inverted	upturn
16.	(d)	Jostle	bump
17.	(m)	Jubilation	celebration
18.	(z)	Occur	transpire
19.	(h)	Panorama	view
20.	(w)	Peripheral	outer
21.	(e)	Reside	live
22.	(l)	Resplendent	dazzling
23.	(j)	Saturnine	gloomy
24.	(p)	Thaumaturgy	magical
25.	(u)	Trepidation	influence
26.	(t)	Unscathed	unharmed

"UPSIDE DOWN" SENTENCE COMPLETION ANS. KEY

1. He **defied** the odds and went on to become a champion.
2. At the concert we **jostled** for position at the foot of the stage.
3. Miraculously, the dog was **unscathed** after being hit by the bike.
4. She often paid her bills after their due date, and **incurred** many late fees as a result.
5. **Chaos** broke out as the standing-room-only crowd was jostled by the stadium ushers.
6. The company was struck by a series of **calamities;** executive fraud, a massive recall, and a class action suit, all of which led to its bankruptcy.
7. Sitting on a dune above the beach, he **gazed** out at the ocean and admired the panorama.

"UPSIDE DOWN" SENTENCE COMPLETION ANSWER KEY cont'd.

8. She's very calm in difficult situations; you have to respect her **equanimity**.

9. The crowd was **jubilant** as each massive balloon rose out of the staging area and joined the parade.

10. During the 19th century it was popular to visit circular exhibit halls that displayed **panoramic** paintings of renowned places or events.

11. Crossing the Tappan Zee Bridge on a clear night, you can see the city lights **glimmering** in the distance.

12. Sparkling like a pile of diamonds a hundred miles away, New York is a **resplendent** beacon.

13. Despite the proof, he was **incredulous** and refused to believe that he was raised by wolves.

14. The **celerity** of the Earth's rotation is 1,070 miles per hour.

15. Humanity's inability to behave humanely is very **disconcerting**.

16. The **constellation** "The Big Dipper" is a group of stars that look like a giant pot in the sky.

17. Their prior partnership was very frustrating, so he approached his new collaboration with the artist with some **trepidation**.

18. **Deviant** behavior is not socially acceptable.

19. Her grandparents now **reside** in Florida.

20. They were looking for **incontrovertible** proof of his complicity.

21. A wizard is skilled in **thaumaturgy**.

22. It was awesome; the roller coaster track turned upside down and **inverted** the cars as we flew into a sharp turn.

23. A stolid woman, she always seems to be wearing a **saturnine** expression on her face.

24. Watching a horror movie in a theater, I was scared senseless when I caught something move quickly through my **peripheral** vision.

25. It doesn't matter how many times I reboot my computer, glitches keep **occurring**.

26. Meteorites hit the moon regularly, leaving its surface pockmarked with **impact** craters.

"UPSIDE DOWN" CROSSWORD ANSWERS

Down
1. impact
2. deviant
3. glimmer
4. defy
5. constellations
6. jostle
7. gazing
8. incur
9. calamity
10. trepidation
11. disconcerting
12. panorama

Across
1. incredulity
2. equanimity
3. jubilation
4. inverted
5. peripheral
6. incontrovertibly
7. resplendent
8. celerity
9. thaumaturgy
10. saturnine
11. unscathed
12. reside
13. chaos
14. occur

"UPSIDE DOWN" SYNONYM SENTENCES ANSWER KEY

1. Her husband better drive with **celerity**, or she'll have the baby in their car.

2. His **saturnine** gaze lays bare his life's hardships.

3. Not knowing what to expect, she approached the exam with **trepidation**.

371

"UPSIDE DOWN" SYNONYM SENTENCES ANSWER KEY cont'd.

4. When World War II ended, **jubilant** crowds packed Times Square.

5. For those who reach Mount Everest's summit, it must be sublime to take in the **panorama** of the entire world below you.

6. Remarkably, he was **unscathed** after falling down the stairs.

7. The facts prove her statements to be **incontrovertible**.

8. Flying over the shore on a bright summer day, I looked down and saw the beachgoers' sunglasses **glimmer** like diamonds scattered across the sand.

9. Although the Web doesn't appear to have a physical form, it actually an vast **constellation** of interconnected computers.

10. The protesters **defied** the government and staged a sit-in near the capital.

11. The subway riders **jostled** one another as they made their way out of the crowded station.

12. Medieval tales often describe astonishing, **thaumaturgical** events.

13. I hate when I bring my car in to be repaired for an intermittent problem, and when I get to the shop, it doesn't **occur**.

14. He decided to **reside** in the city because it was close to his job.

15. Her classic Vette was **resplendent** in bright white livery with blue racing stripes.

16. Her mom said, "Stop **gazing** out the window and finish your homework!"

17. We had so much work to do for the fete that we only took care of the essentials; we blew off doing anything that was **peripheral**.

18. His house was in a state of complete **chaos** after that party.

19. It wouldn't have been such a **calamity** if his parents hadn't come back from their vacation early.

20. It was pretty **disconcerting** to be standing there while they chewed him out.

21. They were **incredulous** that he ignored their instructions not to have anyone over.

22. I think what they were most upset about was the **inverted** ice cream truck in the garage.

23. This episode is definitely going to have huge **impact** on his social life for a few months.

24. His dad, who's pretty melodramatic, yelled, "You have **incurred** my wrath!"

25. I can't believe that he handled it all with such **equanimity**.

26. We don't understand what they're so mad about; it's not like he's **deviant** or anything like that.

MIA JOHNSON GETS INVERTED ANSWERS

Question 1
(c) A catastrophe was going to befall Mia.

Question 2
(d) The author is very happy that Mia did not pass on.

Question 3
(a) On a beautiful summer evening Mia caught a glimpse of a car that was going to hit her.

Question 4
(b) She was in a state of disbelief that some joker just ran a 'STOP' sign, and was about to plow into her.

Question 5
(c) She was fearful of the impending collision.

MIA JOHNSON GETS INVERTED ANSWERS cont'd.

Question 6

(d) Despite her fear of the coming collision, she remained level-headed and thought quickly.

Question 7

(b) The oncoming car smashed into her car, throwing it sideways at great speed.

Question 8

(a) Her car slid sideways with celerity, smashed into a hydrant, and overturned.

Question 9

(c) When Mia opened her eyes she was overturned, suspended by her seatbelt.

Question 10

(d) Beating the odds, Mia was miraculously unhurt, incurring only a few bruises.

Question 11

(a) Following the accident Mia was happy.

Question 12

(b) She shoved her way out of her seatbelt and fell onto the ceiling.

Question 13

(a) Delirious but unscathed, Mia admired the stars shimmering in the night sky.

"MOVE IT" – ANSWER KEYS

"MOVE IT" LISTENING EXERCISE ANSWER KEY

Beset	Cavort	Clout
Context	Devotion	Distraction
Eternity	Euphoric	Fete
Fret	Frolic	Gambol
Grasp	Impression	Indiscretion
Induce	Resolve	Rig
Sublime	Symbiotic	

"MOVE IT" SYNONYM MATCHING ANSWER KEY

	Letter	Vocabulary Word	Synonym
1.	(h)	Beset	inundated
2.	(i)	Cavort	horse around
3.	(e)	Clout	influence
4.	(o)	Context	circumstances
5.	(p)	Devotion	commitment
6.	(j)	Distraction	disturbance
7.	(d)	Eternity	infinity
8.	(c)	Euphoric	elated
9.	(k)	Fete	party
10.	(r)	Fret	worry
11.	(q)	Frolic	play
12.	(b)	Gambol	bound
13.	(f)	Grasp	understand
14.	(l)	Impression	perception
15.	(a)	Indiscretion	tactlessness

"MOVE IT" SYNONYM MATCHING ANSWER KEY cont'd.

	Letter	Vocabulary Word	Synonym
16.	(g)	Induce	pressure
17.	(s)	Resolve	solve
18.	(t)	Rig	manipulate
19.	(n)	Sublime	transcendent
20.	(m)	Symbiotic	mutual benefit

"MOVE IT" SENTENCE COMPLETION ANSWER KEY

1. She was **euphoric** after finishing the SATs.

2. He couldn't **grasp** the ideas presented in the article.

3. The neighbor's party was **distracting** me from my homework.

4. She told him that he needed to **resolve** the problem today.

5. The **fete** to celebrate graduation is being held at my house.

6. He tried to make a good **impression** on his girlfriend's parents.

7. In the 1950's Congress investigated game shows that were suspected of being **rigged**.

8. Taken out of **context**, the senator's sound-bite made him appear ridiculous.

9. **Cavorting** at the fete, the guys tossed their girlfriends in the pool.

10. His bragging went on and on; it lasted for an **eternity**.

11. Puppies like to **frolic** in the open grass.

12. The protesters **induced** her to stop wearing fur by telling her about all of the cute little animals that she would save.

13. Edgar Allen Poe, one of English literature's most renowned authors and a tragic figure, was **beset** by turmoil during his life, and died penniless and alone.

14. Following the revelations of his affair with an intern, former President Clinton became known for his **indiscretions**.

15. The dancers **gamboled** across the stage.

16. The queen is regarded as a political figure, although she has no real political **clout**.

17. A healthy marriage is a **symbiotic** relationship.

18. Man, the beats we heard at the show took you to another place and time; they were **sublime**.

19. I told him, "Don't sit there **fretting** about Thursday's exam, get off your backside and go study!"

20. Martin Luther King **devoted** his life to achieving racial equality.

"MOVE IT" CROSSWORD ANSWERS

Across
1. resolve
2. fete
3. euphoric
4. beset
5. clout
6. indiscretion
7. induce
8. eternity
9. symbiotic
10. grasp

Down
1. rig
2. sublime
3. cavort
4. devotion
5. distraction
6. context
7. fret
8. impression
9. gambol
10. frolic

"MOVE IT" SYNONYM SENTENCES ANSWER KEY

1. The children are **frolicking** in the yard.
2. The street performers **gamboled** across the plaza.
3. He created a **distraction** while she slipped out the back door.
4. My boss says that it doesn't hurt to have friends with **clout**.
5. We watched a beautiful sunset the other evening; it was **sublime**.
6. The kids were **cavorting** in the backyard.
7. He expressed his **devotion** to his girlfriend by proposing.
8. Parents often **fret** about their children.
9. Although the commercials were only 2 minutes long, it felt as though they went on for an **eternity**.
10. Calculus isn't really that hard to **grasp**.
11. After looking at the instructions, I have a pretty good **impression** of what I need to do.
12. The two sisters were forced to **resolve** their differences.
13. He was **euphoric** after receiving his acceptance letter to law school.
14. Urban communities worldwide are **beset** by air pollution.
15. She helped him with his homework, and he helped her with her move; their relationship was **symbiotic**.
16. If you understand the **context** in which the article was written, its point is clear.
17. They **induced** him to do the stunt by offering him a pile of cash.
18. It is against the law to **rig** the lottery.
19. Dumb criminals tend to be **indiscrete**, which makes them easy to catch.
20. The **fete** is at the club on 11th Street and 4th Ave.

BLANDING & JACKSON "MOVE IT" ANSWERS

Question 1
(b) The guys have a mutually beneficial relationship.

Question 2
(d) It is obvious that they are dedicated to entertaining people.

Question 3
(c) Troy expressed that it took a lot of effort to write the song.

Question 4
(a) Ed found it hard to find words that fit the circumstances of the song.

Question 5
(d) They didn't let anything inhibit the progress of their work.

Question 6
(d) They want to get listeners to dance and party.

Question 7
(b) The guys said that "Move It" is a party track, and it fosters an upbeat mood.

Question 8
(c) The theme of "Move It" is easily understood.

Question 9
(a) Ed and Troy want to get into the music industry.

Question 10
(b) Ed and Troy trust that they won't be as careless as other successful artists.

Question 11
(b) Troy and Ed want more chances to record.

Question 12
(d) The guys want to make great music.

Question 13
(d) They want their tracks to be enjoyed by audiences forever.

"EPHEMERAL DAYS" – ANS. KEYS

"E. DAYS" LISTENING EXCERCISE ANSWER KEY

Abscond	Ambled	Antiquity
Appraise	Beatific	Cacophony
Captivating	Conception	Confounded
Dissuade	Elated	Embarking
Endures	Enigmatic	Ephemeral
Erroneously	Flagrantly	Haze
Impart	Intrigued	Licentious
Linger	Modesty	Novelty
Odyssey	Perceive	Profusion
Prolong	Sojourn	Solemnly
Survey	Vague	

"E. DAYS" SYNONYM MATCHING ANSWER KEY

	Letter	Vocabulary Word	Synonym
1.	(e)	Abscond	escape
2.	(o)	Ambled	strolled
3.	(i)	Antiquity	ancient time
4.	(t)	Appraise	evaluate
5.	(x)	Beatific	virtuous
6.	(k)	Cacophony	noise
7.	(a4)	Captivating	entrancing
8.	(y)	Conception	notion
9.	(a6)	Confounded	perplexed
10.	(z)	Dissuade	discourage
11.	(s)	Elated	overjoyed

	Letter	Vocabulary Word	Synonym
12.	(h)	Embark	begin
13.	(u)	Endure	persist
14.	(l)	Enigmatic	mysterious
15.	(j)	Ephemeral	fleeting
16.	(n)	Erroneously	wrongly
17.	(a5)	Flagrant	blatant
18.	(a)	Haze	mist
19.	(g)	Impart	tell
20.	(q)	Intrigued	curious
21.	(a3)	Licentious	immoral
22.	(p)	Linger	loiter
23.	(d)	Modesty	reserve
24.	(b)	Novelty	newness
25.	(m)	Odyssey	journey
26.	(a2)	Perceive	notice
27.	(w)	Profusion	overabundance
28.	(a1)	Prolong	extend
29.	(f)	Sojourn	visit
30.	(v)	Solemnly	seriously
31.	(r)	Survey	review
32.	(c)	Vague	unclear

"E. DAYS" SENT. COMPLETION ANSWER KEY

1. He had the painting **appraised** and was surprised to learn that it was very valuable.

2. It is easy to see (and hear) how the **cacophony** of sounds in NYC can overwhelm some people.

"E. DAYS" SENTENCE COMPLETION ANSWER KEY cont'd.

3. Pablo Picasso, a painter who often portrayed people's eyes on the same side of their heads, is known for his **enigmatic** style.

4. Her **beatific** smile is angelic.

5. The **haze** made it difficult for the driver to see what was ahead.

6. Leaving for their trip, they **embarked** for the Bahamas from JFK International Airport.

7. We decided to **prolong** our date by going dancing after we saw the movie.

8. She **erroneously** believed that she would pass English, and she'll be retaking the class during summer school.

9. The professor **imparted** some of his accumulated wisdom to the class.

10. Telling him that he would wind up flipping burgers, the Principal was determined to **dissuade** my friend from dropping out.

11. After the doctors told her that she had six months to live, she **confounded** them by overcoming her illness.

12. I **ambled** down the beach, stopping occasionally to pick up seashells.

13. Sometimes, it's the **ephemeral** nature of summer relationships that makes them work.

14. I saw an animated cat and mouse flick that **flagrantly** ripped off some classic cartoons.

15. The painting was so beautiful that I couldn't take my eyes off of it; it was **captivating**.

16. Skulking though the alleyway, the jewel thieves **absconded** with the gems they stole.

17. It is extraordinary that William Shakespeare's works continue to **endure** century after century.

18. She was very demure, and her **modesty** prevented her from talking about her achievements.

19. He had never encountered such a device before and was **intrigued** by its novelty.

20. She became totally lost on her way here because the directions weren't complete and were too **vague**.

21. Recognizing that it was futile to try following the vague directions, she said, "Well, I have no **conception** of how to get there."

22. After my friend opened a ketchup bottle by using his belly button, I said, "Well, that was certainly a **novel** approach."

23. The readers **solemnly** recited the names of those who lost their lives on 9/11.

24. Before we rented a tent for the party, I went out to **survey** the backyard to determine out how it would best fit.

25. It was one of those great ephemeral love affairs, two people meeting one another during a brief **sojourn**, enjoying each other's company, and then continuing on their journeys.

26. Las Vegas, which is known as "Sin City," is playing up its **licentious** image to attract tourists.

27. Opening the stereo cabinet, I found a **profusion** of wires, and I realized that I had no idea what I was doing.

28. The Pyramids in Giza, Egypt, date to **antiquity**, and are thousands of years old.

29. Trying to get her laptop fixed, she spoke with four customer service reps, three different technicians, and a software engineer; it was an **odyssey**.

30. I may be wrong, but they look like they're up to no good, just **lingering** in the hallway, furtively looking back and forth.

"E. DAYS" SENTENCE COMPLETION ANSWER KEY cont'd.

31. If they're supposed to be in the building, I **perceive** that they may be waiting for someone to come with the keys to the apartment.

32. She was **elated** when she found out that she had won the car.

"EPHEMERAL DAYS" CROSSWORD ANSWERS

Down
1. erroneous
2. sojourn
3. linger
4. embark
5. captivating
6. modesty
7. amble
8. ephemeral
9. haze
10. novelty
11. antiquity
12. elated
13. prolong
14. beatific
15. profusion

Across
1. confound
2. enigmatic
3. survey
4. odyssey
5. solemn
6. dissuade
7. cacophony
8. impart
9. perceive
10. abscond
11. vague
12. licentious
13. endure
14. conception
15. flagrant
16. intrigued
17. appraise

"E. DAYS" SYNONYM SENTENCES ANSWER KEY

1. He wanted to **appraise** the situation before deciding what to do.

2. Despite her great wealth she was a very **modest**, understated person.

3. I haven't lived in Paris for years, but the memories of my time there **endure**.

4. Working for over three years to get this company started, it has been an **odyssey** to say the least.

5. At the earliest opportunity, I'm going to take a few days off, and the wife and I are going for a quick **sojourn** to South Beach.

6. She wanted to lay out to tan, but a light **haze** was blocking the sun.

7. When he knocked over all of the pots that had been drying, his mom, jarred by the sound of crashing cookware, yelled "What is that **cacophony**!?"

8. Despite his efforts to get her to leave for someplace safe, he couldn't **dissuade** her from staying.

9. We looked at the photo she took of what she told us was the Loch Ness Monster, but all we could make out was the **vague** outline of something in the water.

10. Slipping into the night, the spies **absconded** with a copy of the secret launch codes.

11. The burlesque dancers **licentiously** draped themselves over the show's host.

12. In a low, **solemn** voice, the doctor informed her that her condition was inoperable.

13. With roots that reach back thousands of years, the world's major religions all date to **antiquity**.

14. I was too excited and couldn't sleep because today we're **embarking** on our journey.

15. He's been working on the project for years, but it was originally her **concept**.

16. After their argument, she **erroneously** believed that he would wait for her.

17. I love to **amble** through interesting parts of the city that I don't know yet.

18. Given that his car was gone, I **perceived** that he had already left.

19. I was intrigued by the **novelty** of the technology.

20. The recording star **confounded** her critics by becoming more popular than ever.

"E. DAYS" SYNONYM SENTENCES ANSWER KEY cont'd.

21. He was **elated** when he received his acceptance letter from Columbia.

22. After the tornado she came out of the cellar to **survey** the damage to the house.

23. On our trek through the Amazon, a native priest **imparted** his wisdom to us.

24. Poetry has always been **enigmatic** to her, because she can never figure out what the author is trying to say.

25. The new technology was **intriguing** and sparked my curiosity.

26. Lazy summer days are always too **ephemeral**.

27. I did everything I could to **prolong** my afternoon nap on Sunday, but the din outside kept waking me up.

28. There is a **profusion** of diet gimmicks on the market, but that doesn't mean that any of them work.

29. Dakota is the cutest little kid, and has the most **beatific** smile.

30. I urged her to stay inside where it was safe, but she **flagrantly** ignored my advice and walked out into the hurricane.

31. I always like to **linger** after a movie ends to see if the director did anything interesting during the credits.

32. She was **captivated** by the film's lush imagery.

NINA ZEITLIN'S "EPHEMERAL DAYS" ANSWERS

Question 1
(d) The authors were hanging around the production studio.

Question 2
(c) She thought of the title prior to writing the song.

Question 3

(a) Nina likes a word that means "short-lived."

Question 4

(b) Nina was on vacation when she began writing the lyrics.

Question 5

(a) Ideas and words for the song were written at different times.

Question 6

(a) She found the city magnificent and rich in history.

Question 7

(c) She was excited to begin her visit.

Question 8

(b) Nina had a modest knowledge of the city's outstanding architecture.

Question 9

(b) She was struck by the multiplicity of cultures and the restraint of its citizens.

Question 10

(c) Compared to New York, she found Barcelona somewhat difficult to understand.

Question 11

(d) Nina was captivated by Barcelona and savored walking its bustling streets.

Question 12

(a) Nina would have liked to stay in Barcelona, but she needed to get home.

Question 13

(b) Nina was sad to leave Barcelona, but she was compelled to.

Question 14

(d) She expects that she will remember Barcelona for an indefinite period.

"SUBLIME" – ANSWER KEYS

"SUBLIME" LISTENING EXERCISE ANSWER KEY

Apathetic	Barren	Basking
Berating	Deluded	Din
Finesse	Gait	Hoax
Iridescent	Languid	Lucid
Muddle	Palpitating	Quiver
Random	Savor	Scurry
Shimmer	State	Sublime
Succumb	Unravel	Vindicate

"SUBLIME" SYNONYM MATCHING ANSWER KEY

	Letter	Vocabulary Word	Synonym
1.	(j)	Apathetic	indifferent
2.	(d)	Barren	desolate
3.	(l)	Basking	sunbathing
4.	(h)	Berate	scold
5.	(v)	Deluded	deceived
6	(q)	Din	noise
7.	(b)	Finesse	skill
8.	(r)	Gait	pace
9.	(g)	Hoax	trick
10.	(o)	Iridescent	glow
11.	(e)	Languid	relaxed
12.	(k)	Lucid	coherent
13.	(c)	Muddled	jumbled
14.	(w)	Palpitating	throbbing

	Letter	Vocabulary Word	Synonym
15.	(u)	Quiver	shake
16.	(t)	Random	haphazard
17.	(s)	Savor	relish
18.	(m)	Scurry	scamper
19.	(a)	Shimmer	twinkle
20.	(p)	State	condition
21.	(n)	Sublime	perfect
22.	(f)	Succumb	yield
23.	(i)	Unravel	disentangle
24.	(x)	Vindicate	exonerate

"SUBLIME" SENTENCE COMPLETION ANSWER KEY

1. Looking down at the street from my office window, I watched the people **scurry** as the rain began to fall.

2. She **berated** him for telling her that aliens stole his homework.

3. Questioning him, she thought that his story would **unravel**.

4. Positive that his tale was a **hoax**, she sent him to the principal.

5. Then, all of a sudden, an unusual light with an **iridescent** glow came through the window.

6. We couldn't believe our eyes, but a tall figure that **shimmered** in the light stepped in through the window, and handed the teacher his homework.

7. **Vindicated** by the extraordinary events, he came back to the classroom and said, "I told you that aliens stole my homework!"

8. After a great day of swimming and basking in the sun, we ambled down the beach at a **languid** pace to head back to our hotel.

"SUBLIME" SENTENCE COMPLETION ANSWER KEY cont'd.

9. My grandfather was sent to the hospital with heart **palpitations**.

10. The Confederate army **succumbed** to Union forces in March of 1865.

11. When I go to the beach, all I want to do is **bask** in the sun.

12. Photographs of Mars depict a **barren**, rocky landscape.

13. As the bear slowly approached us, we began to **quiver** with fear.

14. Unable to finish a sentence, it was obvious that her thoughts were **muddled**.

15. After sampling a very fine vintage bottle of wine, the connoisseur remarked, "What a **sublime** finish."

16. Never having encountered such an extraordinary vintage before, he **savored** every drop.

17. His mom said, "He is completely **deluded** if he expects me to pick up after him for the rest of his life."

18. We cannot become **apathetic** and take democracy for granted.

19. I couldn't keep up with my sister as we walked downtown because she has a much longer **gait** than I do.

20. He gave a clear and **lucid** argument supporting states' rights.

21. The speaker was forced to yell over the **din** of the crowd.

22. After 9/11 it isn't uncommon to be subjected to a **random** search at an airport.

23. But, I'm sad to say, that is today's **state** of affairs.

24. He forgot her name, but handled the situation with such **finesse** that she was happy to excuse the gaffe.

"SUBLIME" CROSSWORD ANSWERS

Down
1. lucid
2. basking
3. sublime
4. unravel
5. finesse
6. din
7. deluded
8. apathetic
9. barren
10. random
11. gait

Across
1. muddle
2. shimmering
3. berate
4. savor
5. quiver
6. languid
7. succumb
8. state
9. palpitate
10. scurry
11. vindicate
12. iridescent
13. hoax

"SUBLIME" SYNONYM SENTENCES ANSWER KEY

1. She only slept for a few hours last night and woke up completely **muddled** this morning.

2. Her beautiful hair **shimmered** in the sunlight.

3. He found the hose in knots and **unraveled** it so he could to water the plants.

4. It was an elaborate **hoax**, which took months to prepare.

5. Cold-blooded animals need to **bask** in the sun to maintain their body temperatures.

6. Acquitted by the jury, the defendant was **vindicated**.

7. During hot, humid summer days, I like to keep a **languid** pace.

8. He lacked **finesse**, but he always got the job done.

9. Sometimes, given the overwhelming crises here at home, it's hard not to be **apathetic** about problems elsewhere.

10. The horse trainer was irate when he found out that the mare he just bought was **barren**.

"SUBLIME" SYNONYM SENTENCES ANSWER KEY cont'd.

11. As the Grammy results were read, she **quivered** with anticipation.
12. Following her fall down the stairs, he asked her how many fingers he was holding up to see if she was **lucid**.
13. The mouse **scurried** across the kitchen floor.
14. The **din** of the traffic kept me awake all night.
15. There is something **sublime** about every morning's sunrise.
16. I'm always in awe of the sun's **iridescence** as it breaches the horizon.
17. The horse trotted at a moderate **gait**.
18. To me, events seem pretty **random** and good or bad, you never know what's going to happen next.
19. After he found out that he she conned him, he said "I can't believe that I was so **deluded**!"
20. My heart was **palpitating** after the four-mile run.
21. The teacher **berated** her for coming late to class.
22. When he awoke in a strange and unfamiliar place, he was in a very confused **state**.
23. Exhausted from battling the disease for years, my grandmother **succumbed** and passed away this morning.
24. Great achievements are always comprised of small feats, so I **savor** every accomplishment, no matter how insignificant it might seem.

THE "SUBLIME" PIECE ANSWERS

Question 1

(b) The author was running to get out of the rain and couldn't catch his breath.

Question 2
(a) The doorway light cast a glow that twinkled in the rain drops on the author's jacket.

Question 3
(d) He savors the odd tranquility that occurs when it rains heavily in New York.

Question 4
(c) He was kidding himself when he thought that the rain would stop soon.

Question 5
(b) Keith gave in to the fact that the rain was not going to let up.

Question 6
(a) The author was coherent, but largely unmotivated.

Question 7
(c) The author was having one of those days when you can't get it together.

Question 8
(d) The author was hoping the day would improve, but he didn't expect it to.

Question 9
(b) No matter how down you get, if you keep it together, you can come through.

Question 10
(a) Once Keith got to the studio, he felt better.

Question 11
(c) The author appreciates being part of something creative.

Question 12
(d) He had more energy, and trembled when he heard a high note over the other music in the studio.

THE "SUBLIME" PIECE ANSWERS cont'd.

Question 13

(b) The author chastised himself for letting the rain undermine his mood.

Question 14

(a) The kitchen cabinet did not contain any coffee.

"WIDE OPEN..." – ANSWER KEYS

"WOS" LISTENING EXERCISE ANSWER KEY

Abstain	Affliction	Conjuration
Contagion	Credence	Demure
Effervescent	Enamored	Fallacy
Filament	Fissure	Flagging
Floundering	Forgo	Grave
Lucidity	Manifest	Nemesis
Nostalgic	Obnoxiousness	Obscure
Obtuse	Ominous	Pernicious
Plague	Plausible	Predilection
Reconcile	Refrain	Superfluous
Valor	Volatile	

"WOS" SYNONYM MATCHING ANSWER KEY

	Letter	Vocabulary Word	Synonym
1.	(a3)	Abstain	refrain
2.	(i)	Affliction	cause of suffering
3.	(h)	Conjuration	witchcraft
4.	(r)	Contagion	source of infection
5.	(a5)	Credence	credibility
6.	(l)	Demure	reserved
7.	(a1)	Effervescent	fizzy
8.	(z)	Enamored	smitten
9.	(b)	Fallacy	falsehood
10.	(q)	Filament	thread
11.	(x)	Fissure	crevice

"WOS" SYNONYM MATCHING ANSWER KEY cont'd.

	Letter	Vocabulary Word	Synonym
12.	(f)	Flag	wane
13.	(e)	Flounder	falter
14.	(t)	Forgo	relinquish
15.	(k)	Grave	serious
16.	(c)	Lucidity	clarity
17.	(j)	Manifest	apparent
18.	(d)	Nemesis	arch-enemy
19.	(g)	Nostalgic	wistful
20.	(n)	Obnoxious	insufferable
21.	(a6)	Obscure	vague
22.	(a2)	Obtuse	stupid
23.	(a4)	Ominous	foreboding
24.	(o)	Pernicious	evil
25.	(m)	Plague	outbreak
26.	(a)	Plausible	credible
27.	(s)	Predilection	partiality
28.	(v)	Reconcile	settle
29.	(p)	Refrain	avoid doing
30.	(w)	Superfluous	extraneous
31.	(y)	Valor	bravery
32.	(u)	Volatile	erratic

"WOS" SENTENCE COMPLETION ANSWER KEY

1. The General bestowed a medal on the Private for his **valor** in battle.
2. The bird flu virus is a **contagion** that was thought only to affect chickens and other fowl, but now appears to also be harmful to humans.

3. The Department of Homeland security issued an **ominous** warning to be on the lookout for 'suspicious activity.'

4. She decided to **forgo** her bonus, and instead gave it to charity.

5. He was in **grave** condition after the accident.

6. She was always loud, crass, and **obnoxious**.

7. He plays the tenor sax and has a **predilection** for John Coltrane and jazz from the 1950s.

8. It goes without saying that every super hero needs a **nemesis** to battle.

9. "I'd like to believe that your grandmother ate your homework, but couldn't you at least try to give me a **plausible** explanation?"

10. Surprisingly, human beings' small toes are **superfluous** and do not help us to stand.

11. Some people are just **obtuse**; you can explain something to them a thousand times, but they still don't get it.

12. Although we couldn't stand one another, we sat down face to face, and worked to **reconcile** our differences.

13. Around the holidays I become **nostalgic** for the Thanksgiving dinners that we use to have at my grandmother's house.

14. The hurricane first **manifest** as a tropical storm in the south Caribbean.

15. He was practiced in the art of **conjuration** and referred to himself as a "warlock."

16. Mount St. Helens is a **volatile**, active volcano located 50 miles northeast of Portland, Oregon.

17. After she dumped him for being obnoxious, he made up **fallacious**, hurtful claims about his ex.

"WOS" SENTENCE COMPLETION ANSWER KEY cont'd.

18. While perusing an **obscure** journal that was written around 1850, a researcher uncovered new information about Lincoln's hat.

19. Pressure in the volcanic vent decreased after steam was released through a new **fissure** in the bedrock.

20. Unable to agree on the details of any issue, the peace talks' negotiators are **floundering** in their effort to reconcile their positions.

21. Research shows that children are drinking coffee, but they should **abstain** from consuming large quantities of caffeine until after the age of 18.

22. In light of the fact that his grandmother likes to eat paper, there might be some **credence** to his claim that his she ate his homework.

23. Compelled by an anxious electorate and no employment growth, the candidates have focused on the **flagging** job market.

24. The United Nations has asked China to **refrain** from imprisoning human rights activists.

25. Would-be terrorists are **plaguing** airlines with bomb hoaxes and other efforts to disrupt their operations.

26. According to the Center for Disease control Noise-induced hearing loss is currently the most common occupational **affliction**.

27. She recently became **enamored** with photography, and now she never leaves the house without her camera.

28. Unfortunately, seniors often begin to lose their **lucidity** as they become older and the aging process accelerates.

29. Automotive lighting technology has made significant advances over the past few years, discarding incandescent **filaments** in favor of electro-reactive gases like xenon.

30. When monks first accidentally created champagne in the 1680s, its **effervescence** was an undesirable trait that was regarded as a sign of poor wine making.

31. Their group was reprimanded for spreading **pernicious**, hurtful rumors about other students.

32. Preparing to address the delegates, the keynote speaker adopted a **demure**, restrained tone of voice and a formal posture.

"WOS" CROSSWORD ANSWERS

Down
1. manifesting
2. fissure
3. superfluous
4. filament
5. abstain
6. obtuse
7. grave
8. forgo
9. conjuration
10. enamored
11. contagion
12. fallacy
13. floundering
14. predilection
15. plague
16. refrain
17. demure

Across
1. valor
2. affliction
3. nostalgic
4. obscure
5. nemesis
6. lucidity
7. obnoxiousness
8. effervescent
9. credence
10. pernicious
11. flagging
12. reconcile
13. ominous
14. plausible
15. volatile

"WOS" SYNONYM SENTENCES ANSWER KEY

1. I wish that she would **abstain** from blowing her nose into her shirt, she's grossing me out.

2. There isn't a **filament** of truth to his claim that he's the Queen's mother.

3. He had a difficult time responding to his opponent's arguments and **floundered** throughout the debate.

4. Dr. Evil is Austin Power's **nemesis**

"WOS" SYNONYM SENTENCES ANSWER KEY cont'd.

5. Given the fact that there are an infinite number of galaxies, it is entirely **plausible** that there is intelligent life somewhere in the universe.

6. The band's tour was canceled due to **flagging** ticket sales.

7. She's a pathological liar and I don't put an ounce of **credence** in anything she has to say.

8. Don't you hate when you can't get a song's **refrain** out of your head even though you haven't heard it in three days?

9. My parents love my current girlfriend, but I think that she's too **demure** for my liking.

10. Recording her expenses when they occur makes it is easier for her to **reconcile** her checkbook with her bank statements.

11. The **contagion** was traced to a research lab that was active during the cold war.

12. The event's **effervescent** host welcomed everyone personally.

13. The prevalence of brutality and bloodshed on TV has the **pernicious** effect of desensitizing people to violence.

14. Despite its complexities, she described the process with great **lucidity**, which gave us a better understanding of how it would progress.

15. It is interesting that even the brightest people will believe almost any **fallacy** if it is repeated frequently enough.

16. Predicated upon **conjuration**, Vodun (aka Voodoo) is a religion that has been practiced in West Africa for over 6,000 years.

17. Since we don't have the data yet, we'll **forgo** meeting until next week.

18. An alien variety of seaweed has overwhelmed large areas of the Mediterranean's sea bed, posing a **grave** threat to its indigenous species.

19. Recent leading financial indicators have been extremely **volatile**, underscoring the uncertain state of the economy.

20. I thought that I had made my point clearly, but it seems that he was too **obtuse** to grasp it.

21. Her fiancé is totally **obnoxious**; the first time he came over, he headed straight for the fridge, and then whined that we didn't have any cheese.

22. She's been **plagued** by self-doubt, and she just can't seem to shake it.

23. The **affliction** is weakening his immune system, making him more susceptible to infection.

24. The city's budget woes are **manifesting** a new round of service cuts and tax increases.

25. "Unencumbered by **superfluous** posturing, her performance was raw and inspiring."

26. Away at college, he was swept up by a wave of **nostalgia**, and decided to call some old friends.

27. Although the score was tied, they won the match due to an **obscure** technicality.

28. They're so **enamored** with one another that the entire world around them could crumble, and they would barely notice.

29. With an equal number of classes in favor of, or against, the proposed changes, it exposed a **fissure** in the student body.

30. A fearless warrior, Joan of Arc was renown for her faith and **valor**.

31. Given the growing deficit and declining tax income, the budget situation appears **ominous**.

32. Considering her **predilection** for yellow, I was surprised that she bought a blue car.

NINA Z. LONGS FOR "WIDE OPEN SPACES" ANSWERS

Question 1
(c) The author believes that he may have found a foreboding trend in Nina's songs.

Question 2
(d) Nina seems disposed to writing reflective songs about her bad relationships.

Question 3
(b) She writes songs about relationships with men who aren't good for her.

Question 4
(a) The author cannot square his image of Nina with her heated lyrics.

Question 5
(d) The subject matter of Nina's songs may be considered volatile because she is describing men who are erratic.

Question 6
(b) Nina's vibrant, and sometimes decorous, personality belie the resentment captured by her lyrics.

Question 7
(a) It is possible that she is smitten with guys that are wrong for her, but she can't keep herself from dating loutish, stupid idiots.

Question 8
(c) The author poses that Nina's courage encourages her to date jerks.

Question 9
(a) Nina's ex boyfriends put on a good face at first, then, once they're dating, problems arise as they begin to reveal their true nature.

Question 10
(c) Their attraction to one another wanes, and their relationship begins to struggle.

Question 11

(b) Keith suggests that his inferences may be a misguided belief, and that he doesn't put much weight in his theories.

Question 12

(d) Keith regards his analysis of Nina's work as extraneous, but he also says that there may be some truth to his inferences.

Question 13

(c) The author questions his sanity, and says that he should stop overanalyzing things.

COMBO EXERCISES ANSWER KEYS

COMBO SYNONYM MATCHING ANSWER KEYS

SET #1 ANSWER KEY

	Letter	Vocabulary Word	Synonym
1.	(n)	Accolades	award
2.	(a)	Actuate	motivate
3.	(d)	Beset	overwhelm
4.	(j)	Bested	beaten
5.	(m)	Candor	honesty
6.	(a)	Celerity	speed
7.	(l)	Decree	state
8.	(c)	Devoid	lacking
9.	(p)	Entice	persuade
10.	(s)	Epitome	archetype
11.	(i)	Fallacy	falsehood
12.	(g)	Flagrant	blatant
13.	(e)	Glimmer	shine
14.	(h)	Grasp	understand
15.	(r)	Hoax	trick
16.	(f)	Illuminate	enlighten
17.	(b)	Incredulity	disbelief
18.	(k)	Jeopardize	risk
19.	(o)	Licentious	lewd

SET #2 ANSWER KEY

	Letter	Vocabulary Word	Synonym
1.	(u)	Laborious	backbreaking
2.	(r)	Labyrinthine	convoluted
3.	(i)	Monotony	repetitiveness
4.	(h)	Muddle	jumbled
5.	(k)	Nemesis	arch-enemy
6.	(z)	Obtuse	dull-witted
7.	(m)	Panache	style
8.	(d)	Peripheral	tangential
9.	(o)	Punitive	retaliatory
10	(f)	Quell	suppress
11.	(e)	Rabid	fanatical
12.	(g)	Refraction	change in direction
13.	(b)	Refrain	abstain
14.	(a)	Revelation	discovery
15.	(c)	Savor	relish
16.	(y)	Seclusion	solitude
17.	(w)	Squander	waste
18.	(t)	Surmise	deduce
19.	(v)	Tortuous	arduous
20.	(j)	Trepidation	apprehension
21.	(l)	Ungainly	awkward
22.	(s)	Union	combination
23.	(q)	Vague	indistinct
24.	(p)	Virtuoso	prodigy
25.	(n)	Welter	turmoil
26.	(x)	Waver	hesitate

COMBO SYNONYM MATCHING SET #3 ANSWER KEY

	Letter	Vocabulary Word	Synonym
1.	(d)	Abscond	escape
2.	(h)	Abstain	do without
3.	(r)	Bask	sunbathe
4.	(a)	Cacophony	din
5.	(z)	Complicit	involved
6.	(j)	Demure	decorous
7.	(n)	Effervescent	vivacious
8.	(b)	Finesse	poise
9.	(p)	Gracious	polite
10	(l)	Haze	fog
11.	(y)	Impart	communicate
12.	(f)	Linger	persist
13.	(t)	Manifest	apparent
14.	(v)	Novelty	newness
15.	(x)	Ominous	forbidding
16.	(e)	Pernicious	evil
17.	(w)	Procure	obtain
18.	(c)	Raze	destroy
19.	(g)	Rig	manipulate
20.	(m)	Senescent	aging
21.	(k)	Synchronously	simultaneously
22.	(s)	Toxin	poison
23.	(q)	Tranquil	peaceful
24.	(o)	Underlying	primary influence
25.	(u)	Vantage	perspective
26.	(i)	Volatile	unstable

COMBO SENTENCE COMPLETION ANSWER KEY

1. **Cavorting** at the fete, the guys tossed their girlfriends in the pool.

2. A healthy marriage is a **symbiotic** relationship.

3. He had the painting **appraised** and was surprised to learn that it was very valuable.

4. They **embarked** for the Bahamas from JFK International Airport.

5. Telling him that he would wind up flipping burgers, the Principal was determined to **dissuade** my friend from dropping out.

6. Following the revelations of his affair with an intern, former President Clinton became known for his **indiscretions**.

7. At the concert we **jostled** for position at the foot of the stage.

8. She's very calm in difficult situations; you have to respect her **equanimity**.

9. Sparkling like a pile of diamonds a hundred miles away, New York is a **resplendent** beacon.

10. He is following his dream by **pursuing** a career in law.

11. The presidential candidates are **propagating** their ideas by making speeches throughout the country.

12. He was a total couch potato who had a **sedentary** lifestyle

13. The demonstrator was overrun by government forces and died a **martyr** for his cause.

14. I would never **forsake** my family.

15. He was so embarrassed after pouring a drink down the front of his pants that he **skulked** away from the party.

16. Stalkers are **obsessed** with the celebrities they follow.

17. The beautiful Corvette was a **decoy** to lure customers into the used car lot.

COMBO SENTENCE COMPLETION ANSWER KEY cont'd.

18. The study's outcome is encouraging and **merits** further study.

19. Our team **annihilated** the competition, and we finished the season undefeated.

20. When I brought up the topic she became **pugilistic**, but her tone softened as she came to understand my perspective.

21. I could see the tornado **looming** on the horizon, so we left the house to look for a safe place.

22. The winner voluntarily submitted herself to a physical to **dispel** any allegations that she was using anything to enhance her performance.

23. It is **crucial** that you to follow the directions on the medication's label.

24. She apologized for her **pithy** response to my naive question.

25. Choosing between going away to school or attending college locally and living at home is a **colossal** decision.

26. Thousands packed the canyon of lower Broadway to **extol** John Glenn upon his return as the first American to orbit the Earth.

27. Those who perished on 9/11 were remembered in a **poignant** tribute at the site of the World Trade Center.

28. She could **intuit** that I was worried about my upcoming exam.

29. Given the fact that she can't sing, it is **futile** for her to try out for "American Idol."

30. Feeding a dog chocolate can be **deleterious** to its health.

31. Working for over three years to get this company started, it has been an **odyssey** to say the least.

32. There is a **profusion** of diet gimmicks on the market, but that doesn't mean that any of them work.

33. The bird flu virus is a **contagion** that was thought only to affect chickens and other fowl, but now appears to also be harmful to humans.

34. After the tornado she came out of the cellar to **survey** the damage to the house.

35. He delivered a clear and **lucid** argument supporting states' rights.

36. His mom said, "He is completely **deluded** if he expects me to pick up after him for the rest of his life."

COMBO CROSSWORD ANSWERS

Down
1. paradigm
2. vindicate
3. esoteric
4. perplex
5. traverse
6. languid
7. irate
8. peruse
9. unscathed
10. state
11. succumb
12. stolid
13. endure
14. quell
15. aroma
16. profound
17. cognizant
18. uniformity
19. incite

Across
1. haze
2. neophyte
3. quixotic
4. antithesis
5. vacillate
6. saturnine
7. disconcerting
8. tempestuous
9. acquiesce
10. sublime
11. solace
12. reconciliation
13. slander
14. random
15. captivate
16. gait
17. obscure
18. rectify
19. mired

COMBO SYNONYM SENTENCES ANSWER KEY

1. Considering her **predilection** for yellow, I was surprised that she bought a blue car.

2. "Unencumbered by **superfluous** posturing, her performance was raw and inspiring."

3. The band's tour was canceled due to the **flagging** demand for tickets.

COMBO SYNONYM SENTENCES ANSWER KEY cont'd.

4. Given the fact that there are an infinite number of galaxies, it is entirely **plausible** that there is intelligent life somewhere in the universe.

5. The **din** of the traffic kept me awake all night.

6. Sometimes, given the overwhelming crises here at home, it's hard not to be **apathetic** about problems elsewhere.

7. The new technology was **intriguing** and sparked my curiosity.

8. Lazy summer days are always too **ephemeral**.

9. The recording star **confounded** her critics by becoming more popular than ever.

10. My boss says that it doesn't hurt to have friends with **clout**.

11. Parents often **fret** about their children.

12. They **induced** him to do the stunt by offering him a pile of cash.

13. Although my workout is only an hour long, it seems **interminable**.

14. They were the consummate odd couple; she was outgoing, and **conversely**, he was very shy.

15. The **situation** she found herself in was unsettling.

16. My dad gets totally furious if I eat in front of the TV; I think he's mentally **debilitated**.

17. We stood for the **duration** of their wedding ceremony, and when it was over I couldn't wait to find a couch to crash on.

18. He was **forlorn** over the loss of his puppy, and we couldn't cheer him up.

19. I can't **fathom** how she could deceive her best friend.

20. The new government was in a state of disarray because competing **factions** were fighting for power.

21. The planetarium show made me feel as though I was shooting through the **cosmos**.

22. While the article does bring some new information to light, much of it **borders** on fiction.

23. He considers lobbying to be a **lesser** influence on public policy that it is popularly thought to be.

24. While visiting Rome, we asked our guide to translate a shopkeeper's comments because we couldn't **decipher** what he was trying to say.

25. In video clips, Osama bin Laden reveals a **sinister** smile when he discusses the attack on the World Trade Center.

26. During the spring, many people are **afflicted** by allergies.

27. In her day, Jacqueline Kennedy was quite **comely**.

28. We arrived late to the sale, and the earlier shoppers only left behind the **dregs** of what the store had offer.

29. He decided to **renovate** the house.

30. The girls **scoffed** at his attempt to join the field hockey team.

31. It wouldn't have been such a **calamity** if his parents hadn't come back from their vacation early.

32. The facts prove her statements to be **incontrovertible**.

33. When World War II ended, **jubilant** crowds packed Times Square.

34. Stock prices **fluctuate** day to day.

35. He **wavered** before asking her out on a date.

36. He was traumatized at the circus when he was a kid, and he now lived in **perpetual** fear of little dogs riding bicycles.

ARTICLE EXCERPTS ANSWERS

Question 1
(b) The author was running to get out of the rain and couldn't catch his breath.

Question 2
(a) The doorway light cast a glow that twinkled in the rain drops on the author's jacket.

Question 3
(d) He savors the odd tranquility that occurs when it rains heavily in New York.

Question 4
(b) The author believes that Rodney's primary advantage is his intellect.

Question 5
(c) Rodney's towering verse are the product of great inspiration, and makes other recording artists look inferior.

Question 6
(a) The author feels that Rodney's work dispels the notion that artists who rap are incapable of authoring intellectually challenging material.

Question 7
(b) Timid novices may be befuddled by the complexity of Rodney's work, but appropriately, those who are knowledgeable admire its significance.

Question 8
(d) Those who do not believe that Rodney's work is brilliant are just jealous.

Question 9
(a) She found the city magnificent and rich in history.

Question 10
(c) She was excited to begin her visit.

Question 11
(b) Nina had a modest knowledge of the city's outstanding architecture.

Question 12

(b) She was struck by the multiplicity of cultures and the restraint of its citizens.

Question 13

(b) To gain her love interest's attention she contemplates the use of a lure.

Question 14

(a) Nina appreciates her crush's knowing, sly smile and confident demeanor.

Question 15

(a) On a beautiful summer evening Mia saw a car that was going to hit her.

Question 16

(b) She was in a state of disbelief that some joker just ran a 'STOP' sign, and was about to plow into her.

Question 17

(c) She was fearful of the impending collision.

Question 18

(d) Despite her fear of the coming collision, she remained level-headed and thought quickly.

Question 19

(b) The oncoming car smashed into her car, throwing it sideways at great speed.

Question 20

(a) Her car slid sideways with celerity, smashed into a hydrant, and overturned.

Question 21

(b) Keith & Rodney write music that mixes it up.

Question 22

(a) The artists' music forges it own path, breaking the typical boundaries present in today's play lists.

ARTICLE EXCERPTS ANSWERS cont'd.

Question 23
(d) The author finds the artist's music energizing, and regards it as a metaphorical cure for one's state of well being.

Question 24
(c) The author believes that he may have found a foreboding trend in Nina's songs.

Question 25
(d) Nina seems disposed to writing reflective songs about her bad relationships.

Question 26
(b) She writes songs about relationships with men who aren't good for her.

Question 27
(a) The author cannot square his image of Nina with her heated lyrics.

Question 28
(d) The subject matter of Nina's songs may be considered volatile because she is describing men who are erratic.

Question 29
(b) Nina's vibrant, and sometimes decorous, personality belie the resentment captured by her lyrics.

Question 30
(a) The boyfriend secretly likes her but can't break up with her friend.

Question 31
(b) Mia's storytelling reflects vitality rather than sadness.

Question 32
(c) Political parties and world leaders malign one another.

Question 33
(a) The artists contemplate when people will cooperate and allow peace to flourish.

Question 34

(b) The authors appreciated Adrianne and Lyle's wishes for world peace.

Question 35

(a) The couple's love at risk, the graduate ponders his options.

Question 36

(c) The graduate wonders whether or not he can endure the frustration of being separated from his girlfriend.

Question 37

(a) Avon's protagonist reflects on the enormity of deciding whether or not to end their relationship.

Question 38

(d) He is passionate about his love and praises her flair and sense of style.

Question 39

(c) Avon's character repeats a phrase that his cohorts would understand.

Question 40

(b) The graduate increasingly misses his girlfriend, and he cannot subdue his longing for her.

Question 41

(d) Although it is a difficult decision, the graduate concludes that he and his girlfriend should break up.

Question 42

(c) His path unclear, he struggled with the confusion of youth.

Question 43

(a) Joe moved between jobs while he was finding himself.

Question 44

(d) During his period of indecision he wasn't suffering.

Question 45

(a) Joe did not want to fanatically chase fame and fortune.

ARTICLE EXCERPTS ANSWERS cont'd.

Question 46

(b) Joe was a great mechanic that worked on Porsches.

Question 47

(c) Troy expressed that it took a lot of effort to write the song.

Question 48

(a) Ed found it hard to find words that fit the circumstances of the song.

Question 49

(d) They didn't let anything inhibit the progress of their work.

Question 50

(d) They want to get listeners to dance and party.